How to Bullyproof Your Classroom

2nd Edition

K–5

Caltha Crowe

Center for Responsive Schools, Inc.

All net proceeds from the sale of this book support the work of Center for Responsive Schools, Inc., a not-for-profit educational organization and the developer of the *Responsive Classroom*® approach to teaching.

The stories in this book are all based on real events in the classroom. However, to respect students' privacy, names and many identifying characteristics of students and situations have been changed.

© 2021 by Center for Responsive Schools, Inc.

All rights reserved. No part of this book may be reproduced in any form or by any electronic or mechanical means, including information storage and retrieval systems, without permission in writing from the publisher, except by a reviewer, who may quote brief passages in a review.

ISBN: 978-1-950317-14-1
Library of Congress Control Number: 2021945840

Photographs by Jeff Woodward and © Alice Proujansky

Center for Responsive Schools, Inc.
85 Avenue A, P.O. Box 718
Turners Falls, MA 01376-0718

800-360-6332
www.crslearn.org

Contents

INTRODUCTION	What Is Bullying? What Can Classroom Teachers Do About It?	1
CHAPTER ONE	Gateway Behaviors: What to Do When Mean Acts Emerge	15
CHAPTER TWO	Helping Children Get to Know Each Other	41
CHAPTER THREE	Creating Classroom Rules	63
CHAPTER FOUR	Teaching Children How to Work Together	85
CHAPTER FIVE	Outside of the Classroom	113
CHAPTER SIX	How to Prevent Cyberbullying	145
CHAPTER SEVEN	Sample Lessons for Teaching Children About Gateway and Bullying Behaviors	169
	Primary Grade Lessons	183
	Upper Elementary Lessons	213
EPILOGUE	The Challenge of Kindness	245
APPENDIX A	Children's Literature to Use in Bullying Prevention Work	247
APPENDIX B	Resources	261
REFERENCES		270
ACKNOWLEDGMENTS		284
ABOUT THE AUTHOR		287
INDEX		289

INTRODUCTION

What Is Bullying? What Can Classroom Teachers Do About It?

His mom snapped photos as Paul climbed the high steps onto the school bus for his first ride to school. Paul stepped into the aisle and headed toward the back. But as he walked down the aisle, looking for a seat, he tripped and sprawled onto the floor. His lunch box snapped open and yogurt from his lunch smeared on the bus flooring and down the front of his new shirt. He found a seat and sat, looking determinedly down at his lap, tears streaming down his face. Next to him, Sam, the only other kindergartner on the bus, whispered, "Cry baby." Paul continued to look down.

Paul's first bus ride to school set a pattern of abuse from Sam. When kids their age rode the bus, Sam told them not to sit with Paul. Sometimes he snatched Paul's jacket or hat. Soon, other kids joined in with the bullying. They laughed, grabbed Paul's hat, and passed it around the bus. This mean behavior continued daily for the next eight years, escalating from name-calling to poking, pinching, shoving, and tripping.

Paul was a different child at home than he was at school. At home, Paul loved to bike ride, go fishing with his dad, watch movies with the family, or trade jokes with his mom. At school, his teachers noticed that he didn't socialize with the other children. As Paul got older, he did his homework each night. But at parent-teacher conferences, his teachers reported that Paul often didn't turn in his homework.

Despite regular home-school communication, the problem persisted. Paul was too sad and fearful to remember his homework or pay attention in class, and his academic progress was sporadic. His parents talked with him about why he was having such a hard time with school, but Paul never said anything about the bullying. Even though the bullying was persistent and deeply distressing, Paul, like many children who are targeted for bullying, was too ashamed and afraid to tell an adult.

In middle school, Paul finally confided in a trusted guidance counselor. The guidance counselor confronted Paul's tormentors. In time, Paul healed from the years of bullying—he made friends, enrolled in martial arts, and took on a leadership role.

But not all children recover so well. News reports recount too many stories of children who commit violent acts against themselves or others in response to persistent bullying.

Paul's story is played out every day in schools around the world. A child, like Sam, picks on another child, engaging in behaviors like name-calling and other mistreatments. Adults are unaware of the mean behavior and therefore do not intervene. When adults do not step in, children assume that the behavior is okay and the meanness escalates, with classmates encouraging the mean behavior through watching, laughing, and even joining in. After many years of being treated in this way, adolescents often can't imagine that their life will ever improve.

Children's lives in school don't need to be this way. Educators in many schools and classrooms teach children how to be kind and inclusive. In these classrooms there are clear rules about how to treat one another, lessons to help children recognize bullying and other mean behavior, and protocols to help them treat children who are bullied respectfully and report the mean behavior to trusted adults.

The focus of this book is on preventing bullying—by identifying and intervening in the small, mean behaviors that can escalate into full-blown bullying and by creating an environment where kindness rather than meanness prevails.

What Is Bullying?

The federal government defines bullying as unwanted aggressive behavior between school-aged children. They define it as a way that a child with physical or social power abuses a less powerful child. Bullying behaviors are also behaviors that are repeated or have the potential to be repeated (StopBullying.gov 2020).

I begin by sharing the federal definition of bullying for the simple reason that this is a book about preventing it. But there's perhaps a less obvious reason for teachers to understand how bullying differs from other kinds of mean behavior: For the safety of the bullied child, bullying requires a different set of responses from adults than aggression that grows out of conflict between equals. I talk about this in the chapters that follow.

Bullying can be physical, relational, or both

Bullying can consist of an act or series of acts of physical violence, such as hitting, pinching, tripping, shoving, or spilling things on someone. Bullying can also consist of acts of relational aggression such as purposely excluding someone or spreading rumors about someone.

Relational bullying can be direct or indirect. When Matt says to the other children in his class, "Let's call Mia 'Fluffernutter,'" and they chant "Fluffernutter, Fluffernutter" softly in the cafeteria so that Mia can hear while the adults can't, that's direct relational aggression. If Matt had told everyone, "Don't play with Mia," and Mia couldn't figure out why no one would play with her, that's indirect relational aggression. Matt might escalate the aggression by adding an indirect cyberbully piece. For example, he might encourage classmates to anonymously reject Mia in an electronic role-playing game. All of these acts are bullying because they are assertions of power by Matt over Mia and all are abusive behaviors.

Scope of the problem

Bullying is pervasive and worldwide, and is not rooted in any one culture. Children bully other children in rural, urban, and suburban schools, and at every income level. The Olweus Bullying Prevention Program, created by

Dr. Dan Olweus (the Scandinavian psychologist who originated modern bullying prevention programs), issued a report in 2019 using data gathered from a sample of 245,000 elementary and high school children in the United States who responded to the Olweus Bullying Questionnaire (Luxemberg, Limber, and Olweus 2019). This questionnaire is administered to students whose school is preparing to begin the Olweus Bullying Prevention Program. In the questionnaire, bullying is defined, in child-friendly terms, as negative, hurtful behavior that occurred repeatedly and involved an imbalance of power. Questions are multiple choice and the responses use specific language that is designed to minimize subjective reporting. For example, a question might ask if a particular behavior occurred once a month, two or three times a week, and so on, rather than using terms such as "seldom" or "frequently." Questions cover a range of bullying behaviors that fall into three general categories:

- Direct bullying (physical aggression or name-calling)
- Indirect bullying (exclusion or rumor spreading)
- Cyberbullying

Data showed that for children in grades three to five, 22 to 27 percent of the children reported being bullied by others at least two to three times in the previous month. In the database, 7 to 14 percent of children in grades three to five admitted to bullying others in the past month (Luxemberg, Limber, and Olweus 2019). Other researchers report that as many as 33.7 percent of elementary school children in the United States say that they have been bullied at some time (Bradshaw, Sawyer, and O'Brennan 2007).

Bullying behavior frequently starts as early as preschool or kindergarten when children begin to establish power relationships (Alsaker and Valkanover 2012; Yerger and Gehret 2011). Multiple studies have demonstrated that many children continue to be targeted year after year. Olweus reports that 39 percent of elementary school girls and 45 percent of elementary school boys who reported being bullied said that they had been bullied for more than a year. Fifty percent of the high school students who reported being bullied had been bullied for more than a year (Olweus and Limber 2007).

Who is part of a bullying interaction?

The child doing the bullying

Bullying is about power—gaining power, asserting it, and maintaining it. It's difficult—and not very useful—to assign a "bully personality profile." In the past, children who bullied were often described as children who were outcasts, on the fringes. In contrast to that, some studies have shown that children who bully repeatedly are often the popular kids, with high self-esteem (Menesini et al. 2003). One study shows that students who engage in bullying behavior are often in the middle of the social hierarchy and use bullying as a way to achieve higher status (Faris and Felmlee 2011).

The common characteristic is that the child who bullies sees assertion of power as desirable and social-emotional or physical aggression as the best or only way to rise in the social hierarchy.

Other studies have found that children who repeatedly bully show moral disengagement (Gini, Pozzoli, and Hymel 2014) and a lack of empathy (Zych et al. 2019). They often think that what they're doing is just fine and it's the bullied child's own fault that they are different and therefore deserve being treated meanly. The children who bullied felt that they deserve power and that "the loser" deserves the treatment they are receiving.

The child who is targeted

Although all children have the potential to be bullied, some are more frequently bullied than others. Children who are shy or less assertive than others have few strategies for protecting themselves. Children who are different in any number of ways may be bullied frequently. Jo Ann Freiberg, formerly the Connecticut State Department of Education bullying consultant, reported that her caseload of children being bullied overwhelmingly consisted of those with special needs (J. Freiberg, personal communication, June 2010). Looking different, acting different, or having self-protection skills that are less developed than those of their classmates all made the children in her caseload more likely to be bullied.

Children who do not conform to gender stereotypes can also be bullied. "She plays with the boys" or "He's gay" might be the opening gambits

(GLSEN 2012). Children who may be targeted include those who are overweight, who dress differently, whose family incomes are different (either lower or higher) from those of their classmates, or children whose skills and interests are simply different from those of their classmates (GLSEN 2012; Olweus and Limber 2007).

> ### Use Language That Focuses on the Action, Not the Person
>
> Everyone has the potential to engage in mean behaviors. For most, it's a transient action. But some people can get stuck in the mean behavior. When we use terms like "the bully" we risk stereotyping children and helping them stay stuck in that role. For that reason, throughout this book I use phrases that focus on the action rather than the person—for example, "bullying behavior" and "the person doing the bullying." These phrases communicate a belief that the person can do better and open the door for change.
>
> Similarly, terms like "the victim" risk stereotyping a bullied child as weak or helpless. It's only a few steps from calling someone "the victim" to blaming them for playing that role. If instead we refer to the "person who is bullied," then we place responsibility on the person doing the bullying and free from blame the person who is bullied.

Studies show that there are a small number of children who go back and forth, who sometimes instigate mean behavior and who sometimes are the target of mean behavior (Olweus 1993; StopBullying.gov 2017b). These are often the children who have poor social skills, are quick to anger, lack self-control, and have few or no friends to support them. Marie, who is often picked on or ignored, discovers that if she spreads gossip about Kaitlyn she's suddenly the center of attention in the classroom. However, next week Marie may be targeted when Kaitlyn rallies friends to gang up on her.

Witnesses to the mean behavior

Bullying is a social act. Researchers have found that 85 percent of bullying incidents include not just the child who bullies and the child targeted but also an audience: the children who witness the mean behavior. These bystanders are an important part of the equation. Often, the child who bullies will be trying to appear powerful to the audience as much as to the child bullied. In many cases, bullying needs this audience if it is to thrive; one way to thwart the bullying is for the audience to show disapproval (Craig and Pepler 1998).

The Olweus Bullying Prevention Program describes multiple roles that bystanders might play. At one end are those who actively join in the bullying. At the other end are those who try to help the child who is targeted. Most bystanders fall in between. Some don't take an active part but support the bullying through laughter or other signs of approval; others simply watch. Some quiet bystanders might be uncomfortable with the bullying behavior, but they don't intervene (Lambe et al. 2019; Olweus and Limber 2007; StopBullying.gov 2017b).

Even if bystanders only watch, the message to the child doing the bullying is that their behavior is acceptable. On the other hand, if bystanders show disapproval, the message is quite the opposite and can have a powerful effect. In a classic Canadian study, researchers used hidden video cameras and microphones to observe children on the playground. They found that 57 percent of the time when peers intervened in bullying incidents the mean behavior stopped in an average of ten seconds (Craig and Pepler 1998).

All too often, bullying prevention policies focus on how to teach the children who are bullied to stand up to bullying. This is not a realistic approach. We don't expect people who are robbed at gunpoint to stand up to the criminals, for example, and we don't expect people who are targets of domestic abuse to "just walk away" or to "tell the batterer to stop." We need to make bullying as socially unacceptable as domestic abuse or armed robbery. We need to teach children to take care of each other—we need to turn bystanders into allies.

Adults

Adults are often unaware of bullying behavior in schools and classrooms. In study after study, adults underestimated the prevalence of bullying (National School Climate Survey, n.d.; O'Brennan, Waasdorp, and Bradshaw 2014). In the Canadian study of Craig and Pepler (1998), they observed behavior on the playground and in classrooms. The researchers recorded an average of one bullying incident every seven minutes, with adults intervening in only 4 percent of these incidents. Even more alarming is the fact that when researchers observed classrooms, they noted that when adults were present in the room they intervened in only 14 percent of the incidents that occurred—despite the fact that 71 percent of these same adults reported that they "nearly always" intervened in bullying incidents.

The Olweus Bully Prevention Program's 2019 survey of nearly a quarter million school children found that over a two-month span 34 percent of high school students and 44 percent of middle school students reported that bullying incidents had happened in their classrooms with a teacher present but not intervening. Only half of the third, fourth, and fifth graders surveyed reported that their teachers intervened in such situations (Luxemberg, Limber, and Olweus 2019).

What Can We Do?

A wealth of research as well as the experiences of classroom teachers tells us that there's a lot that they can do to prevent bullying in their classrooms and in their schools (Bear 1998; Espelage and De La Rue 2012; Kasen et al. 2004; Katz and Chard 2000; Pepler and Craig 2007; Wang, Berry, and Swearer 2013; Yerger and Gehret 2011). Taking the following steps will decrease the likelihood of unkind behavior and increase the likelihood that students will stand up for each other and report unkind behavior to the teacher.

- First, teachers can build a classroom community where everyone feels valued and included. They can help students build strong, positive relationships with each other and with the teacher, and they can establish rules that guide children toward kind, friendly, and inclusive behavior.

- Once the rules are established, teachers can take the time to help children understand how the rules apply to a range of school situations and make sure children know that teachers hold them accountable for their behavior.

- Teachers can also increase their observation and awareness of the small, mean behaviors that can develop into bullying.

- Finally, teachers can give students the tools they'll need to address mean behavior when they witness it.

Much of the current research and writing focuses on schoolwide practices to address bullying. And indeed, a schoolwide approach is optimal. But even if your school has not instituted schoolwide changes, there is still much you can do in your classroom and in collaboration with grade-level team members to create a safe climate for learning.

My experience in over thirty-plus years in elementary schools is that children can meet the expectations of the classroom, even when those expectations are quite different from those outside the classroom. Moreover, children can take what they learn in the classroom out into the world around them. As you change your classroom, you might just be taking steps toward changing your school.

Strategies to Prevent Bullying

In writing this book, I drew on my many years of experience as a classroom teacher as well as on the wealth of thinking and research on how to prevent bullying. For much of my teaching career, I used the *Responsive Classroom*® approach to teaching. One of its missions is to give teachers the tools they need to create and maintain safe, caring, and joyful classrooms and to teach children to be kind and caring outside the classroom walls as well.

Many of the social-emotional learning strategies of the approach are effective ones for bullying prevention. In the following chapters you'll find information about helping children get to know each other through the structures of a daily Morning Meeting, creating positively stated rules that are connected to students' learning goals, using Interactive Modeling and role-play to help children apply expectations to specific situations, and responding quickly and calmly to misbehavior.

If you are already familiar with the *Responsive Classroom* approach, I hope you'll gain a new appreciation of how consistent use of *Responsive Classroom* strategies can be an effective tool in your bullying prevention efforts.

And if you are not implementing the *Responsive Classroom* approach, I believe you can find ways to adapt these strategies to your own classroom structures. If you'd like to learn more about the approach, you'll find rich resources at www.responsiveclassroom.org.

Topics covered in this book include the following:

Addressing gateway behaviors. I begin the book by talking about gateway behaviors—those small acts of disrespect or unkindness that we often let slide, giving children the message that these behaviors are acceptable (Englander 2013). We hear one child call another child names. We notice two children sitting close together in a way that excludes another child. We hear about one child taking another child's cookie at lunch.

Although these are small acts, lack of attention to such behaviors can lead to full-blown bullying. It's important to notice and respond to these behaviors appropriately, nonpunitively, and calmly. Keeping the response nonpunitive is especially important—there is research that shows that when children are exposed to aggressive punishments, they become more aggressive (Divecha and Brackett 2020; Olweus and Limber 2007).

The goal is to firmly show children that meanness is unacceptable, to teach them more appropriate social skills, and to help them begin to develop habits of kindness. To learn more about this, see Chapter One.

Building a positive and safe classroom community from day one. Research indicates that bullying happens less frequently in classrooms where all children are included in activities (Divecha and Brackett 2020; Espelage and DaLaRue 2012; Gottfredson 2000; StopBullying.gov 2017a). It also indicates that bullying happens less frequently in classrooms where the teacher shows warmth and responsiveness to children (Elledge et al. 2016; Olweus and Limber 2007; Wang, Berry, and Swearer 2013). Researchers have discovered that these variables account for widely divergent amounts of bullying behavior in the same school and even among various classes at the same grade level (Henry et al. 2000). I'll present a number of strategies in Chapters Two, Three, and Four that will help you create a safe classroom community.

Creating rules. Rules are essential guideposts to children's behavior and are a key ingredient in most evidence-based bullying prevention programs (StopBullying.gov 2017c; Swearer et al. 2010; Wang, Berry, and Swearer 2013). Rules set the standard for how children treat each other, their classroom, and their work. But for rules to be effective, teachers need to do ongoing work with students to help them understand how the classroom rules apply to day-to-day situations. For more information about creating and applying rules, see Chapter Three.

Teach children to report. To effectively address bullying, we need children to become allies who protect the child being bullied by reporting to an adult.

Without adequate teaching about what and how to report, children are reluctant to report bullying to trusted adults in school. Research has shown that younger children are more willing to report incidents of bullying than older children (Yerger and Gehret 2011). Nonetheless, in the database of more than 245,000 responses to the Olweus Bullying Questionnaire in 2019, 55 percent of the third through fifth graders (the youngest children in the sample) who reported being bullied in the previous two months had not reported it to a teacher (Luxemberg, Limber, and Olweus 2019). The good news is that this is an improvement from when the questionnaire was administered in 2010, when 70 percent of third graders had not reported being bullied to a teacher.

One factor in children's reluctance to report bullying to adults in school is that all too often we give mixed messages: on the one hand, asking children to tell us about bullying, and on the other hand, chastising them for "tattling." It's important to help children understand the difference between telling the teacher about small behaviors that they can let go of or resolve independently and reporting mean behavior to a trusted adult to keep someone safe. To learn more about this, see Chapters Three and Six.

Addressing outside-the-classroom behaviors. Research shows that a lot of bullying and pre-bullying behavior occurs in areas of the school outside of the classroom, such as the hallway, playground, lunchroom, and school bus (Olweus and Limber 2007; Ttofi and Farrington 2011). It can also spill into the cyber world, both at school and outside of school. School rules and anti-bullying protocols are an important piece of addressing bullying in these areas. But there's also a lot that classroom teachers can do to help children apply the kind behaviors they're learning in the classroom to other parts of the school and the electronic world. In Chapter Five, you'll learn about specific strategies for helping students be better citizens.

Teaching digital citizenship. Elementary school students do engage in cyberbullying. However, it is nearly always an extension of classroom bullying rather than a stand-alone behavior (Luxemberg, Limber, and Olweus 2019). As students begin to use electronic devices, teaching about safe and friendly use of these devices is vital. In Chapter Six you'll learn about how to connect kindness in the classroom to kindness in the electronic world.

Working with parents. Communication with parents is a critical element in preventing bullying. Parents can let teachers know about children's behavior at home that might indicate problems at school and teachers can let parents know about classroom bullying prevention strategies. One international meta-analysis of bullying prevention programs found that a strong parent component was an important part of every successful bullying prevention program (Farrington and Ttofi 2009). You'll find information about working with parents in each chapter.

> ### About the Term "Parent"
> Students come from a variety of homes with a variety of family structures. Students might be raised by grandparents, siblings, aunts, uncles, or foster families. I want to honor all these people for devoting their time, love, and attention to raising children. However, it's hard to find just one word that adequately encompasses all these caregivers. For simplicity's sake, I use "parent" to refer to anyone who is a child's primary caregiver.

Teaching children about bullying. Children need to know what bullying is and how to prevent it. Direct teaching may help a child who is tempted to bully to stop and think. It may empower a child who is targeted to seek help. The most effective lessons about bullying, however, focus on helping children who witness bullying to be an ally of the child who is bullied. Children can learn to avoid laughing at the bullied child's expense, to befriend that child and comfort him, and, most important, to tell a responsible adult.

To have a positive classroom and school climate free from meanness that might escalate into bullying behaviors, we also need to directly teach children some of the subtleties of social discourse. What is the difference between laughing for fun, say at a silly joke, and laughing at someone's expense, which violates our rule to be kind? Why is it important to refer to people by their names rather than unfriendly nicknames that they may not like?

For more about this, including lesson plan ideas, see Chapter Seven.

Final Thoughts

Teachers have an important opportunity—and an obligation—to curb mean behavior. The elementary school years are a period during which adults can make a big difference. Children in grades K–5 are more willing to turn to adults for help solving relationship problems than are their older peers. Furthermore, children's attitudes toward school and learning are formed in the early years of school. By creating a climate of safety and inclusion in elementary school classrooms, teachers can support children in taking risks and discovering the joys of learning in their current lives and in the years to come.

CHAPTER ONE

Gateway Behaviors: What to Do When Mean Acts Emerge

Arriving at school in the morning, fifth graders take down their chairs as Ms. Hernandez collects homework and oversees lunch sign-up. Max approaches Jason. "Did your mom let you watch *Game of Thrones* last night or did she make you go to bed early?" he asks. "Naw," Jason replies, a little abashed, "She told me I had to go to bed." Max smirks. Clearly uncomfortable, Jason turns away. In the competition for who gets to be the most grown-up, Max wins because he stayed up late on a school night. Moreover, he got to watch a violent, adult-rated TV show. Is Max's behavior bullying? No, of course not. But it is a first step in social competition.

Next door, as children trickle into their third grade classroom, Missy whispers to Laticia, "Eww, that purple hair is ugly. You'll never get a boyfriend." Is that bullying? Maybe. We'd need to know more to be sure. Whether or not it's bullying, it's certainly social aggression.

When small aggressive acts are left unchecked, they can grow to permeate a classroom and become the accepted mode of interaction. Mean acts and words become the norm. Only a few steps separate competition about who has more privileges at home to openly calling Jason a "baby" and then to excluding Jason from games at recess. It's even fewer steps from directly insulting Laticia about her hair to repeatedly insulting her and organizing other girls to do the same.

Once such disrespectful behaviors are normalized, they can take on a life of their own in classrooms. Classmates may watch and even laugh at the cruelty, rewarding the child who initiates these behaviors with attention and social cachet. This encourages the child behaving meanly to escalate the unkind behavior.

Barbara Coloroso, in *The Bully, the Bullied, and the Not-So-Innocent Bystander* (2016), paints a picture of a typical bullying scenario. Children are playing on the playground. The child planning to bully brushes up against another child as if by accident. When no one comes to the targeted child's defense, the child who is bullying snatches his classmate's ball and throws it away. If no one objects to that, things escalate, first into name-calling, then shoving, hitting, and more. The bullying becomes chronic as the child doing the bullying feels powerful in his cruelty and the child who is targeted blames him- or herself.

Stephen Wessler, an attorney and retired school violence prosecutor for the state of Maine, reports that every school violence case he prosecuted, including those that led to death, began with mean words (Wessler 2003).

"We Need to Focus on the Small Stuff"

If we catch the small initial behaviors, referred to as "gateway behaviors" by Elizabeth Englander of the Massachusetts Aggression Reduction Center (MARC), and nip them in the bud, they won't have an opportunity to grow and blossom into out-and-out bullying. As Englander says, "We need to focus on the small behaviors that express contempt." The first step in meeting this challenge is to watch for the subtle acts of aggression that may be going on in our classrooms. Next, we must stop the inappropriate behavior quickly, respectfully, and consistently (Englander 2017).

In the two examples presented at the beginning of this chapter, neither teacher was aware of the comments. A great deal of research demonstrates that teachers are often unaware of both small acts of social aggression—gateway behaviors to bullying—and out-and-out bullying (Craig and Pepler 1998; Englander 2013). Often educators are unsure of how to intervene when they do see or hear questionable behavior (Berguno et al. 2004; Biggs et al. 2008; Duong and Bradshaw 2013). When children notice that their teachers do not intervene, they conclude that social cruelty is acceptable (Gini et al. 2008). Children make comments under their breath, give a classmate a quick kick when the teacher's back is turned, or pass notes with mean comments. Amazingly, we teachers often miss these behaviors even if we're in the classroom when they happen. The National School Climate Center (n.d.) notes that students "report feeling significantly less socially and physically safe than adults realize."

Although it's true that teachers miss many mean behaviors, it's also true that such behaviors often happen during less supervised times of the school day and in less supervised areas.

School, however, doesn't need to be this way. In this chapter I will describe strategies that you can use to hone your skills of noticing mean behaviors. I discuss how to tell the difference between what's developmentally appropriate and what's a gateway to bullying. Finally, I provide guidelines for stopping the gateway behaviors.

Observe Student Interactions

If teachers are to reduce or prevent bullying, they first need to notice the many small, mean-spirited acts that can lead to it. Making time to observe your students' interactions might seem daunting in a day already packed with responsibilities. Nonetheless, by making small adjustments to daily routines, you can find time for quick observations. Here are some ideas:

- **Use arrival time to observe students' interactions.** It's tempting to use arrival time to do administrative tasks such as lunch count and homework check-off. However, you can give students responsibility for such tasks. If you spend time observing, you'll gain valuable information about students. With such an arrangement, Max and Jason's teacher might have noticed their interaction, and Missy and Laticia's teacher might have heard their whispered conversation.

- **Make time to observe during lunch.** If you eat lunch with your students, rotate where you sit so that you can see how a variety of students treat each other. If you're not on duty during lunch, I suggest that you get to the lunchroom a couple of minutes before it's time to pick up your students. Use this time to quietly observe and learn about what the students are doing. One day, I arrived at the lunchroom a few minutes early to hear Joey say to Michael, "Look at your ugly pasta." Bullying? No, but possibly mean and hurtful in a way that could escalate if we don't investigate further and intervene if the teasing is truly mean and not playful.

- **Use informal moments during choice time, indoor recess, or independent work time to observe the social culture of the classroom.** Notice who gravitates toward whom and who is alone. Both are indicators of a climate of inclusion and exclusion, clues that might alert you to behaviors that are potential gateways to bullying. A fully inclusive classroom protects against bullying.

Assess Your Observations

For your observations to be useful, you'll need to assess what you're seeing and hearing so you can understand what it's telling you about your classroom and then guide possible interventions. What follows are some key things to pay attention to.

Notice children's words

Is the tone mean and insulting?

Take the case of Joey, Michael, and the "ugly pasta" described earlier. Teasing can be mean and hurtful or it can be a bonding experience between close friends. Ask yourself, who is enjoying the joke? Who is made uncomfortable? Body language can provide clues. Is the joke followed by shared laughter or is only the person who made the joke laughing? Do the children lean in together or does the person joked about pull away?

Jokes about someone else's body (the purple hair), family ("Your mother . . ."), abilities ("You read like a baby"), and food (the ugly pasta) are often meant to demean. On the other hand, jokes about shared events leading to shared laughter can solidify friendships.

In the "ugly pasta" situation, I first spoke privately with Michael to ask how he felt when Joey made the comment about his pasta. "It hurt my feelings when he made fun of my food," he said. I then had a serious private talk with Joey. For a few weeks, I kept a close eye on the two boys, watching for further signs of mean behavior, and found that the early intervention appeared to stop it.

Is code being used to indicate who is "in" and who is "out"?

Besides mean words and casual insults, no matter how small, there are more subtle things to listen for. Children's conversation reveals a lot about who is "in" and who is "out." One year, some boys in my third grade class started calling each other "Bubba." I noticed that some boys, though, were not called "Bubba" and were left out of the "Bubba" inner circle. I followed up this observation with a class discussion about nicknames. I explained that sometimes the use of nicknames can be hurtful or a means of excluding others. We agreed that in school we'd call everybody by their given name. My students took this decision seriously and, going forward, were careful to use each other's names correctly.

Notice children's interactions

Who's in charge? Who's included? Who's left out?

When students work together in small groups, whether for reading, writing, math, science, or social studies, take a minute to observe their interactions. Notice who gets a turn and who is left out, who takes charge and who sits back. These moments will give you rich information that will help you protect your classroom climate, keeping it kind, inclusive, and safe.

If someone is chronically left out, listen to conversations around that child. What are the other children saying to or about the isolated child? If one student is consistently in charge, listen to the words and tone that child uses to maintain control.

One day, I sat quietly on the side while a group worked on a social studies project. Manuel and Sarah were planning their diorama while Justin sat and listened. Were Manuel and Sarah excluding? Was Justin sitting back and letting them do the work? As I observed Justin over time, I noticed that no one spoke to him, and no one made a place for him in the circle, much less sought him out for work and play.

I came to discover that Justin, seemingly surrounded by classmates, was nonetheless an ignored child in the social life of the classroom. Aware of that fact because of my observations, I arranged for Justin to partner with children who might share interests with him. For reading, I partnered him with Allan, who also loved to read Dragon Masters books. I noticed that Justin really enjoyed working with his kindergarten buddy and so did Miguel. I arranged for the two of them to help the kindergartners with their snowsuits at the end of the day. Soon, Miguel, Allan, and Justin were seeking one another out in the classroom. Justin was moving into the circle of our community.

Investigate why a child is isolated

Are one or more of the students in your classroom, like Justin, always alone? If there's an opportunity to choose partners, are these students the last chosen? Where is the isolation coming from? Finding answers may take a bit of investigating, including a conversation with the child who is isolated.

Be sure to check in with the child privately. My experience and that of many experts who work to prevent bullying is that children who are targeted for bullying are so intimidated that they're unlikely to be truthful in front of the children who are being unkind (Olweus and Limber 2007).

When I noticed that Suzy was always alone on the playground, I asked her about it in private. "Clarisse doesn't like me anymore," she explained. It turned out that Clarisse had told all the other girls not to play with her. I knew I needed to act on that information.

I had a private talk with Clarisse. I told her that I'd noticed that Suzy was alone

> ### If You Suspect Bullying, Do Not Use Conflict Resolution
>
> In the situation involving Suzy and Clarisse, I did not use the strategy of a student-to-student conflict resolution meeting. When one child tells others not to play with a classmate, this is not a conflict to be resolved between the child doing the telling and the one being excluded. It's an aggressive act that needs to be stopped. Conflict resolution meetings are a strategy used between equal participants to help them learn to listen to each other. When there's a difference between real or perceived power, the behavior may be a gateway behavior or even actual bullying. In the situation such as the one with Suzy and Clarisse, it's unfair—and possibly dangerous—to the child who is targeted to expect them to take part in a conflict resolution meeting (Burke 2019).

on the playground. I asked her what she'd noticed about who was included in the group of girls who played together. Her response was, "Suzy's a baby; we don't like to play with her." I let her know that it wasn't okay to exclude Suzy. "Suzy's a member of our classroom community. You need to include her in games on the playground, just the way you include others," I said.

I also told her that I'd heard from a couple of sources that she had been telling others not to play with Suzy. I didn't open it up for discussion. I simply said, "Our rule says we'll be kind to all. It's not okay to tell others not to play with someone. I know that you can be kind and include everyone. I'll be watching to make sure that you do."

Just as I had with Justin, I helped other girls in the class connect with Suzy by arranging suitable reading and writing partnerships. I also used some strategies with the whole class, such as revisiting our classroom community-created rule to be kind, and leading a role-play on how to include everyone. Soon Suzy was back in the mix of girls playing together on the playground.

Keep in mind that a child sitting alone does not always indicate they've been excluded. For example, one day I arrived to pick up students in the lunchroom. As I stood and watched for a minute, I saw Halima sitting alone at the edge of the group. Later on I asked her, privately, about her lunchroom seat. "I like to sit there because then I can talk with Dorthea, my friend in Mrs. Kelly's class," she explained. So she wasn't being excluded; she was just making a choice.

Consider children's stage of development: Is this typical behavior? Is it okay behavior?

Was the spate of "Bubba" nicknames in my classroom a developmentally predictable behavior? Perhaps. Nevertheless, it was exclusionary and thus not acceptable in our classroom any more than exclusionary child-created "clubs" were.

In contrast, some developmentally predictable behaviors may look unkind but are actually okay, and not necessarily destructive to the classroom feeling of community. When two eleven-year-old girls pick each other out as "best friends" they're learning how to have a close friend, an important part of life. It's important to make sure that they are friendly to all their classmates and continue to work with children who are not part of the dyad, but no one would benefit from trying to prevent the selective friendship.

How do you know whether or not children are engaging in cruel behaviors, a step along the continuum toward bullying? How do you know how to respond? Here are some things to look for.

Look for equity

Kindergartners will sometimes express displeasure by saying "You can't come to my birthday party," never mind that the birthday is six months away, in the summer, and no party is planned. Usually "You can't come to my birthday party" is said, for example, after a tablemate snatches a crayon or takes someone's place in line. It's one way that a five-year-old knows to express displeasure.

If the "You can't come to my birthday party" insult is an equally expressed back and forth between two children, then it's probably not a step along the bullying continuum. It does, though, call for some social skills instruction on what to do if someone snatches your crayon or cuts in front of you in line.

On the other hand, if there's one child who is consistently told that he's not coming to anyone's birthday party, consistently told that he can play only if he'll be the dog, or is usually the one chased on the playground, then there's a power imbalance that might very well grow into bullying.

> ### Consider Erring on the Side of Caution
>
> It can be difficult to tell whether seemingly mean words are hurtful or not, and whether they are the first steps toward bullying or they are bonding events between equals. In the end, for the sake of emotional and physical safety, you may decide to simply tell students, "We only use kind words in this class." Children can trade insults in fun at home.
>
> You may also decide to simply say, "In this class we keep our bodies to ourselves." Rough-and-tumble play can be reserved for situations outside of school. You may decide to say, "In this class, everyone needs someone to play with, so we include everyone unless they want to be by themselves."
>
> Such guidelines will not only clarify for children what is—and is not—acceptable, it will minimize the number of judgment calls you need to make in assessing their interactions.

Look at children's facial expressions and body language

Watch to see whether children's expressions are friendly, neutral, or grudging. Look at their bodies. Do they lean into their partner or away? Is their posture open and welcoming or closed?

Many eleven-year-old boys love to trade insults. If two boys are engaged in such a contest, and each is giving as good as he gets, the situation has met the standard of equity. If they're both laughing and smiling, they're probably engaged in verbal play rather than taking a step toward bullying.

The six-year-old boys' equivalent to older boys' trading of insults is rough-and-tumble play. When first graders burst onto the playground after a morning of concentrated academic work, they butt and roll like puppies. It is the six-year-olds' equivalent to older boys' trading insults. It's likely not an expression of social aggression—unless there's one boy who's always getting knocked over while the others are doing all the knocking. Are they all laughing and smiling or is there one who doesn't look like he's enjoying this type of play?

Pay attention to children who might be at risk of being targeted

Any child has the potential to be targeted by bullying behavior. Nonetheless, some children are more likely to be targeted than others.

Children who look different from others

Is the child overweight? Do they wear glasses? Does the child dress differently from their classmates? Whether the difference in appearance is the result of family income, body type, or parenting styles, when children are perceived to be different from their classmates they might be at greater risk for bullying (GLSEN 2012).

Children who don't conform to gender stereotypes

The girl who prefers to play football, for example, or the boy who likes to wear dresses are at greater risk for bullying. Keep your eyes open to see if such children are being excluded, surreptitiously insulted, or nudged out of the way (GLSEN 2012).

Children receiving special education services

Many researchers identify children receiving special education services as being at a high risk for bullying because they may seem a bit different or more vulnerable to their classmates (Freiberg 2009; Olweus and Limber 2007; StopBullying.gov 2021b). It's important to make sure that children receiving special education services are included and treated respectfully (GLSEN 2012).

When I began teaching, one of my colleagues told me that I'd need to have "eyes in the back of the head." Those eyes need to be wide open to protect the at-risk child.

Pay attention to children who might be at risk of engaging in bullying behavior

Anyone has the potential to engage in meanness and bullying behavior. Nonetheless, there are some risk factors indicating who may more easily fall into that role.

The child in the middle

If bullying is about gaining and maintaining social power, then it's important to watch children in the middle of the social hierarchy who might be trying to gain power as well as those children who have gained power through sometimes subtle cruelty and are seeking to maintain it.

The "popular" child

Research over the last two decades has shown that popular kids are often the children who bully (StopBullying.gov 2021b). Often these popular children are liked by adults as well as by other children. It's easy to miss the fact that someone so likeable is being cruel. The popular child may be articulate, funny, physically attractive, good at sports, and have lots of friends—qualities that may be as attractive to adults as they are to children.

This is why it's important to observe students' behavior objectively. By paying attention to the child whom you like so much, you may be inadvertently making too many allowances for their unkind behavior.

Mrs. Sharpe is a school librarian in a small rural school. She sees all students in the school once a week for library class and therefore knows every student well. "There's a boy in sixth grade, Jackson, that everyone picks on," she told me. "The children take off their shoes when they sit on the library carpet," she continued. "They're all sitting there and suddenly they start to say, 'Eww, Jackson's feet smell.' Well, all of their feet smell, but they're all blaming Jackson."

I asked her if someone in particular started the insults and she said that she'd watch and see. A few weeks later she told me, "I've been noticing. It's always Wayne who starts it off. Once he starts in on Jackson, the others follow. They all want to be Wayne's friend. I don't blame them. I'd like to be Wayne's friend, too. He's smart, he's funny, and he's good at sports."

It's important to notice children who might be at risk. It's also important not to make assumptions. Any child can be targeted. Any child can find themselves drawn into aggressive behavior. If you watch objectively, then you'll put yourself in the best position to be the most helpful to all students.

Intervening: Stop Small Behaviors Before They Become Big Problems

Once you've done some observing to better understand students' social interactions, the next step is to use that understanding to stop behaviors that might be gateways to bullying when it's still relatively easy to do so. Sometimes teachers are unsure whether they should step in when someone says, "Your pasta is ugly." Isn't he just expressing his opinion? Well, yes, but he's also possibly being unkind. What about, "Your purple hair is ugly and you'll never get a boyfriend"? That's certainly an unkind statement, and one about a part of the targeted child's body—her hair. It is also a potential opening move in a chain of escalating events and is very much worth stopping.

In the following pages I'll spell out strategies for stopping such small mean behaviors. Classroom and school rules, teacher language, fair and respectful consequences, and teacher modeling all play a part.

Stop gateway behaviors quickly

It's important to intervene as soon as you notice unkind actions or hear unkind words. Elizabeth Englander promotes the "nine second" response: Spend the first two seconds noticing and the next seven seconds briefly and firmly responding (Englander 2013).

Although it may take you more than two seconds to figure out what's going on when a student rolls their eyes or makes a mean joke at the expense of another, Englander's point—that a quick response is important—fits with my experience working with children. A quick response makes it clear to the child engaging in social cruelty, the child targeted, and any nearby students that mean behavior and exclusion are unacceptable in the classroom (Englander 2013).

In research conducted by MARC, students reported that the most damaging thing adults did in response to gateway behaviors was to ignore them (Englander 2013). When adults miss the opportunity to respond quickly, they often end up looking as if they're ignoring the behavior (Gini et al. 2008). Bystanders then think that the behavior is acceptable, and children who say or do unkind things don't have an opportunity to learn about the impact of their behavior and how to change it. In some cases, the targeted children start to believe they somehow deserve the bad treatment. Not responding quickly sets up conditions for mean behaviors and bullying to flourish.

Refer to classroom rules

One of the challenges of these gateway behaviors is that it's not always clear what to say and how to stop them. This is where classroom rules can play an important role. In Chapter Three, you'll learn about a process for establishing classroom rules that children connect to and believe in as well as the reporting of rule-breaking. If children are invested in the rules and understand that they help keep everyone safe, then the rules can provide a solid framework for stopping small cruelties.

"Our rules say to be kind; that statement was not kind" is a short and simple way to refer to the rules and stop the behavior. Another approach is to give the student the opportunity to reflect on their behavior. A teacher might say, "Think about our rule to be kind. How can you be kind right now?"

Whichever of these approaches you use, you are avoiding a power struggle with the student by referring to the rules. It's the rules that are saying to stop the mean behavior, not the teacher.

Use brief, matter-of-fact language to remind and redirect

Short, simple statements are most effective in stopping small unkind comments or actions. "Stop, that was not a kind statement; reset and say it kindly" is clear and succinct. It's tempting to go on and on, telling children about all of the ramifications of their actions. You can be sure that as you go on and on they will tune you out.

> **Some Language to Try**
>
> *Stop, reset, refresh.*
>
> *Use kind words.*
>
> *Our rule says . . .*
>
> *Think about our rule . . . ; how can you follow it?*
>
> *In our class, everyone gets to play.*
>
> *In our class, we keep bodies to ourselves.*

A matter-of-fact tone will allow children to listen. In contrast, a blaming or shaming tone will lead children to feel belittled and resentful. The same words can sound calm or shrill, straightforward or sarcastic. Statements such as "That sounds unkind" or "Keep your feet in your own personal space" will be heard best if they're stated calmly.

Try coming up with some potential statements that you might use when you hear unkind comments or see unkind actions. Practice them. That way, in the actual situation, you'll have some phrases and a matter-of-fact tone of voice that will come naturally.

For more information on reminding and redirecting language, see *The Power of Our Words: Teacher Language That Helps Children Learn*, 2nd edition, by Paula Denton (see Appendix B).

Model respectful and assertive responses to meanness and bullying

Research on bullying shows that classmates can—and sometimes do—step in and effectively stop bullying and gateway behaviors. But why don't they step in more often? There are many reasons, but one of them is that students aren't sure whether or not the behavior they're witnessing is okay. When they see adults letting it go, they learn that they should also do so. On the other hand, when you practice respectful and assertive ways to stop cruel behaviors, you set a standard of kindness and let students know that they also shouldn't let mean behaviors go.

Furthermore, you're showing children how to take a respectful and assertive stance against meanness and bullying. The Olweus Bullying Prevention Program states, "When children see adults taking positive action against bullying behavior, it empowers them to do the same" (Olweus and Limber 2007, 33). By their actions, teachers can give a clear message that any kind of mean behavior is unacceptable.

At the same time, it's important to model respectful behavior toward all students, including the child who is being unkind. If you stop mean behaviors with disrespect, a harsh tone, or sarcastic words, then you can escalate the climate of disrespect. When you calmly and kindly redirect students who are exhibiting mean behavior, you model behaviors that promote a climate of respect.

Here are two ideas for how to do this:

- "Go public" with redirections and interventions for unacceptable behaviors.
- Use logical consequences to show students that you expect them to take responsibility for their actions and change their behavior.

I'll explain each in detail in the following pages.

"Go public" with redirections and interventions for unacceptable behaviors

When Julia announced loudly "I'm not sitting near Louis; he smells," Mrs. Cohen responded firmly, in front of the whole group: "Everyone in this class is part of our community. Our rules say we will include everyone. Julia, make a space for Louis in a friendly way." Mrs. Cohen's firm, respectful, and direct tone and words showed the class that exclusion was unacceptable. She did not belittle or threaten Julia. Nor did she take Julia aside to give the redirection. Research shows that such adult behaviors as belittling, threatening, or taking the student aside will promote bullying (Englander 2013; Olweus 1993; StopBullying.gov 2017a).

When Mark called Harry "Hair Ball" during a math lesson, Mrs. Larsson firmly said, "Mark, reset and use Harry's name when you speak to him." The next day, Mrs. Larsson held a class meeting about using people's names as they want them to be used. She didn't humiliate Mark by saying that the meeting was about his behavior. She didn't humiliate Harry by announcing to those who might not have heard that someone had called Harry "Hair Ball." She simply said, "We have an important issue that we need to discuss." Children who had heard Harry referred to as "Hair Ball" knew perfectly well why they were having the meeting. Those who had missed the name-calling just knew that Mrs. Larsson cared a lot about people's names being used in a respectful manner.

Use logical consequences to teach students to take responsibility for their actions

Bullying is a serious matter, and it is of vital importance that teachers protect children by stopping mean behavior in its tracks. Logical consequences are one tool that will stop mean behaviors and help students learn a different way to behave.

Keep in mind, however, that logical consequences are not a form of punishment. Unlike punishment, which can give a message of "You're bad," logical consequences send the message that children have the potential to stop mean behaviors and make positive changes. The goal of logical consequences is to teach children a better way to behave, not to shame them or make them feel bad.

The research shows that taking a punitive approach to bullying, which began in the 1990s and continues in some states today, is ineffective or, in some cases, actually promotes bullying (American Psychological Association 2008; StopBullying.gov, n.d.). When children are treated punitively, they have a model of disrespect. In addition, when children are punished, their resentment can escalate.

To use logical consequences effectively, in a non-punitive way, use the following guidelines:

- Be sure consequences are related to the misbehavior
- Deliver consequences respectfully
- Be sure consequences are proportionate to the misbehavior

Be sure consequences are related to the misbehavior. Consequences related to the misbehavior help children make the connection between their actions and the consequences. Gateway behaviors to bullying are, by their nature, social. They encompass spreading unkind rumors, calling children cruel names, and excluding children from play. Even when the behaviors are physical ones such as hitting, hair pulling, and pinching, they are, at the root, a social assault. For that reason, many consequences will involve removing the child who has engaged in these behaviors from the social situation.

If a child is mean to others on the bus, she'll need to sit next to the bus driver for a few days. If a student throws a ball directly at another student during physical education, he'll lose the privilege of throwing the ball for the day. When Martine and Lucy tell the other girls not to play with Suzanne at recess, their teacher, Mr. Stegman, explains that they will both lose the privilege of playing with others at recess the next day. In addition, he separates Martine and Lucy so they lose the opportunity to socialize with each other.

In all these cases, the teacher will check in with each child about the misbehavior and then discuss and practice more pro-social ways to behave before the children regain the social privilege that they temporarily lost.

Exclusionary behaviors are about how children choose whom to be with and whom to leave out. For that reason, it's often a logical consequence for children to lose the privilege of choosing, whether partners, teams, or work groups. Despite class meetings about fair teams, the class athletes—Malik, Andrew, and Finn—arranged things so that they were always on the same kickball team at recess, playing against the less athletically accomplished students. In response, Mrs. Young told them that they'd lose the privilege of picking teams and she would make the team assignments for a few days.

Besides being social, gateway behaviors to bullying are also, by nature, unkind. For that reason, logical consequences might involve practicing acts of kindness. If an older child bothers the kindergartners on the school bus, the consequence might be for them to go to the kindergarten room and, under the kindergarten teacher's close supervision, kindly listen to kindergartners read before dismissal.

Deliver consequences respectfully. Consequences that are calmly and respectfully delivered model better behavior skills (StopBullying.gov 2017a). Children who bully have sometimes been subject to disrespectful treatment themselves. That's the model they're familiar with. It's important to show them a better way. Furthermore, if you humiliate children, they will be resentful and possibly focus on revenge rather than how to do better next time. Mr. Stegman was calm and matter-of-fact when he explained, "You won't be able to play together at recess tomorrow, Martine and Lucy."

Be sure consequences are proportionate to the misbehavior. When you use consequences to underscore the importance of friendly and respectful behavior, it's important that those consequences be proportionate to the misbehavior. Mr. Stegman didn't tell Martine and Lucy to take a break, as he sometimes did when students didn't follow the rules in a game of tag. Telling others not to play with Suzanne was far more destructive than breaking the rules of a game. Nor did he tell them that they'd miss recess for the rest of the year, which would have been disproportionately punitive.

For more information about logical consequences, see *Teaching Self-Discipline: The Responsive Classroom Guide to Helping Students Dream, Behave, and Achieve in Elementary School* (see Appendix B).

When children deny culpability

Perhaps you've heard the denials: "But I didn't do anything—you just like to pick on me." Studies have shown that many children who bully do not feel remorseful about their behaviors. Some believe that they have every right to insult, exclude, or otherwise harass others (Davis 2007a; Gini, Pozzoli, and Hymel 2014; Olweus 1993). When Mrs. Sharpe spoke with Wayne about his badgering Jackson, his response was, "But Jackson's such a dork. He deserves it."

It's important not to engage in the "I didn't do anything" discussion. Simply stating class and school rules, employing a consequence, and then moving on gives the right message: We do not treat people that way in this community.

Perhaps you've heard the complaints as well: "But it's not fair; other kids do that and you don't say anything." This is why it's vitally important to make sure that consequences are delivered evenhandedly. When Mikal and Jerome, usually kind to all, tried excluding others on the playground by giggling wildly and saying, "Don't play with Sam, he's a jerk," Mr. Stegman calmly explained to them that they wouldn't be able to play with others at recess tomorrow, and he'd be watching them during the next week to make sure that they were kind to everyone. When Martine and Lucy showed similar exclusionary behavior, the consequences were the same as Mikal's and Jerome's. The children could see that the rules and consequences apply to everyone.

Strategy in Action

In the Midst of Change, a Second Grade Teacher Responds to Misbehavior

Over the summer, the school district where Mr. Harrison teaches second grade went through a redistricting. This fall many children are attending new schools. Along with changing bus routes and new faculty configurations, everyone is dealing with different student groupings. Who will be friends with whom? Who will be "in" and who will be "out"? Who will be popular?

It's November. Although Mr. Harrison had spent time at the beginning of the year building community, he's noticing an increase in mean behaviors. For example, three boys have begun to roll their eyes whenever another boy speaks in class. Parents are starting to report mean comments about classmates on social media from the same boys. Mr. Harrison knows that he needs to put a stop to this behavior. He has a serious talk with the three boys, making sure to stay calm and nonjudgmental. He refers to classroom rules and points out that the class has agreed to take care of each other. He listens carefully to each student's point of view. Then he says, "I expect you to follow our classroom rule to take care of each other. That means that you will be respectful listeners when anyone in the class is talking. I will be watching to make sure you do that. I know you can."

Mr. Harrison has also noticed that four girls in his class have started calling themselves "The Cliquettes." He heard one girl say to another, "I'll be your friend if you don't play with Leslie."

He knows he needs to talk with the girls and decides to meet individually with each one because he doesn't want to reinforce their exclusive bonding. When he talks with them, they each nod their heads and agree to do better. The next day, though, he sees Shavonne wandering the room to "sharpen her pencil" while whispering to various girls. He finds a note crumpled up on the floor that says, "You're ugly. You can't be one of the cute girls."

Mr. Harrison can see that he needs to do more to stop the Cliquettes' mean behavior immediately. He begins by separating the four students, realigning table groupings so that they sit far away from each other. He also informs other teachers who work with his class that these girls will be separated for a period of time. Next, he tells each girl why he will be separating her and that he will be watching her and noticing incidences of kind and inclusive behavior. They'll meet in a few days to evaluate how things are going.

Mr. Harrison continues to intervene in small acts

After these incidents, Mr. Harrison realizes he needs to use firm and immediate consequences for the smallest acts of disrespect. The first time a student rolls his eyes or passes an unkind note, Mr. Harrison will stop the behavior with clear language, referring to classroom expectations followed by a consequence. "Max, stop that. In this class we use respectful body language," will be Mr. Harrison's first response to his eye-rolling. If Max continues, Mr. Harrison will calmly and respectfully separate Max from the group.

Mr. Harrison revisits community-building activities

Mr. Harrison also decides to bolster the class's work on community building. He'll revisit some of the activities that he used with his students in the beginning of the year. The children will play singing and clapping games that get them moving around, relating to nearly everyone in the class. He'll infuse academics with a community-building focus as well.

Mr. Harrison decides that this would be a good time for a whole-class poetry unit. Children will search poetry books for favorite poems to share with classmates. They'll memorize some poems as a class and recite them chorally. They'll write poems and share them with classmates, all under close supervision to keep things friendly and kind.

Mr. Harrison also decides that this would be a good time for the whole-class math unit on graphing. Children will interview each other about favorite hobbies, with careful emphasis on asking kind and respectful questions. They'll create graphs and share them with the class.

Throughout these community-building activities, Mr. Harrison uses language to nurture a climate of caring among his students. "What have we learned about classmates today?" he asks after children have concluded interviews about their hobbies. He then reinforces caring behaviors with such language as "I've noticed people listening to each other so carefully."

Soon, Mr. Harrison's comprehensive approach proves to be effective. By reestablishing expectations of positive behavior and responding quickly and directly to misbehavior, he is able to create a kind, caring classroom community.

Communicating With Parents About Misbehavior

In the chapters that follow, I talk about ways to keep the channels of communication open and how to build trust with parents. This includes talking with parents about your efforts to create a safe and caring classroom, your approach to establishing classroom rules, and how you respond to misbehavior. In addition, be sure to invite parents to ask questions and share information that could help you effectively teach their child. This is important work that needs to begin in the first days of school and continue throughout the year.

One area of communication that needs particular tending is about bullying and gateway behaviors. Teachers need to hear from parents when they see or hear about mean behaviors between their child and others in the classroom or in the school. And teachers need to keep parents informed about behaviors they see in school and how they're responding. If you regularly give parents this information and the opportunity to share what they know, they'll be more likely to trust that you care and that you want the best for their child. And if a bullying situation that involves their child should ever come up, it will make the communication go more smoothly.

Over more than thirty years of teaching, I've come up with some guidelines for how to keep communication about these difficult situations open and positive.

Hearing parents' concerns

Unkind behavior, especially bullying behavior, often goes on under a teacher's radar. The spitball is tossed or the hair is pulled when our backs are turned. The student is "uninvited" to the birthday party in the hall or on the way to boarding the school bus. We have no firsthand information about what children do to each other in the online environment. Research shows, and my experience supports, that parents are more likely to know about bullying and other mean behavior than teachers are (Axford et al. 2015). Parents also know about bullying situations that happen at home, on social media, or in the community that can spill over into the classroom.

If parents don't let you know about these behaviors, then the meanness can spiral out of control. However, if you've established clear channels of communication, parents can provide valuable insight into students' lives both inside and outside of school and be your ally in bullying prevention work.

Listen, assess, and communicate your observations to parents

When parents contact you with information about mean behaviors they've observed at home, in the community, or in cyberspace, listen and assure them that you will carefully observe the students involved to see if the mean behaviors are occurring in the classroom. You then need to follow through with a text or email to set up a phone call with the parents to let them know what you've observed and how you are going to respond. For more about communicating with parents about outside-the-classroom mean behaviors, see Chapter Five.

Parents will also hear about and report to you any incidents that happen at school. It's important to take these reports seriously, even if you think the child is embellishing a small incident. For example, Janine might complain to her parents that "Lori rolled her eyes at me in school today." Janine's parents are concerned and call you. You need to take their report seriously and then observe carefully.

If you see no such put-down behavior when you watch and instead observe that Janine and Lori actually work well together, you can respectfully let Janine's parents know. Your observations might reassure Janine's parents that the eye-rolling was a small, one-time incident.

You also need to let Janine's parents know that you will continue to watch Janine's and Lori's interactions, and that you will want to know right away if they hear anything more about disrespectful behavior. When you communicate your appreciation of their reports and emphasize your commitment to respectful behavior in the classroom, you increase the likelihood that parents will stay in contact and let you know about potentially harmful events.

Set the stage so parents feel it's okay to report concerns

Note that in this example about Janine and Lori, the positive outcome was possible because Janine's parents felt comfortable bringing a complaint to the teacher in the first place. It's important to set the stage so that parents feel it's safe and productive to approach you with a potential problem. In Chapters Two, Three, and Four you'll learn about how to establish open, trusting communication with parents in the first days and weeks of school.

Notifying parents about student misbehavior

Just as teachers need to hear from parents about outside-the-classroom behavior, parents need to hear about the mean behaviors that occur in the classroom. How you let them know, though, makes a big difference in how supportive they will be as you and your school work to solve the problem. Here are some things to remember.

Wait until you're calm

If you're angry or annoyed about a student's behavior, then wait until you've calmed down before contacting the parents. I'll never forget the moment in my classroom when Jimmy pinched Christa on the bottom. I went right to the telephone and called his mother. My frustration and annoyance crackled right through the air waves. Jimmy's mother was understandably protective of him. Although I eventually repaired my relationship with Jimmy's mother, she never did see the bottom-pinching incident quite the way I did.

Begin with the positive

No matter how negative the event, it's always possible to begin with something positive. Madelyn is circulating around the classroom loudly whispering "You dork" to her perceived "enemies." It's still possible to start your conversation with her parents by saying, truthfully, "Madelyn's reading skills have improved in the past month," or "Madelyn always has a joke or a cheerful comment for me when she arrives in the morning." More than anything else, parents want to see that you like their child. With that established, they can more easily hear about their child's imperfections.

Avoid labeling

No one wants to hear that their child is a bully. If you use that word, you'll set up parents to feel defensive and stop listening to what you're hoping to communicate. It's better to describe the behavior as specifically and concretely as possible. "Yesterday, during social studies, Mike told Jamie his map looked 'stupid' and that he didn't want Jamie to be part of his work group" is specific and succinct. Leave out embellishments such as "with a mean smile on his face" or "in a bossy way." Be matter-of-fact. If you convey that Mike made a mistake that's been made by many other children, you're far more likely to enlist his parents' cooperation than if you convey indignation and outrage.

Provide evidence

If parents are skeptical about your report, concrete evidence may help. When a group of third grade girls started directing "Don't sit next to Katie on the bus," the bus company actually had a digital video of the behavior to share with the parents of the children involved. Of course, not every school bus has a camera to monitor student behavior. You may, however, have the actual note a child sent, or other physical evidence.

Inform parents but retain responsibility for solving the problem

Once everyone understands what happened, it's unreasonable to put the burden of solving the problem on the parents, just as it would be unreasonable for them to expect you to get their child in bed on time. It's more realistic to hope for support, or at least a lack of resistance, while you and your school solve the problem.

It's also important to let parents know how you are going to respond. For example, "Because Faye told others not to sit with Katie, she cannot ride the school bus for a week" or "Mike will need to work alone during social studies for a few days."

Maintain confidentiality

When several children are involved in an incident, parents often want to know what consequences you're employing with the other children. Don't violate confidentiality by going into specifics. It's fine to simply say that you are addressing the problem with every child. At the same time, be clear with parents that you are required to follow school, state, and federal policies on matters of privacy (U.S. Department of Education 2020). Educators are not allowed by federal law to discuss discipline matters regarding students who are not their child.

KEY IDEAS

- **"Focus on the small stuff"**—notice and stop small acts of exclusion, mean words, and seemingly casual swipes before they become major incidences of bullying that are far more difficult to turn around.

- **Take time to observe students** both in the classroom and in other settings so that you're aware of the behaviors they're engaging in.

- **Use respectful consequences** immediately for small "gateway" misbehaviors.

- **Listen carefully** to parents' concerns.

- **Notify parents** about children's misbehavior.

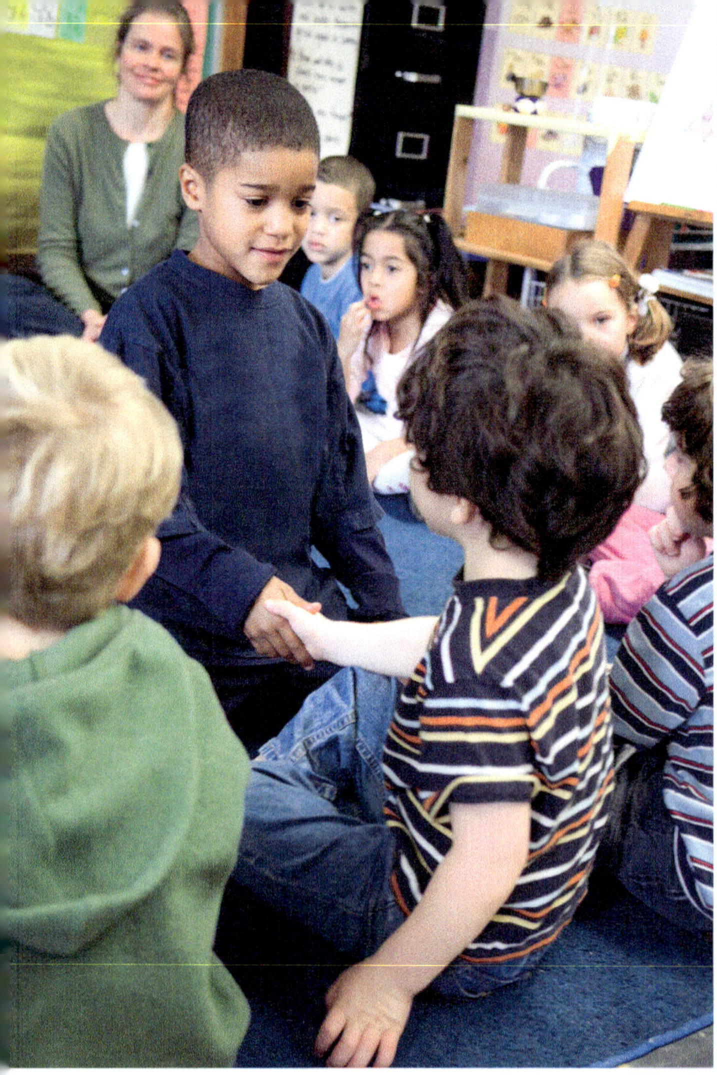
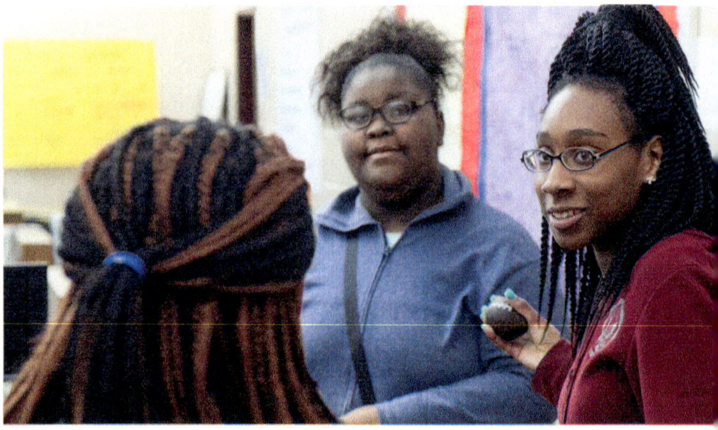
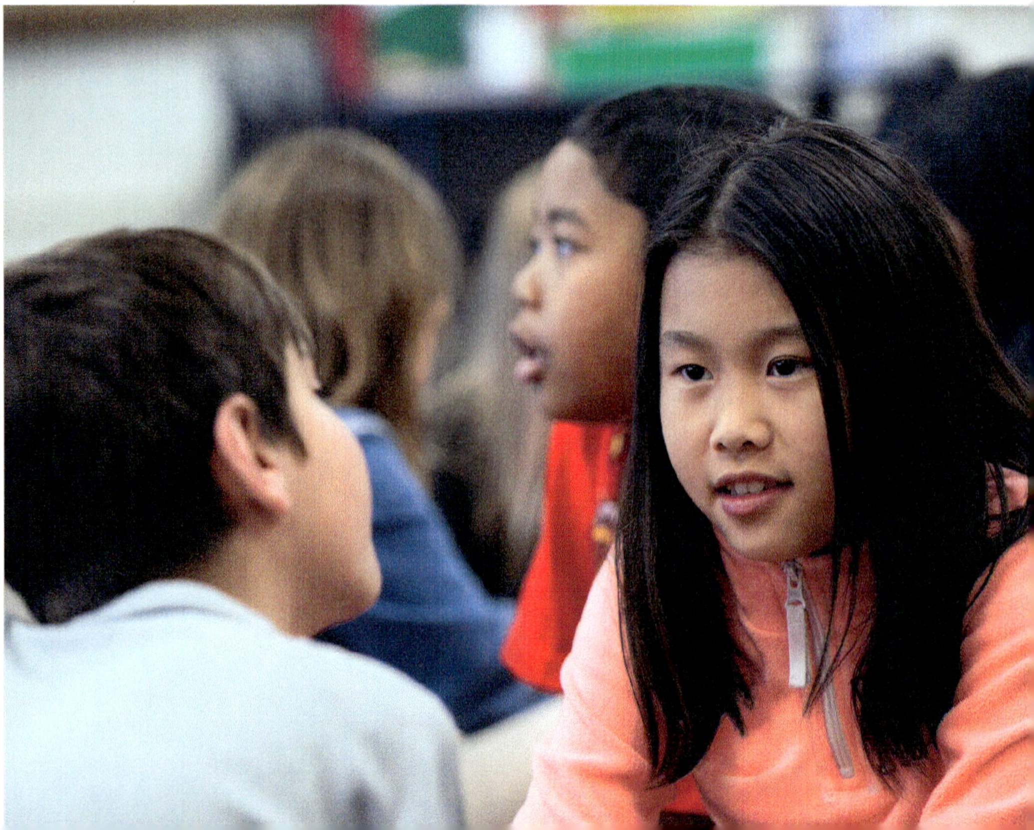

CHAPTER TWO

Helping Children Get to Know Each Other

The students in Mrs. Meyer's third grade class are getting ready for the morning. James is sharpening classmates' pencils. He pauses for a quick high five with Lenore as she enters the classroom. Shari, busy checking people's homework, stops to congratulate Kendra, who often forgets her homework. "You remembered, today!" she says. Lewis, who uses a wheelchair, is approaching the classroom door. Markeith sees him and checks the furniture to make sure that there's enough space for Lewis's wheelchair and then goes to meet him at the door. "Hi, Lewis," he says. "Did you watch the game last night?" He knows that Lewis is an avid basketball fan.

Mrs. Meyer's students welcome each other into the classroom each day. She takes deliberate steps to ensure that her students know each other's names and greet each other kindly and respectfully. She structures opportunities for students to share information about their lives and to have fun together. She knows that teachers who reduce or prevent bullying are teachers who focus on creating a positive climate in their classrooms and in their schools, a climate where every student is known, honored, and respected.

From day one, teachers like Mrs. Meyer take steps to build a strong, inclusive classroom community. They pay attention to how children treat each other. They help children get to know each other and how to work and play together. They set expectations of a positive experience where each student will work and play with every other student. And the teachers will continue to work to build a strong and inclusive community throughout the year.

The importance of these efforts is backed by the research on bullying, which shows that children are less likely to engage in bullying behaviors if they feel connected to their peers, to their teacher, and to their school as a whole (Cohen et al. 2015; Hinduja and Patchin 2014; Wang, Berry, and Swearer 2013; Zych, Farrington, and Ttofi 2019). Research also shows that children who are targeted for bullying are often the children who are isolated from the group (Pellegrini 2010; Rodkin and Gest 2010).

Teachers can begin with the most basic step of helping children learn each other's names and giving them opportunities to learn about each other's lives. When we do this, we are also helping them practice empathy, value differences, and understand the importance of being friendly to all, even if they're not going to be best friends with everyone. We then can encourage and support them as they make hard decisions about behavior.

In this chapter, I will focus on the following topics:

- Helping children to learn each other's names
- Helping children to get to know each other through structured greetings, sharing, and whole-group activities
- Integrating "getting to know you" activities into academic structures
- Communicating to children's parents about creating a caring and inclusive classroom and that you want to work with them in ongoing ways to achieve this goal

Begin With Learning Each Other's Names

It's easy to assume that children will take the initiative in meeting their classmates. However, in my experience, children may know only the names of others who live in their neighborhood, who ride their bus, or whose families are family friends or relatives. Those are the children they speak to, sit with, and play with on the playground. Without deliberate "getting to know you" structures, the children who are comfortable with each other get to know each other better while other children stay on the margins of the social networks in the classroom, which can leave them vulnerable to the type of mean behavior that may lead to bullying.

Use name tags or cards in the first weeks of school

Making sure that everyone learns everyone else's name is the first step toward creating an inclusive classroom. In many schools, children and adults wear name tags for the first six weeks or so of school. In addition, children label their tables, desks, and lockers or cubbies with personally decorated name cards, and children's names are prominently displayed on attendance charts.

The use of name cards or tags is valuable at all grade levels, not just the primary grades. Sometimes we assume that older children won't need name tags because they know each other from previous years. Some children will know each other, of course, but others may not. In addition, older children will often gravitate toward those children who are familiar, whose names they know, and whom they've seen before. The children whose names they don't know could become the marginalized children, those children who might be targeted for bullying.

To make the name tags in early grades, when children are just learning to read, teachers might take a photo of each child as they arrive for meet-the-teacher day. Teachers can then augment each child's name tag with a small copy of their photo. Older students might want to decorate their name tags with drawings of their favorite activities, symbols that indicate something about them, or other decorations that make the name tags their own.

Structure opportunities to practice kind behavior

The introduction of name tags also provides an opportunity to begin guiding children toward kind and helpful behavior. Mrs. Velasquez greets the earliest arriving of her third grade students with directions to find their cubbies, put away their belongings, find their labeled seat, and begin to decorate their name tag. As subsequent children come in, she asks the early arrivers to show the new arrivals how to complete these routines.

Down the hall Mr. Rinaldi, a kindergarten teacher, places name cards on tables. As children arrive in the classroom, he greets them warmly at the door and directs them to find their name at a table. Miss Snyder, the music teacher, is there to assist, guiding children toward their name card, helping them get started coloring a picture, and directing them to help each other. "Julius, this is Natasha," she says as Julius finds his name card next to Natasha's. "Natasha, would you show Julius where the crayons are?" she asks.

Through these small steps, Mrs. Velasquez and Mr. Rinaldi send a powerful message: "In this classroom, we help each other. In this classroom, everyone is important. In this classroom, kindness rules."

Help Children Get to Know Each Other

Learning names is an important first step. But to prevent bullying, we as teachers need to go beyond simply making sure that children know each other's names. We need to help them get to know each other in a climate of safety and support, and we need to build an inclusive community where everyone belongs and where everyone has a role, just as Mrs. Meyer did in the opening paragraphs of this chapter. The best strategy that I have found to create this caring climate is the *Responsive Classroom* strategy of Morning Meeting (Rimm-Kaufman and Chiu 2007). In Morning Meeting, everyone in the classroom community gathers in a circle each morning to greet each other, share news about their lives, take part in an activity together, and read a posted message from the teacher.

In the following pages, I'll provide information on helping children get to know each other better by using strategies based on Morning Meeting structures. If you don't use the *Responsive Classroom* strategy of Morning Meeting, you can still adapt these ideas to fit your classroom schedule and structure.

Set up greeting routines

There's great power in beginning every day with each child greeting classmates and being greeted in turn. Setting up a whole-group structure for this kind of beginning is an important way that you can help children get to know each other and feel that they belong. At the start of the year, these whole-group greetings can be as simple as a friendly "Good morning," coupled with a classmate's name, making its way around the circle. As children become comfortable with this basic greeting, you can add a handshake or a high five.

As the year progresses, you can add other challenges such as having children greet each other across the circle, combined perhaps with tossing a ball or other soft object. Whatever structure is used, as each student's name is stated, the student is brought into the circle of the community. When everyone is part of that circle, the potential for any individual to be treated meanly is dramatically reduced.

Build in time for greeting, every day

A daily morning gathering such as Morning Meeting is a highly effective structure for ensuring that students greet each other every day. However, if you choose not to use such a structured daily gathering, you can set aside a few minutes for a quick greeting early in the school day.

Mr. Rinaldi waits until everyone has arrived. Then he gathers the children in a circle on the rug and leads the class in a simple song that uses each child's name. "Where oh where is our friend Natasha?" Mr. Rinaldi sings. The tone is set: Natasha is our friend. Children who feel ready join in as he repeats that line three times. Natasha may stand, wave, or simply smile to show where she is. Students then sing "Way down yonder in the paw paw patch" before Mr. Rinaldi sings "Where oh where is our friend [classmate's name]" to name the next student, and on they go until everyone has been named.

State the purposes of greeting

Greeting each other every day is a powerful way to bring everyone into the classroom community, but it could backfire if children greet each other in ways that further unkind agendas. To keep greetings safe, teachers need to teach the purposes and skills of greeting each other respectfully and inclusively.

The first step is to tell children why they are greeting each other every day. Be explicit about building a sense of safety. For example, you could say: "We'll greet each other every morning so that everybody feels welcome in our class." When children understand the purpose—that greeting each other contributes to everyone's feeling included in the classroom community—they will be more likely to stay invested in keeping the greeting safe and friendly.

Throughout the year, teachers should periodically remind children of the purposes of greeting. "Remember our rule to be kind and friendly as we greet each other this morning," a teacher might say. Or, "Remember, we greet to make everyone feel welcome. What does it sound like when someone makes you feel welcome? How can you make your greeting partner feel welcome this morning?" Children need frequent reminders to keep that positive energy flowing, regardless of the expected behavior.

> **Some Language to Try**
>
> *We'll greet each other every morning so that everybody feels welcome in our class.*
>
> *How can you help your greeting partner feel welcome this morning?*
>
> *How might it feel when someone greets you with a smile?*
>
> *How can we make sure that everyone is safe and taken care of while we share?*
>
> *What can we do as we sing the B-I-N-G-O song to make it fun for everyone?*

Teach and practice the skills needed for greeting everyone in a respectful, friendly way

Children need to learn how to be respectful and friendly to those they don't know or don't know very well yet. Show children what a respectful, friendly greeting looks like and sounds like. Model how to greet someone with a smile. For more on this, refer to the *Responsive Classroom* strategy of Interactive Modeling described in detail in Chapter Four.

To build students' investment in being respectful and friendly, help them tap into their own thoughts and feelings by reflecting with them. Two questions that students might ask themselves are "How might it feel when someone greets you with a smile?" and "What can you do to make your greeting partner feel welcome in school?"

Ms. McCabe's fifth grade class gathers in a circle at the start of each day for Morning Meeting. Throughout the year, Ms. McCabe introduces a variety of greetings. With each new greeting, she takes time to discuss how to do the new greeting in a respectful, friendly way. "What does a friendly greeting look like?" Ms. McCabe asks. "How do we shake hands in a friendly way?" "What does a gentle high five feel like?" Even fifth graders need to know exactly what is expected if they are to maintain a climate of respect for all. After the class has successfully completed a greeting, they briefly reflect on how they felt as they greeted and were greeted.

Plan and structure greetings that include everyone

One of the purposes of greetings is to build an inclusive climate so it's important that children greet a variety of classmates each morning. When Mr. Sailor says to his students, "Greet three people whom you haven't spoken with yet this morning," he's making sure that his fifth graders greet someone who is not their best friend. Mrs. Ianello has her first grade students count two people around the circle, greet the third, and then take the third person's place while that person begins another round of greeting. By doing this, she is mixing up her students, ensuring that each student greets someone other than the person they chose to sit next to. Such practices foster an atmosphere of inclusion, which is vital to preventing bullying.

Continue with greeting all year long

To maintain an atmosphere of welcome and friendly inclusion in your classroom, it's important to keep the greeting routine going all year long. You'll likely find that students miss greeting each other if you skip a day. Certainly, if I had ever forgotten to begin the day with our greeting, the students would have quickly reminded me.

Children often bully children whom they perceive as outsiders. Knowing each other's names and then using people's names in a welcoming word or friendly way every single day is one part of the systematic effort teachers can make to prevent the formation of a culture of "outsiders" and "insiders" that can allow bullying to develop.

Help children get to know each other through structured sharing

Structured sharing is another important way to help children get to know each other. In the *Responsive Classroom* strategy of Morning Meeting, each child tells the class something about themselves by talking briefly on either an assigned or a self-chosen topic. For example, the teacher might name a topic that applies to everyone, such as "What I want to be when I grow up," "Something that I'm good at," or "Something that's hard for me." Assigned topics can also be academic, such as a favorite story, a favorite place to do homework, or a favorite mathematical operation.

Alternatively, individual children might choose their own topics, such as something they found on the way to school (a bird's egg or feather, a pretty stone), the death of a pet, their favorite ice cream flavor, or other topics of great interest to children at different ages.

Two or three children might share a few sentences at each session or everyone might have a chance to share a word or phrase.

The purpose of sharing is to bring everyone, equally, into the classroom community, so whether or not you use the *Responsive Classroom* strategy of Morning Meeting, it's important that all students have an equal chance to share over a period of time. This might be over a week or a month depending on how much time you have available.

Teach children how to share in a way that connects with their classmates

For sharing to be successful, teachers need to take the time to teach children some specific sharing skills that will help them connect with their listeners: speak loud and clear, make eye contact, and keep their sharing brief but informative. After you teach those skills, children will actually want to listen to one another, will learn about one another, and will begin to build empathy for one another. Without attention to these skills, sharing can turn into an exercise where one child gets to talk but no one listens and learns about the child.

Modeling is an effective way to teach these skills that are so vital to successful sharing. Mr. Rand begins a modeling session in his third grade class by sharing something about himself. "This year we're going to get to know each other by sharing about ourselves. We're going to share public news, things that we want everyone to know. I'm going to tell you a little bit about my favorite after-school activity," he says. "I'll tell you about my favorite activity in a way that is efficient but gives you some information about me. I love to coach soccer for my son's soccer team." Mr. Rand goes on to elaborate with a few sentences about coaching soccer. Then he asks his students what they noticed. Did he share something public? Was he efficient? Did they learn something about him that they didn't know before?

Students chime in with observations about Mr. Rand's sharing. Tomorrow a student in the class will share some public news about themselves.

Teach children how to listen respectfully to others' sharing

When teaching children how to listen to each other, it's important to remind them that the purpose of sharing is to get to know each other and that listening carefully helps them to do that.

Furthermore, it's important to break down the skills involved in listening and teach these skills separately, even for older children. You need to model looking at the speaker, being quiet while the speaker talks, keeping attention focused on the speaker, and remembering what the speaker says.

Teachers can hold children accountable for listening by expecting them to report back what they learned. Playful formats make this task pleasurable. "Listen carefully because afterwards we're going to play a game called 'Who Remembers?'" explains Mr. Wu, a fourth grade teacher.

The class shares "What I like to do after school" in an around-the-circle format. Mr. Wu begins by saying, "After school I like to go to the gym." Sammy, sitting next to Mr. Wu, uses Mr. Wu's sentence stem and says, "After school I like to watch TV." Next, Frannie says, "After school I like to ride my bike." Once the class has finished, Mr. Wu asks the class, "Who remembers who likes to watch TV?" Many hands go up. Children are eager to share that Sammy likes to watch TV. Playing "Who Remembers?" doesn't put anyone on the spot, but it does give many children a chance to share what they heard. It elevates and honors listening to each other.

When children share about themselves, they're opening themselves up to the group, which can feel risky. To increase safety, it's important to teach children how to respond with friendly interest and respect.

"Today people are going to begin sharing about what they want to be when they grow up," explains Mrs. Smarz, a second grade teacher. "You're going to get to share what you want to be when you grow up and you're going to learn what classmates want to be when they grow up. This is important information. How can we make sure that everyone is safe and taken care of while we share?"

Children chime in with ideas. "We can listen to them," says Marty. "We can show an interested face," says Pauline.

"Sometimes someone's idea can strike us as sounding funny," elaborates Mrs. Smarz. "What might we do if that happens?"

"We can make sure we don't laugh," says Jenine. "I don't want anyone to laugh at my idea."

"If we don't laugh," asks Mrs. Smarz, "what will we do?"

"Hold your laugh inside and just make a friendly smile?" asks Santiago.

"Good idea," says Mrs. Smarz. "Okay, let's go. If people forget and do start to laugh, I'll stop the sharing so that we can keep everyone safe."

With this type of preparation, the students know that they have decided together to respect one another's feelings. Gateway behaviors such as snickering about someone else's personal information have been headed off. And everyone knows that if those behaviors emerge, Mrs. Smarz will stop the activity.

Consider limiting the use of "props" such as toys

Children sharing about material objects can become a "bring and brag" session that highlights the income differences among students. When a child brings in an elaborate toy to share, children whose families can't afford such toys can feel left out and further marginalized in the culture of the classroom. Children whose families can afford such toys are linked together. The drawing of such class lines in a group can potentiate bullying (Sweeting and West 2001).

If you think that young students need a prop to support their sharing, you might allow objects that students made or found, or provide other kinds of guidelines for choosing appropriate objects to share. Mrs. Doukali, a kindergarten teacher, has her students share a favorite book. That way, if someone doesn't bring a book from home, she can help that child pick out a book from the school library.

When you keep the focus of sharing on learning about each other rather than displaying possessions, you help children know and understand each other and in the process develop empathy for others who may, on the surface, seem a little different.

Build in time for sharing even if you don't have a Morning Meeting

If you don't have a daily Morning Meeting, you can give students opportunities to get to know each other through sharing. Sharing could occur after lunch, during snack time, or at the end of the day. It might occur as frequently as every day or as infrequently as once a week. Regardless of frequency or time, it's important to structure these sharing sessions carefully and to teach children the skills they'll need in order for them to be interesting sharers and respectful listeners.

The more students know and understand each other, the stronger their connection to school and to their classroom community will be, and the more likely the students are to avoid bullying behaviors and to protect classmates who are targeted.

Use whole-group activities to build connections

Whole-group activities provide another opportunity to bring all students into the circle of community. In a *Responsive Classroom* Morning Meeting, group activities may be serious or lighthearted. They may involve the direct practice of an academic skill or the practice of a skill that is less obviously academic. The important thing is that everyone is able to do the activity and that everyone participates equally in a way that is non-competitive and fun. As children laugh together at a silly game or concentrate deeply to read a poem chorally, in unison, with fluency and expression, they are building those all-important feelings of connection to one another.

Ms. Farnum's fourth grade class is sitting in a circle and each student has written a little-known fact about themselves on an index card. Ms. Farnum makes a point of saying, "This is a fact that you'd like to share with all of your classmates." The children circulate, find a partner, and read their fact to their partner. They switch cards, find a new partner, and read a fact about their previous partner to their new partner. "Did you know that Saul takes violin lessons?" Nora reads to Josie. They switch cards again and Josie tells Leo about Saul and his violin lessons.

Mrs. Singh's first grade class sings together, "There was a farmer who had a dog, and Bingo was his name-o." As they sing, they spell out B-I-N-G-O, leaving off one letter in each round of the song. Their faces are smiling, their bodies move softly to the music, and as they enjoy singing together, they are incidentally practicing some spelling skills. Singing together builds community.

Ms. Robatille's fifth and sixth graders have come to the circle with their homework, an index card on which they've written a current event that they've read about in the news. Ms. Robatille begins a rhythm, "snap, snap, clap, snap, snap, clap," snapping her fingers and clapping her hands. The students join in. They snap twice together and then clap. The first student reads his current event. The class begins the pattern again, and after the next clap, the second student around the circle reads her current event. The activity is lively and engaging. Children listen intently, both to learn about each other's current events and to keep up with the pattern. In the rhythm of snaps, claps, and listening, they are one community.

The feeling of closeness engendered by this type of cooperation protects against bullying. Research shows that marginalized children are most likely to be targeted (Card and Hodges 2008; Pellegrini et al. 2010), and these daily cooperative activities, where every child has an equal role, protect against such marginalization. Research also shows that if children are targeted, that targeting often stops quickly when a peer intervenes (Pepler, Craig, and O'Connell 2010; Salmivalli, Kärnä, and Poskiparta 2010), and peers are more likely to intervene when they know and feel empathetic toward the child being targeted (Thornberg and Jungert 2013).

Plan group activities that foster inclusion

Whole-class activities taught and supervised by the teacher are a great tool for building the feeling of closeness and empathy that helps prevent bullying. It's important to plan group activities carefully if they are to foster closeness. Activities that help children get to know each other build community. For example, when children play the guessing game "Fact or Fiction," where they share two facts that are true about themselves and one fact that is made up, the class guesses which ones are true and which one is fictional. Children learn more about each other while also having fun.

Activities where children all laugh together engender warm feelings of community. Miss Levine's third grade plays "What Are You Doing?" Sean, the first child in the circle, stands in front of Marissa, who is seated next to him. Sean jumps up and down on one foot. Marissa asks, "What are you doing?" When Sean replies, "Brushing my teeth!" everyone laughs at the intentional mismatch. It's then Marissa's turn to pantomime brushing her teeth while announcing that she's doing a different action, such as swimming. The next child will then pantomime swimming while stating that she's doing some other action. As the action moves around the circle, the children laugh together while break dancing, twirling around, and doing jumping jacks.

Activities where the group as a whole creates something positive build these same feelings of closeness. Doing a choral reading of a poem can provide a sense of group cohesion. As the class breaks up into small groups to devise gestures to go with various lines of a poem and then reads the poem chorally while sharing their gestures, each small group is contributing to the effort of the class as a whole, creating a beautiful and dramatic reading of the poem. To get you started, sources of tried and true games and movement activities can be found in Appendix B.

Teach and supervise group activities

To keep group activities inclusive and kind, it's important to carefully teach and supervise the activities. As with greetings, if you introduce the activity by stating its community-building goal and then reflect with children about ways they might meet this goal, you will increase their investment in making the activity kind and safe for everyone.

Mrs. Singh, in the earlier example, teaches the B-I-N-G-O song carefully. She starts out by explaining to the first graders, "We sing together to have fun together. What can we do as we sing to make it fun for everyone?"

"Everyone needs to sing," says Jamie.

"Sometimes kids make mistakes when they're learning a new song," says Mrs. Singh. "How can we take care of each other if someone makes a mistake?" she asks.

"Don't laugh at them," contributes Suzanne.

"What will we do if we don't laugh?" Mrs. Singh continues.

"You could say, 'That's okay,'" says Petar.

"You could just ignore it and keep singing," says Monique.

This type of preparation heads off any unkind behaviors that might emerge and keeps the activity fun and safe for everyone. Without this type of preparation, the activity could potentially turn unkind and divisive, contributing to an atmosphere where bullying could take root and flourish.

It's also important to think about the various parts of an activity and plan to protect against possible unsafe moments. When Ms. Farnum cautioned her students to write down facts they'd like to share with everyone, she was protecting them from sharing a fact that may be too private, and one that could lead to subsequent unkind teasing.

Build in time for whole-group activities every day

I encourage you to build in time during the day when you and the children do these kinds of fun activities together. Group activities can provide a quick, energizing break between more focused academic tasks or serve as a transition between academic blocks. These activities do not need to take a lot of time and in fact can be done in two to three minutes.

> **Interactive Modeling**
>
> The *Responsive Classroom* strategy of Interactive Modeling lends itself to teaching children new greetings and activities, how to share respectfully, and how to be respectful listeners during other people's sharing. It's also a good strategy for teaching other skills discussed in this book. You'll find a detailed description of Interactive Modeling in Chapter Four.

Children who have been taught to function as a cohesive whole in the classroom have less need to create a feeling of cohesion by picking on an "outsider." They already have that feeling of cohesion. When they do see a classmate being picked on, isolated, or taunted, they are far more likely to step in and take care of the person being targeted because they are part of their group. Having even just one friend can protect a child against bullying (Englander 2013; Hodges et al. 1999). Being part of a cohesive group, and feeling connected to school and the people in it, is even more protective against bullying (Espelage and De La Rue 2012; Orpinas and Horne 2010). We as adults have the power to create that feeling in our classrooms.

Ideas for Greetings, Sharings, and Group Activities

Greetings

- "Good Morning, [classmate's name]" (passed around the circle)
- Across the Circle Greeting (walking across the circle to greet a classmate)
- Ball Toss Greeting (tossing a ball to the person you're greeting)
- "Where, Oh Where, Is Our Friend, [classmate's name]?" (sung by the class to each classmate)
- High Five Greeting (share a high five with the person you're greeting)
- Skip Greeting (everyone skips two neighbors and greets the third person in the circle)

Sharing topics

- What I want to be when I grow up
- Something I'm good at
- Something that's hard for me
- Favorite after-school activity
- A favorite book of mine

Group activities

- Trade One Fact
- B-I-N-G-O Song
- Snap, Snap, Clap (naming current events to a beat)
- Fact or Fiction (students name two facts and one fiction about themselves; others guess which are facts and which is fiction)
- What Am I Doing? (pantomime game)
- Choral reading of a poem

Infuse Academics With "Getting to Know You" Activities

Dedicating time to "getting to know you" activities is one step toward building that all-important feeling of connection to classmates and teachers. Building such activities into academic lessons is another step you can take. Simple graphs and charts, Venn diagrams, and questionnaires all lend themselves to "getting to know you."

Use surveys and graphs to share information at any grade level

Teachers can create simple surveys that ask students questions such as number of siblings or favorite hobbies. Later, children can graph the information. This kind of activity is appropriate at any grade level, including kindergarten.

Kindergarten teacher Mrs. Hauer creates a chart that asks "Do you have a brother or sister?" followed by "yes" and "no" columns. The children write their names in the correct column. Next, they'll indicate how many siblings they have and the class will make a graph of this data. They're learning about each other and at the same time becoming familiar with the concept of charts and graphs.

Use Venn diagrams to learn about each other and discover areas of shared interest

Ms. Lim's third grade students work with randomly selected partners to create Venn diagrams, a skill that's part of the third grade math curriculum. The middle section, where the two circles intersect, is for "Things we have in common." The outer, nonintersecting parts of the circles are for "Things that make us unique."

Stacia and José work together on their Venn diagram. Stacia writes her name and "red hair" in the nonintersecting part of her circle and José writes his name and "black hair" in his nonintersecting part of the circle. They take turns writing as they fill in the middle intersecting part, adding "third grader," "like pizza," "like math," and "like recess." As they talk they discover that Stacia likes to read Junie B. Jones books and José likes to read the Magic

Treehouse books, and they add these to their own outer circle. Later on, they'll each share with the class one thing that they learned about the other. All the Venn diagrams then go up on a bulletin board so that all students can learn about one another.

Strategy in Action

A Fifth Grade Teacher Weaves Together Academics and "Getting to Know You" Activities

It's the first day of school. As Ms. Fillion greets the children, she offers each student a slip of paper from a jar. Each slip has a question written on it: "Are you left-handed or right-handed?" "How many siblings do you have?" or "What's your favorite food?" and so forth. She directs each student to a stack of clipboards, each with a class list clipped to it. The students begin to mix and mingle, carrying a clipboard and a pencil. They introduce themselves to their new classmates and interview each other about the question on their paper, writing the answers next to each student's name on the class list. Ms. Fillion watches the students and notices that they are smiling and laughing. She can see that they are enjoying speaking with new classmates and learning about each other. As the children move about the classroom, they are practicing the skills of conversation.

Once the class lists are full, Ms. Fillion gives a signal for attention and brings the students to a circle of chairs. She begins with a greeting. "We'll do a greeting every day," she explains. She models greeting Mercedes with a friendly, "Good morning, Mercedes." Students notice that she smiled and made eye contact.

"What might you do if you don't know someone's name?" asks Ms. Fillion.

"You could look at their name tag," suggests Rosa.

"We're ready to go," says Ms. Fillion and the class begins to greet each other around the circle, Mercedes greeting Leo, Leo greeting Rosa, Rosa greeting Felipe, and so on.

Next, Ms. Fillion asks a few students to share what they've learned about their new classmates. "Alejandro has seven brothers," Maria shares with the class.

"We have seven kids who are left-handed," Frankie announces.

"Fifteen kids like pizza best," proclaims Elena.

The students are beginning to learn about each other. At this point they're just scratching the surface. They will get to know each other more deeply in the coming weeks, setting the stage for an inclusive community where students will treat each other with care and respect.

The next day, at math time, the students begin to create graphs from the information that they gleaned the previous day. Elena's graph is about fifth graders' favorite foods, Frankie's graph is about their class's hand preference, and Maria's is about classmates' siblings.

When the graphs are finished, Ms. Fillion reviews the skill of summarizing. Then the fifth graders practice this skill as they write well-organized paragraphs to summarize the data on the graphs.

Ms. Fillion is ensuring that the students get to know each other. She's giving a clear message that everyone in the class is important. In doing this, she's taking first steps in setting the expectation that everyone will be treated with kindness and respect. She's engaging in vital community-building practices while she teaches math and writing skills that are part of the fifth grade curriculum. By interweaving community building with academic skills, Ms. Fillion is taking a step toward preventing bullying in her classroom community.

Enlist Parents in Bullying Prevention Efforts

The problem of bullying is a tough one, and it's unlikely that we'll be able to solve it without allying with children's parents. In fact, international bullying prevention research shows that forging a strong home-school connection is one of the most important things that we can do to prevent bullying (Bradshaw 2015; Espelage and De La Rue 2012; Zych, Farrington, and Ttofi 2019). Bullying will continue to go on under our radar until we enlist parents in the effort to keep us informed about children's sense of safety in our classrooms. The first step in building this alliance is to talk with parents early in the year about your plans for creating a safe, caring classroom and your desire for open communication with them.

Be explicit that you care about inclusion and kindness

During your very first contact with children's parents, make it clear that your goal is to make the classroom a safe place for their children. Let them know about the steps you will take to help children get to know each other and to build community. Be explicit that you care about inclusion and kindness. You may be able to give parents this information directly at back-to-school night or you may decide to communicate with them through a letter home, an email, text, or follow-up phone call. Whichever format fits with your school and wider community, the message needs to be clear: I care about making school a safe place for learning.

Let parents know that you want to hear from them

Some parents may think that teachers are unconcerned about meanness and bullying. I have heard friends and other acquaintances say "She doesn't care" when speaking of their child's teacher. When they find out that I'm a teacher, they tell me tales of their child's mistreatment in school and ask, "Do you think I should tell her teacher? What if she takes it out on my child?" Unless teachers explicitly tell parents that we want to know, they may not tell us about mean ways that their child is being treated in school.

A kindergarten teacher talks to parents at back-to-school night

The kindergartners' parents are seated at back-to-school night, listening to Mr. Rinaldi discuss the upcoming year in kindergarten. He describes what the first days will be like and the ways in which he will help children feel welcomed and begin to get to know each other. Mr. Rinaldi also talks about teaching children how to get along with each other and teaching them how to meet school behavior expectations. He then says, "If your child is to have a good start in school, it's important that he or she feels safe here in our classroom. Sometimes children will tell parents things that they don't tell their teacher. If your child tells you about anything in school that is causing him to feel sad, to feel hurt, or to feel otherwise unsafe, please tell me about it. Please do not hesitate to contact me. Your child's comfort and safety in school is the most important thing to me." Mr. Rinaldi ended the evening with this powerful message.

A third grade teacher writes a letter and calls parents early in the year

Third grade teacher Mrs. Velasquez doesn't have the type of sit-down opportunity with parents that Mr. Rinaldi does. She does, however, write a letter that she sends home on the first day of school. She welcomes parents to the classroom community, describes some of the community-building activities the children will do in the first weeks of school, and explains about opportunities for parents to join the class for specific activities. She ends the letter by stating clearly and explicitly, "In this classroom I expect all children to be kind to each other. I'm counting on you to help by telling me if you suspect that anything unkind is going on."

Over the next few weeks Mrs. Velasquez takes her class list and texts a couple of parents each afternoon after school. She mentions something positive that she's noticed about the child, such as "I've noticed that Amaya enjoys math so much" or "Garrick is so helpful to Bree," a child in the classroom who has multiple disabilities. She also asks the parent if they have any concerns about their child's experience in third grade so far and invites the parent to set up a phone call if they would like. She's setting up channels of communication that will maximize the likelihood that parents will let her know if mean behavior or bullying is going on.

KEY IDEAS

- **A safe and kind classroom** helps prevent bullying.
- **Structures you put in place** on day one are an important ingredient in creating safe, kind classrooms.
- **Begin with learning each other's names**.
- **Use greeting, sharing, and whole-group activities** to help children get to know each other and build community.
- **Combine "getting to know you" activities** with academic activities.
- **Parents are potential allies** in bullying prevention. Take steps early in the year to communicate with parents about what you will do to prevent bullying and invite their participation.

You've worked hard all
year to make your 3rd grade
goal. Think about what
you did this year to
meet your goal. What
strategy did you use that
helped you reach your goal, or
greeting - explain
model it
share - we have sign ups
introduce sharers
activity - movement, song,
read aloud
message - you read, they read
together
Plan
what do they know how to do
already?
what will you need to model?
what words will you use to
keep them on task?
Tt
Uu
UNCOVER
TIGER

CHAPTER THREE

Creating Classroom Rules

Students in Mrs. Fox's first grade classroom gather in a circle on the meeting rug. It's the first week of school. So far this week, they have talked about what they want to learn in school this year and they are now talking about the rules they'll need to help them reach their learning goals.

"Why do we need rules?" Mrs. Fox asks.

"So that we can have fun," pipes up Sylvie.

"How do rules help us have fun, Sylvie?" asks Mrs. Fox, not quite sure where this is going.

"Because if we don't have rules kids might bully each other and then school wouldn't be fun," Sylvie replies.

Sylvie is right, of course. Rules provide a foundation on which we can build a classroom community and give children guidance about behavior expectations. Without common understandings about how to behave and how to treat each other, the classroom community will be adrift and full of the potential for mean behavior.

For these reasons, rules are an essential component of bullying prevention efforts. Most evidence-based bullying prevention programs include establishment of anti-bullying rules that let students know that mean behavior is unacceptable. Furthermore, these programs employ daily references to the established rules. Whether children read these rules chorally at the start of the day, hear their teachers mention the rules in the course of learning routines or lessons, or reflect on them at the end of the day, the rules are always there, front and center (Hinduja and Patchin 2014; Swearer et al. 2010).

In my experience, by going one step further and cocreating rules with students you will add the power of student investment in the rules. Children who have worked together to create their rules will believe in the rules, and they will want to follow them as well as help each other follow them. In this chapter, I share information about how to cocreate rules with students so that they see the rules as an important tool for keeping the classroom safe and kind.

You may instead decide to create classroom rules yourself and present them to the children early in the year, or you may decide to use previously established schoolwide rules in your classroom. If you choose to follow one of these paths, you can still build student investment in the rules by reflecting with students about how the rules will help keep everyone safe, how they will help everyone be kind, and how they will help everyone learn. No matter which approach you follow, it's important to establish classroom rules early in the year, build student investment in the rules, and keep the rules alive, day to day.

In addition to providing guidance to the classroom community about acceptable behavior, rules that children believe in will help teachers avoid power struggles with certain children. For example, children who bully often resist adults setting limits about bullying and other mean behaviors. When teachers refer to rules that are supported by everyone in the classroom, children will be reminded that the rules are setting the limits and therefore the children are less likely to slip into a power struggle with the adult who's enforcing the rules. "Our rules say to be kind; that wasn't kind" seats the locus of limit setting with the rules rather than an adult whim. It also is a reminder that rules apply to everyone—that in this classroom, being kind is the socially acceptable choice.

In the following pages, you'll find ideas for increasing the effectiveness of rules. Specifically, you'll learn about:

- Bringing children into the rules creation process
- Keeping rules general, few in number, and stated in positive terms
- Helping children apply the rules to daily life
- Responding to children's reports of mean behavior

Bring Children Into the Rules-Creation Process

Over many years of teaching children in a variety of grades and in a variety of settings, I have found that cocreating rules with students in the first days and weeks of school brings the power of a shared vision into the classroom. I have used many methods for teaming with students to create classroom rules but I finally settled on the method that many *Responsive Classroom* teachers use as the most straightforward way to build student investment in the rules.

I began by helping each student articulate a learning goal for the year. For example, when I elicited goals from third graders, Alycia said that she wanted to become a better reader and read lots of books. Matt said he wanted to learn new math facts. Sometimes goals were social goals. Shane, who hadn't had many friends the year before, said that he wanted to make a new friend. We decorated the walls with their pictures of themselves attaining their goals. The room was full of hopes for our year together.

With goals named, I then asked, "If we are all going to achieve our goals, what rules do we need?" As students brainstormed a list of rules, they had a lot to say. Past hurts were remembered as Pauline said, "No hitting," and as Samuel said, "Call people by their own names."

I helped students reframe the "no" or "don't" rules into positives by asking questions such as "If we're not going to hit people, what will we be doing with our bodies?" Pauline suggested, "Bodies to ourselves." Investment was building as everyone got their ideas out and listed them on the large piece of chart paper in the front of the room.

We then began a process of sorting that long list, grouping the ideas by categories, and naming each category as a rule. We spent fifteen minutes or so each day for a week, distilling our rules and naming them. The time that we spent increased student investment as they proudly said, "We're working really hard on this." (See the table that follows for an example of this categorizing process.)

Brainstormed Ideas, Sorted Into Categories	Rules
Responsibility for self Pay attention Do your work Listen to each other and to the teacher	Take care of our own learning
Responsibility toward others Keep our bodies to ourselves Include everyone Use kind words Call people by their own names Listen to others' ideas Cooperate with teammates	Be kind to all
Responsibility for the environment Take care of materials Clean up after ourselves Take care of other people's things	Keep our classroom and school beautiful

Eventually we came up with three to five sentences, each naming a class rule. If the students did not mention kindness and inclusion, then I made sure to bring it up. For example, I might say, "Do we have a rule that will protect people from mean words?" or "Do we have a rule that will help everyone have someone to play with?" Children easily came up with a rule that would help them feel safe and included.

We posted the rules prominently in the classroom and everyone signed their name at the bottom, testifying that they endorsed our rules.

You may not feel ready to engage in this process, or you may feel that your students aren't ready to think about rules in this way. This isn't a problem—there are many ways to modify the process while still retaining student engagement and investment. For example, students can name the goals and the teacher could create the rules based on those goals.

Another option would have the teacher create the rules and then the children discuss topics such as "How will these rules keep us safe?" and "How will they help us learn?" As students reflect, they think about their wishes for a safe learning environment in school.

My colleague Donna Skolnick had her second grade students get into small groups and prepare short plays about how each rule would create a classroom that would be "the way we want our school to be."

As long as you involve your students in some part of the process of creating the rules, you are on your way to having rules that will become the touchstone for life in the classroom community and a foundation for bullying prevention.

For more information about this approach to rules creation, see *Teaching Self-Discipline: The Responsive Classroom Guide to Helping Students Dream, Behave, and Achieve in Elementary School*, by Caitie Meehan, Cory Wade, Earl Hunter II, Laurie Badge, and Suzy Ghosh (see Appendix B).

Keep Rules General, Few in Number, and Stated in Positive Terms

In the process described earlier, I talk about creating a brief list of general rules stated in the positive. On the surface, it may appear that this approach to the rules won't be strong enough—to tackle something as serious as bullying, creating a long list of "don't do it" rules may seem to be more effective. However, when teachers post a long list of explicit and detailed rules addressing all possible misbehaviors, it's all too easy for a child who bullies to pick at these rules and say, for example, "But there's no rule against pinching someone's nose so that must be okay." In addition, a list of rules stated in the negative can feel constraining and restrictive to children, something to find the wiggle room around rather than something to draw inspiration from.

Rules stated in the positive are more effective than rules stated in the negative. Rules such as "We will be kind to everyone," "We will take care of our classroom environment," and "We will be responsible learners" help children know what to do rather than what not to do. The positive framing of these rules also allows children to build a vision of a caring community and communicate that together we will create a classroom that is safe, inclusive, kind, and joyful. The rules will then more likely be something that everyone wants to respect in order to help maintain that feeling of safety and inclusion.

Help Children Apply the Rules to Daily Life

Providing the rules is a first step. For ongoing effectiveness, however, it's important to keep the rules alive, front and center, in children's daily school life. One way to do this is through ongoing reminders and conversations with the children about how the rules apply to specific situations.

For example, a rule such as "Be kind to everyone" provides an anchor for the class. To prevent the inevitable mean behaviors that can lead to bullying, though, it's important to be explicit about application. Before a group activity, a teacher might ask, "If our rule says 'Be kind to everyone,' how will we make sure everyone is included during our group activity?" When a teacher has noticed exclusionary behavior, she might say, "Sometimes people leave others out on purpose. That is not okay in this class. We have a rule that says 'Be kind to everyone.'"

These conversations can be brief and can happen at any grade level. In Mr. Rinaldi's kindergarten class, there are three rules: "We will be kind," "We will do our work," and "We will take care of our classroom." These three simple rules cover most of the challenges of kindergarten. He begins by asking children to think about what being kind might look like and sound like. "Pretend you are sitting at the table and drawing. You are using the blue crayon. The person sitting next to you asks to use the blue crayon to color in the sky in his drawing. What could you do that would be kind?" asks Mr. Rinaldi. Children offer ideas for how they might handle such a challenge, and then take time to draw pictures of themselves doing kind things. On subsequent days the children discuss the second and third rules, and then create drawings about doing their work and taking care of the classroom.

After Mr. Rinaldi has introduced and discussed the rules with the class, he is careful to refer to them frequently over the course of the school year. For example, when the children line up to go out to recess, he says, "Who can remind us about Paul's picture of being kind on the playground?" Lori raises her hand and says, "He showed kids playing together. Everyone gets to play."

Conversations about rules might also focus on helping children understand exactly what some of the more general words mean. The rules in Mr. Shane's second grade classroom are "Be respectful," "Be responsible," and "Be safe." Mr. Shane knows that his students will need lots of practice if they are to understand what "respectful" and "responsible" mean as well as how "be safe" applies to the school setting. He knows that adults often use "respectful" when speaking to children as if it means "Follow adult directions," and he wants to clarify the deeper meaning of that word.

Remembering the dictionary definition of respect ("To have regard or esteem for"), Mr. Shane starts out by saying, "Another way of describing 'be respectful' might be 'treat everyone so that they know they're important to you.'" Mr. Shane then leads the class in a discussion of what second graders might do to show their classmates that they're important. Mr. Shane records student ideas on a chart.

Laticia says, "We can help each other find things."

Tommy says, "We can share pencils."

Then, to expand the class's thinking beyond material objects and toward less tangible things such as how they speak to one another, Mr. Shane says, "How could we use kind words to show someone that they're important to us?"

Mikey quickly replies, "We could ask, 'Do you want to play?'" and Sylvie suggests, "Do you want to eat lunch with us?"

Mr. Shane agrees, saying, "Those certainly sound like kind words."

Later on, as the students get ready to go out to recess, Mr. Shane says to the class, "Remember Mikey's idea about how to be respectful—be sure to ask anyone who's alone if they want to play." When the children come in from recess, he tells them, "Put your thumb up if you remembered to ask someone to play." Mr. Shane is bringing the rules to life for the students.

In both Mr. Rinaldi's class and Mr. Shane's class, the conversations will continue throughout the year in one-on-one conversations as well as in whole-group discussions.

Explicitly make the connection between rules and bullying or mean behavior

It's important to directly and explicitly connect the classroom rules to unacceptable behaviors such as bullying and gateways to bullying. If we don't do so, the students may not understand that these behaviors are not acceptable. Because the students see or have seen others behaving unacceptably, by not connecting these behaviors to the rules they may think the behaviors must be all right (Swearer et al. 2010).

Furthermore, there is evidence that teachers miss many mean behaviors that occur under their radar (Craig and Pepler 1998; Ostrander et al. 2018). In some cases, teachers don't see "popular" children as ones who might bully others (Rosen, Scott, and DeOrnellas 2017), and sometimes teachers don't intervene because they don't know what to do (Maran, Tirassa, and Begotti 2017). When we don't stop these behaviors, children may imagine that we think the behaviors are acceptable. Teachers need to be absolutely clear that mean behaviors are never acceptable.

Let's say you and the children have created a classroom rule about kindness and inclusion. The children have agreed to follow this rule and are invested in doing so. You've discussed possible applications of this rule by raising questions such as: "What would being kind look like on the playground?" "What would you do to follow our rule to be kind when you see someone who has no one to play with?" "How can you be kind to a new reading partner whom you don't know well yet?"

The next step is to raise the issue of mean behavior explicitly and directly. You might say, "Sometimes kids leave someone out or call someone mean names because they want to show that they're more important than that person. This is not kind. When someone does that, they are not following our rule."

Especially when working with older children, it can be helpful to name the behavior as "bullying" and to define what bullying is. You might say, "Bullying is when someone is mean to someone else, especially someone who is less powerful in the classroom. Bullying might be using mean words or leaving someone out on purpose, or hitting, kicking, poking, and pinching someone. Bullying might be to someone's face or it might be behind their back."

Base your decision to explicitly connect mean behaviors to the word "bullying" on whether or not this is a familiar word to your students. Communities may vary when considering if "bullying" is an often-used word. If the community where you teach does not use the word "bullying," you can simply use the term "mean behaviors." It may or may not be helpful to introduce the word "bullying" as a pathway to kindness.

Notice that I'm suggesting to describe "bullying" and mean behavior explicitly as a breach of the class-created, positive vision of "We will be kind." Student investment in "We will be kind" then leads to student investment in "We will not bully."

It might be helpful at this point to write on a sentence strip "We will not bully" and attach it to the class rule "We will be kind" as a visual reminder of this application of the rule and to make it clear to children that bullying behavior is not acceptable.

> **Some Language to Try**
>
> *If our rule says "Be kind to everyone," how will we make sure everyone is included during our group activity?*
>
> *Those certainly sound like kind words.*
>
> *Remember [Mikey's] idea about how to be respectful—be sure to ask anyone who's alone if they want to play.*
>
> *How can you be kind to a new reading partner whom you don't know well yet?*
>
> *Sometimes kids leave someone out or call someone mean names because they want to show that they're more important than that person. This is not kind. When someone does that, they are not following our rule.*

Use children's books to begin a discussion of rules

Many high-quality picture books for children of all ages describe bullying behaviors in an accurate and accessible way. Reading such a picture book aloud and discussing it with the students as you read is another way to open up a discussion about bullying and how class rules can protect students from bullying. The slight remove of a picture book leads to a discussion that children can engage in without dwelling on the fact that perhaps they have done some of the acts described in the book.

In Katie Couric's accessible book *The Brand New Kid* (2000), classmates reject Lazlo, the "new kid" in school. Listeners' faces are sad as they hear about the mean things that the children in the story are doing to Lazlo. Ellie has a moment of empathy and asks Lazlo to play. Listeners' faces brighten visibly as Lazlo gets a smile on his face. This shared literature experience has given the class a common understanding that they can live by the classroom rule to be kind and protect each other from bullying.

Appendix A includes an annotated bibliography of picture books that I recommend because they present accurate information about bullying behavior and are appealing to children. In Chapter Seven, I offer lesson plans that will help you talk with students about mean behavior and bullying. Included are specific discussion questions to use as you share some of these picture books with students.

Help children connect the rules to cyberbullying

Cyberbullying occurs among young children. Children use digital devices, without supervision, at younger and younger ages. Once they have access to phones or lightly supervised computers or tablets, some elementary school students send each other mean texts, emojis, or use social media to engage in social cruelty or bullying toward classmates. When bullying begins at school it can escalate through the use of devices that can be accessed 24/7 (Englander 2013). For that reason, it's important that educators directly teach the importance of digital kindness.

In Ms. Jones' third grade each child has a school-provided tablet for use in school. Each tablet includes the application SeeSaw, which enables students to keep a digital portfolio of their school work.

Ms. Jones introduces how to save writing work on SeeSaw and how to make helpful comments on others' writing using the application. The third graders have already learned how to have in-person peer writing conferences that are helpful and kind. Cyber comments are the next step.

First, though, Ms. Jones reviews the classroom rules that children have cocreated:

> Help each other and be kind
>
> Be serious about our experiences
>
> Be responsible with and respect all materials

She decides to create a new list of rules for the class's SeeSaw accounts that are connected to their class rules, the same way they connected "We will not bully" to their class rules.

She gathers her students in a circle. "Today we're going to start using our SeeSaw apps for comments about classmates' writing. First, we need to think about how to keep ourselves and others safe in the SeeSaw environment. Let's look at our rules and see how they can help us."

Sara raises her hand. "'Help each other and be kind' will be important," she says.

"How might we help each other and be kind while making comments about others' work on SeeSaw?" Mrs. Jones asks.

"We can make sure we say kind things," says Larry.

Mrs. Jones records this idea on chart paper.

"We're going to use SeeSaw to give each other feedback about school work,"

Mrs. Jones explains. "What if you need to give someone constructive criticism?" she asks.

"Maybe we can say, 'Be honest but be kind,'" says Maya. "If we need to say something that might sound unkind on SeeSaw we can say it in person."

Mrs. Jones writes this idea down on the same chart.

"We also need to remember that it can be easy to say something mean to someone when we can't see their face and don't know how we're making them feel," says Mrs. Jones (Englander 2013). "How can we help ourselves be kind when we're typing a message?"

"How about make a picture in your mind of the person?" suggests Jenny. "Imagine how your comment will make them feel."

Mrs. Jones adds this information to the SeeSaw rules chart.

Before the children go to work she says, "Remember, be honest but be kind." As the children write, take pictures of their writing, and post those pictures, Mrs. Jones reminds them frequently of their SeeSaw rules.

The class is invested in cyber safety. They see the connection between the class rules that they worked so hard to create, their SeeSaw rules that they're creating as a class, and the class's climate of safety and kindness. (For more on cyberbullying, see Chapter Six.)

Strategy in Action

Ms. Robatille Tailors the Rules-Creation Process for Fifth and Sixth Grade Students

Ms. Robatille teaches a combined fifth–sixth grade class. The sixth graders were with her the previous year, but the fifth graders are new to the class. She knows that she needs to begin the year by setting expectations and creating rules with the newly formed combination class. Ms. Robatille also knows that the sixth graders are at the normal development stage of separating from adults and establishing independence. For this reason, she needs to handle rules creation carefully so that the sixth graders will take a positive leadership role as the new fifth graders are incorporated into the group.

The students at this school have engaged in some form of rules creation at the beginning of the year at each grade level since kindergarten. Ms. Robatille wants to make the rules creation process feel fresh and important to the students and not simply a ritualized re-creation of something that they did when they were five years old. To engage all of the students fully, she makes lots of connections between the rules, students' personal goals, and the real life of the classroom.

She begins with a discussion of students' strengths and challenges

Ms. Robatille begins with a discussion about what students are good at. The students are excited. The class hears about sports and academics, family life, and friends. Next, she says, "There's always room for improvement in whatever we do." The class begins to discuss what might be a challenge for students in fifth and sixth grade. She's careful to protect the eleven-year-old students, who tend to be sensitive, by keeping the topic to "students in general" rather than "what might be challenging for you." She finishes this discussion with the concept of a personal goal: "What might you work on improving in school this year?"

Students name goals

Over the course of the next week, students name their goals. Some are academic, such as understanding fractions better, and some are social, such as mentoring a younger student or making a new friend.

Students and teacher create rules connected to the goals

During the second week of school, the class begins to brainstorm lists of potential rules that might help them achieve their goals. Ideas are as concrete as "No interrupting" and "Take care of computers," or as general as "No excluding" and "Help others when in need."

After their hard work creating a list of possible rules, Ms. Robatille notices that the students need an activity break. The class goes outside to play a game of soccer. Upon returning to the classroom, they discuss what contributed to their game going as well as it did. Children mention that they supported and encouraged each other, used teamwork, and included everyone. Ms. Robatille adds these comments to the class list of potential rules.

Over the next few days the class combines and tweaks their list until they have created four overarching class rules: "Respect each other and yourself," "Respect the classroom and each other's property," "Use teamwork," and "Be safe."

A game provides an opportunity for applying the rules

At the end of the second week of school, the class goes outside to play a game of kick ball with another class. Before they leave the classroom, Ms. Robatille asks students to remind everyone of one important classroom rule they might need to take into consideration while playing the game. She makes a point of saying, "What rule will help you treat each other fairly and kindly and stop mean behaviors?" Immediately, many hands go up and students eagerly chime in: "Use teamwork." When she asks them what teamwork might look like and sound like, they say, "Encourage and support each other" and "Let everyone have a turn."

Afterward, Ms. Robatille asks her students what they noticed during the game. Mia says, "I saw James help David up when he fell." Another says, "Kendra did a nice job helping Matthew [a student with a diagnosis of autism] run around the bases."

Fifth and sixth graders alike feel invested in their rules. They see the connection between the rules posted on the wall and their daily classroom life. The rules are theirs, and they will help the students have a good year. Ms. Robatille feels that the time that she has devoted to the process was well worth it. Together they have taken the first steps toward a kind and cooperative multiage community.

Talk With Students About How and When to Report Rule-Breaking or Mean Behaviors

Rules provide an essential framework for positive behavior. No matter how carefully the rules are established and practiced, though, children will still sometimes engage in mean behavior and bullying. Unfortunately, much of this behavior can happen behind a teacher's back. Because we can't stop meanness and bullying behaviors that we don't know about, we need children to alert us.

In study after study, children say that their teachers "don't do anything" about bullying (Craig and Pepler 1998; Englander 2013). Their perception is that teachers don't care, so children learn not to tell us about it. This situation has been inadvertently created by teaching students not to tell. If we could do only one thing to stop bullying in school, the most effective step would be to change the school culture about tattling.

Replace "Don't tattle" with "I can see you know our rule"

When children begin school, often at five years old, they rely on the authority of the adult in charge. They want to know what is allowed and what isn't, and they expect to get this information from their teacher. As children learn the rules, they begin to incorporate them through what psychologist Lev Vygotsky called "other regulation" (Vygotsky 1978). In other words, they report to the teacher every time they see someone not following the rules that they themselves are trying so hard to follow. This "other regulation" is a way for them to learn the rules—they're practicing the rules by correcting others, and they're leaning on the teacher's guidance as they practice their knowledge of the rules.

For example, Charlene pushes ahead in the lunch line to create a spot for herself at the front. "Teacher, teacher," sings out Josie, "Charlene cut in line." That constant other regulation about small things can feel pretty irritating to the adults to whom the children are reporting small infractions. The adults often respond by saying, "Don't tattle."

The problem is that young children don't necessarily know the difference between telling about relatively minor problems like Charlene's cutting in line and reporting instances of mean or intimidating behavior such as, for example, Charlene's telling Josie that she has to surrender her dessert every day at lunch. Even adults sometimes have trouble discerning whether any particular behavior is a minor "just let it go" behavior or something that needs a firm response.

My colleague Chip Wood, who first drew my attention to Vygotsky's concept of other regulation, suggests responding to young children's telling about small behaviors by saying, "I can see that you know our rule against cutting in line" or "Thank you for letting me know that you know our rule." These responses honor children's impulse to tell about things that are important to them while not getting overly involved with relatively minor behaviors such as cutting in line.

Teach children how and when to report mean behaviors

It's also important to teach children directly that it is important to talk to a responsible adult when they see or experience behaviors that could escalate into bullying. Children of all ages can learn to report behaviors that are mean, hurt feelings or bodies, or are dangerous or destructive.

Notice that I use the word "report." I'm not suggesting that children need to "report" in an official way as part of a state-law mandated anti-bullying protocol. Instead, I'm using the word as a replacement for "tattling" or "telling." The taboo against tattling is so strong in our culture that it's better not to use language such as "tell a responsible adult" because the word "telling" has such negative associations for children (as in "I'm gonna tell on you") and sounds too much like "tattling."

To give children the message that we care about their safety, we need to err on the side of listening when they come to us with grievances that, at least at first, sound like tattles. Abolishing the word "tattle" from our own vocabularies would be a powerful first step. We need to show our students that we do care. Otherwise, mean behavior and bullying will continue to flourish out of our sight, and teachers will be oblivious.

Be sure there's a response when children report mean behaviors

Another way that adults sometimes give children the message that it's better not to report mean behaviors is by handling their reporting in a way that doesn't fix the problem or, in some cases, makes the problem worse (Twemlow et al. 2006).

Once you teach students to report mean behaviors, they will try out that reporting. It's important that the adults they report to respond assertively and sensitively. All too often, adults at school will respond to children's reporting of a problem by responding with "Work it out yourself." This practice can make bullying worse. If you suspect bullying, then you need to intervene to stop the behavior and protect the child who is targeted.

If children are asking for help, you need to investigate. What happened? If it's a minor conflict among equals, such as who among a group of friends gets to go first in Four Square, you can carefully help the children practice the skills of conflict resolution. If it's an act of meanness, then it's time to intervene immediately to stop the meanness. However, as I discuss in Chapter One, if you suspect a power difference, don't have the children do a conflict resolution talk.

Responding doesn't mean that you have to share the resolution of the problem with the child who reports it unless they're reporting something that happened to them. If they're reporting something they've witnessed, then it's fine to say, "I'll take care of this right away." If they're reporting something they've experienced, then they'll need more reassurance about how you're going to keep them safe. It's also helpful to say to the child who has experienced meanness or bullying, "If the problem continues, let me know." You may think you've dealt with the situation when in fact the behavior may continue.

In Chapter Seven, you'll find lessons for explicitly teaching children about meanness and bullying. These include lessons about how, when, and what to report. Before you teach these lessons or talk with students about reporting mean behaviors outside of the classroom, it's important that you figure out whom the students need to report to when you are not present. If you have the same recess staff every day, then check in with one of the recess supervisors, explain the lessons that you're about to teach, and make sure that the staff members will pass any information about bullying or gateway behaviors to you.

The same advice applies to the cafeteria or other outside-the-classroom settings at school. Schools are full of reporting logjams. The recess supervisor may have heard about the mean behavior and the cafeteria supervisor may have heard about it, but they haven't communicated with each other or with the child's classroom teacher.

Keep information confidential

Equally important is to keep information that children report to you as confidential as possible. When you speak with a child who is exhibiting mean behavior, it works best to say, "Several different people have told me . . ." or "It's been reported to me . . ." to avoid naming the child who reported the behavior. This is particularly important because children who engage in bullying behaviors might retaliate if they think that someone—either the child who is targeted or a bystander—"told" on them. Confidentiality protects the reporter.

Clarify what happened before you confront

Children who bully will often deny that they were involved so you should make sure that you know the facts. Start by asking the child or children who are reporting the mean behavior a few questions to get a clearer sense of what happened. Have them describe the behavior. When and where did it happen? Was it mean? In what way? What felt unsafe about it? What felt hurtful? Specific information will give you a clearer picture of whether the behavior being reported is in fact mean.

Situations can get complicated so be sure to listen carefully. For example, a group of girls in second grade had actively excluded their classmate Missy for months. They had called her mean names, spit on her on the bus, and refused to sit near her. When Missy, in her misery and frustration, said to the girls "I'm going to get a gun and shoot you," they reported this fact to their principal, Ms. Platz. She listened carefully to Missy when she was sent to the office for using threatening words. By asking specific questions, Ms. Platz uncovered what had led up to Missy's threatening words. Being fully informed allowed Ms. Platz to handle the situation fairly and effectively.

Once you know the facts, it's important to be clear, firm, and descriptive when you talk with the child involved in the mean behavior. Be clear and firm in your own mind about the consequences of the behavior—you don't want to get caught up in negotiating. If you allow for any wiggle room, the child who bullies may well take it.

When children deny their involvement in mean behavior, I've found it helpful to keep in mind the main goal: to keep the child who's been targeted safe. That means protecting that child from the one engaging in the mean behavior. Keep in mind too that the child who is being mean is the one who needs to be removed from the situation, and not the child targeted. For example, a teacher might calmly say, "People have reported that you called Paul a 'loser' and told him that you'd punch him if he tried to join the game. As a result, you'll be out of the game for a few days until you can treat Paul as an equal member of our class." Over the next few days, the teacher checks in with the child to make sure he understands how to treat Paul fairly and rejoin the game. This isn't about punishment—this is about keeping Paul safe in school.

Communicating With Parents About Rules

To convince parents that you are sincere in wanting to work with them on the important issue of preventing bullying, you need to let them know about some of the specific steps that you're taking to create an atmosphere of kindness and safety. Sharing information about how you create and support classroom rules is a simple and concrete way of doing this.

Let parents know that you value classroom rules

First, it's important to let parents know that you view classroom rules as a strong and positive foundation for building a safe, caring classroom community. In your early communications with parents about how you will keep the classroom safe for all students, let them know that the class will have rules to guide children's behavior. Reassure parents that the rules will keep their children safe. When the parents understand that the rules are meant to keep everyone safe, they are far more likely to let you know if they think that something unsafe is going on.

Let parents know the process you will use for creating rules

Unfortunately, many adults' experience with school rules might have been negative—long lists of things "not to do" often accompanied by a list of what would happen if the rules were broken. Letting parents know about your process for creating positive rules can help reassure them that their child's experience will be a positive one.

Communication about how you will create rules can happen during visits such as back to school night, or via texts, emails, phone calls, or a letter sent home to parents. If you're going to work with the students to create the rules, briefly explain some of the steps that the class will complete and offer a brief explanation of the power of cocreating rules with students.

Telling parents that children have "written and made drawings about their hopes and goals for the year" and that children have "thought about what rules might make their hopes and goals come true" conveys that the rules come from the classroom community rather than from an outside authority figure. Explaining that the children "spent time creating the rules" and are "proud of the work that they've done" lets families know that the children are invested in their hard work to create meaningful rules.

Ask for parents' thoughts about learning goals for their children

You begin to build the lines of communication when you tell parents about what you're doing in the classroom. The lines of communication become even stronger if you ask their opinions, creating two-way communication. Formation of a child's learning goals for the year is a key opportunity for parent input.

Many teachers send letters home early in the year asking parents to suggest one school-based goal for their child. This is a practice that I used for many years in my own teaching. I found that parents' goals told me a lot about my new students. For example, when parents replied that they hoped their child would become more independent about homework completion, I had some information about what might be happening at home around homework. When a parent said that she hoped her child would learn to love math or reading, I understood something about the child's current attitudes toward those subjects.

Sometimes goals were unrealistic, such as when a parent suggested that they'd like their first grader to understand square roots by the end of the year. Even unrealistic goals, however, gave us a point to begin a conversation. Whatever adult family members articulated as a goal, the important thing was that two-way communication had been established. Beginning our conversations around a positive topic such as goals for the year stood us in good stead if it became necessary to discuss more sensitive topics.

Share classroom rules with parents and let them know how you will help children apply the rules

Once the class rules are created, send a copy home with each student. Many teachers ask parents to sign a copy of the rules and send it back to school to indicate that they have read the rules.

It's also important to let parents know that the rules are not empty statements written beautifully on chart paper. Let them know that you will be talking with students in an ongoing way about how the rules apply to specific situations, including bullying. And reiterate that you want to hear about any unsafe behavior that is going on. Knowing the rules can help parents be stronger partners in bullying prevention.

KEY IDEAS

- **Classroom rules are a foundation** for bullying prevention efforts.
- **Find ways to bring students** into the rules-creation process; cocreating rules with students is a powerful way to do this.
- **Connect the rules** to students' learning goals. This increases students' investment in the rules.
- **Keep rules general,** few in number, and positive—a long list of negatively stated rules can work against bullying prevention efforts.
- **Talk with students** about how the rules apply to specific situations, including situations of meanness and bullying.
- **Encourage students** to report mean behaviors they experience or witness.
- **Replace "tattling,"** which has negative connotations, with "reporting" or "talking to an adult."
- **Work with other school staff** to ensure that children's reports of mean behavior will be heard and acted on.
- **Communicate with parents** about your approach to classroom rules.

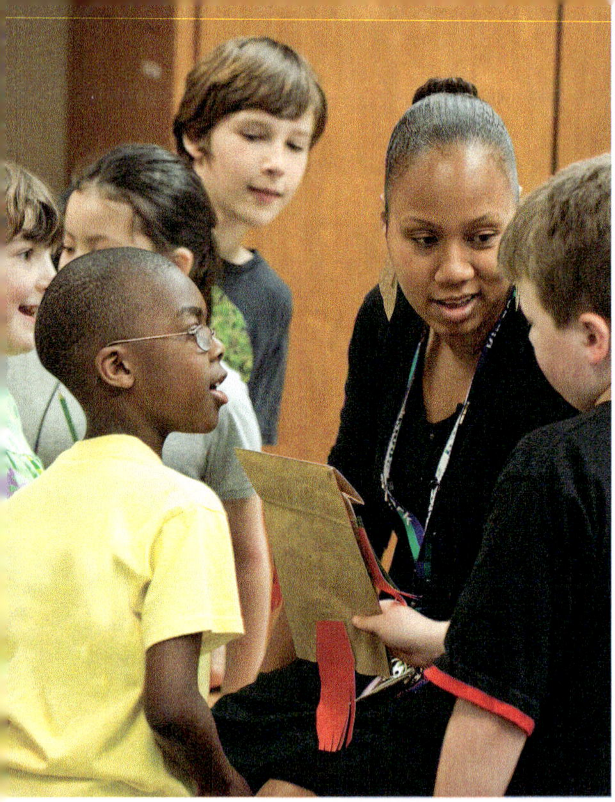

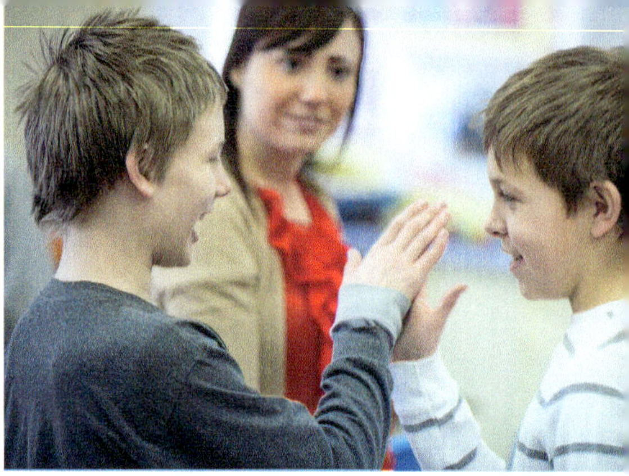

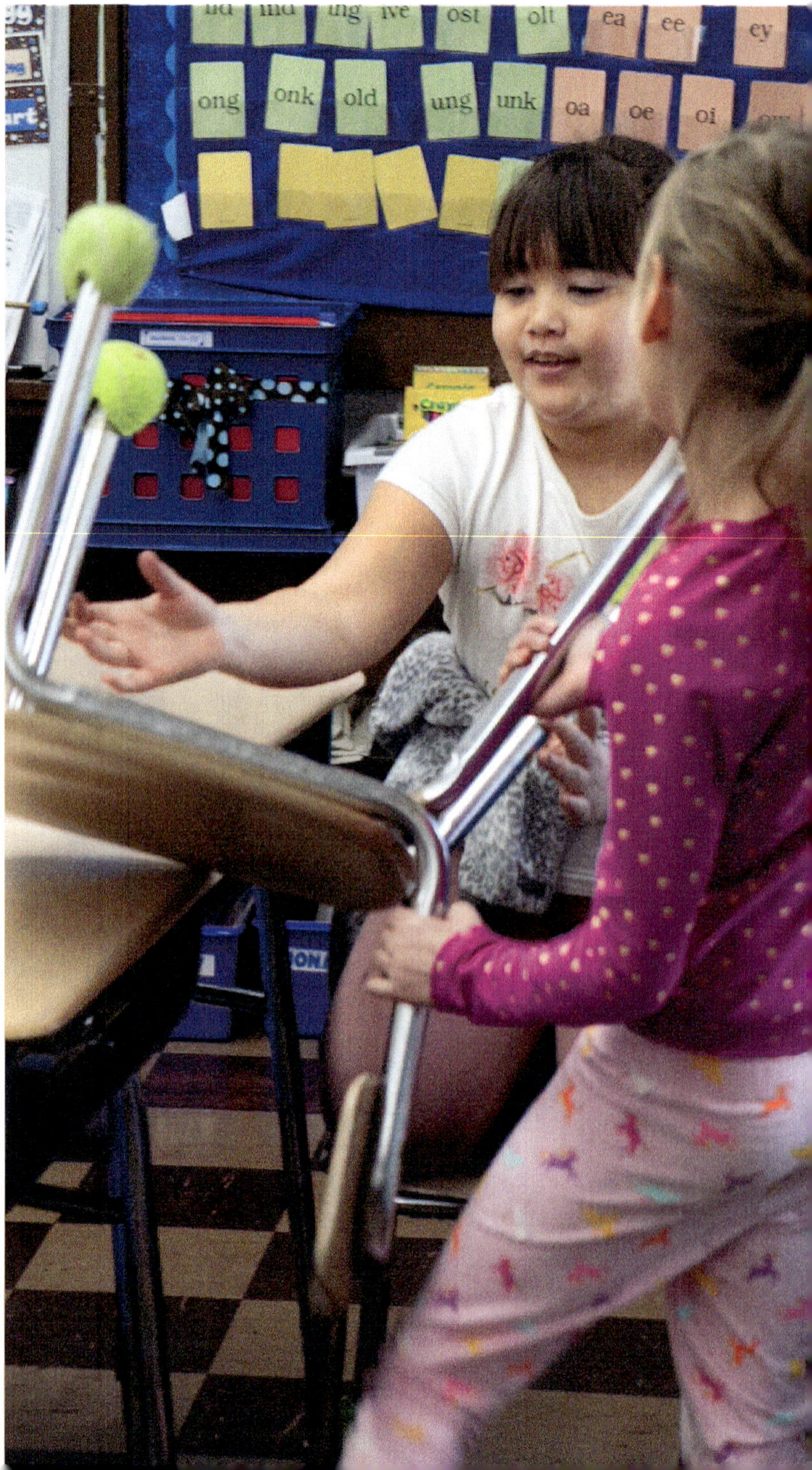
ost
olt
ea
ee
ey
ong
onk
old
ung
unk
oa
oe
oi

CHAPTER FOUR

Teaching Children How to Work Together

Third graders Mandy and Garrick are writing partners for the day. They sit facing each other, ready to review Garrick's most recent draft of his story "Fishing With My Dad." As Garrick reads the draft aloud, Mandy's face and body posture show that she's listening. She offers relevant comments and suggestions, just as her teacher has taught her to do. Garrick asks questions to be sure he understands her suggestions and makes notes in the margin of his paper. When they've finished talking, he eagerly sets to work creating a final draft of the story, incorporating many of Mandy's suggestions.

Earlier, Garrick was the coach as Mandy read her draft. Like Mandy, he sat quietly, looked attentively at Mandy as she read aloud, and offered her helpful comments. Working together in this collaborative and respectful way has helped Mandy and Garrick bring their stories into focus and strengthen their writing and thinking skills. It has also given them an opportunity to practice being respectful listeners, a skill they can transfer to other school situations.

There's another benefit to this collaborative work: Children get to know each other. Mandy is not the only student who has seen Garrick's story—Garrick has shared earlier drafts with other classmates as they helped him work through the revision process. One morning, as students arrived at school, they rushed to tell Garrick about a piece on fishing that would be on TV that night. "Garrick loves to fish," many of the children announced. They know this because of the work they've done with Garrick on his story.

A key to a strong community is having each student willing to work with every other student in a respectful way. Whether it's working with a partner or in a small group, children need to know how to work together cooperatively if a climate of kindness and inclusion is to prevail in the classroom. However, it's not enough to simply group children together and expect them to work collaboratively. In fact, bullying may increase in classrooms where the teacher does not provide sufficient attention to the composition and functioning of the cooperative groups. When socially powerful children are grouped with children who are ostracized, the group may provide a rich climate for bullying behaviors (Vaillancourt, Hymel, and McDougall 2003). In our opening story in this chapter, the teacher carefully considered which children would make effective writing partners while keeping in mind whether any particular pairing might feel unsafe to certain children.

In my experience, another key factor is whether or not the children are taught, explicitly, how to work together respectfully. For example, Mandy and Garrick's teacher took steps to teach the students and model for them how to give and receive feedback on their writing before sending them into group work. She had the children practice how to listen carefully, use body language that communicates respectful interest, ask clarifying questions, and give an opinion in a kind yet honest way. That's a lot of skills—skills that children don't necessarily bring to school, and therefore ones we need to deliberately teach.

When students work together in small groups without explicit instructions, things can soon go awry, even when we assign tasks such as group leader and timekeeper. Without explicit instructions, some students become overwhelmed, sit back, and do nothing. Other students, in frustration, take over, ordering their classmates to action. Irritation mounts. Soon the arguing begins. Over time, a negative climate takes root in the classroom community. Mean comments and exclusion are regular events and disrespect is the norm.

To prevent this, it's important to break down the skills needed for small-group work and teach each skill explicitly. To be able to work together smoothly, children need to know how to take turns speaking, listen to their partner or group members, respond to what partners or group members say, and keep their words, tone, and body language friendly and respectful. Thus the circle of respect grows stronger.

First, Observe the Students

To discover which cooperative work skills students need, carefully observe the children as they work as well as in their casual interactions. As you watch, analyze which skills students have as well as which skills they're missing. You can then break down the missing skills into steps that are appropriate for the children's age (see Strategy in Action on pages 91–92 for an example of breaking down skills for first graders). Doing so enables you to make the instructions in partner and group work skills pointed and effective.

Questions to guide your observation

Do all students interact in a friendly and respectful way with one another?

Notice who interacts with whom. Does each student interact with a number of others during the course of the day? Are some students frequently on their own? Do certain students gravitate to each other over and over? Do students divide up by gender, race, or the neighborhood where they live? If you do notice divisions in your classroom, it's time to teach and practice how to be friendly to everyone.

> **Work respectfully with your partner or group:**
> - Sit with your partner or group
> - Look at the person who is speaking
> - Wait until the speaker finishes speaking before sharing
> - Respond to what your partner or the speaker says
> - Share your ideas when it's your turn

What do you notice about students' body language?

Watch students as they work together. Do they face each other or turn away? Does one group member slowly inch toward another group, as if trying to slide into more appealing company? Does one group member roll on the floor, inattentive, while his partner talks? If children aren't using respectful body language, you need to teach and practice what respectful body language looks like.

Do students listen and respond to each other's words?

Listen in on their conversations. It's common for children to conduct parallel conversations, each talking away, sometimes simultaneously, without much regard for what the other is saying. More often than not children will need direct teaching about how to have a conversation before they can successfully work in a small group. Provide direct instruction and modeling about how to listen to what another student says, followed by how to respond directly to the content of a partner's words.

Do students share materials gracefully?

Observe students to learn how they manage materials. Do they share writing implements and art materials, or do they snatch them away from each other? Do they hold books and pictures so fellow group members can see, or do they take care only of their own need to see the materials? If you notice students having difficulty with sharing, take the time to teach them how to share.

Second, Teach the Skills Needed for Successful Group Work

Observing children and gathering information about group and partner work skills is an ongoing process. As you identify areas that need work, you can use a number of strategies to teach and support needed skills. In the following pages, I'll explain how to use each of these strategies:

- Model desired behavior
- Role-play ways to respond to potentially tricky situations
- Continually name and reinforce ideal behaviors
- Use anchor charts to remind students of newly learned skills
- Use the "fishbowl" strategy to reinforce small-group skills
- Coach individuals and small groups
- Provide structures for taking turns within a small group

Model desired behavior

The *Responsive Classroom* strategy of Interactive Modeling is one of the best strategies I know for teaching children the skills needed for successful group work. In Interactive Modeling, the teacher and a few students demonstrate the expected behavior while the rest of the students watch carefully and then name what they observed. In the final step, everyone has an opportunity to practice the behavior while the teacher coaches them. Interactive Modeling takes only a few minutes, and because the student is actively engaged in the process, the new learning that occurs is significant.

Here are suggested steps in Interactive Modeling used to prepare fourth grade students to listen respectfully to a partner when working together on a science project.

1. **Tell the class what you're going to model and why.** As a way to increase student investment in doing this behavior, it's important to connect the behavior to the classroom rules. You might introduce the modeling by saying, "Our rules say to 'take care of each other.' When you work on a project with a classmate, you need to take care of each other by listening to each other's ideas. Today you're going to work with a partner to begin to turn one of your 'wonders' about earthworms into an investigation. To make a good start on planning your investigation, you need to listen to your partner's thoughts and ideas." Setting the skill in the context of planning a project such as their first scientific experiment helps increase student investment in the skill.

2. **Prompt all students to watch carefully as you demonstrate the skill.** For example, you might ask a student to talk while you listen carefully to what the student says (help the student prepare something to say ahead of time). To instruct observers, you might say, "Notice what I do with my body and my face to let Thea know I'm listening to her." It's important that the teacher plays the key role here to ensure that the modeling shows the desired prosocial behavior.

3. **Ask students what they noticed about your behavior.** Be sure to highlight the desired actions. "What did you notice about my careful listening?" the teacher asks. A student might say, "You looked right at your partner"

or "You nodded your head seriously as your partner spoke." Asking students for their observations like this maximizes the likelihood that they will be engaged—and take in the learning.

4. **Ask one or two students to model the same behavior.** You might say, "Yasmine, would you show the class careful listening as Thea talks to you about her ideas?" The teacher has talked to Yasmine ahead of time to help her practice careful listening so that she'll be ready with some helpful behaviors. If children have some familiarity with the behaviors being practiced, you can ask for volunteers in the moment.

5. **Ask students what they noticed.** Students might say that Yasmine looked at Thea as she talked, that she nodded sometimes, and that she said "Hmm" quietly sometimes.

6. **Give everyone a chance to practice while you watch and coach.** Assign a simple discussion topic and then form partnerships. You might count off by 2s, having the ones listen to the twos first and then have the twos listen to the ones while you circulate around the room, prompting children to use careful listening. "Remember to look right at your partner, Timmy," or "Listening body language," or "Classroom rules say to take care of your partner" are all words you might use as you remind and redirect.

7. **As students practice, provide feedback using reinforcing language.** Reinforce signs that students are listening. Feedback can be for the whole class: "I see lots of students looking at each other's faces to show that they are listening." You can also give feedback privately to individual students. For example, you might quietly say to Germaine, "Your eyes are on Rosita. That shows that you're listening to her."

Some Language to Try

Our rules say to "take care of each other." When you work on a project with a classmate you need to take care of each other by listening to each other's ideas.

What do you notice about my careful listening?

Yasmine, would you show the class careful listening as Thea talks to you about her ideas?

Remember to look right at your partner, Timmy.

I see lots of students looking at each other's faces to show that they are listening.

Model only what to *do*

In Interactive Modeling, the emphasis is on what *to* do rather than what not to do. You needn't show sarcastic or disrespectful responses. Children are well aware of negative behaviors—they don't need to see them modeled. They already see cruel and sarcastic responses on television situation comedies or hear unkind words in popular music so they already have these soundtracks in their minds. Our job is to give them a different, more positive soundtrack.

When we give students a model of what to do, we provide them with the actions and the words they can use to be kind. When they use those actions and words, they feel the power of positive connections with their classmates. Those positive student-to-student connections are protective against bullying behavior.

Strategy in Action

Ms. Guerin Teaches First Graders How to Read With a Partner

First grade teacher Ms. Guerin is getting ready to introduce partner reading. She begins by watching children during arrival time free choice as they sit on the rug and look at books. To successfully read with a partner, the children will need to share the book so that both can see the pages. With this in mind, Ms. Guerin pays special attention to the children's use of this skill as she observes. She sees that the children enjoy reading together, but often one child holds the book while her partner, struggling to see the page, peers over her shoulder.

On the basis of her observations, Ms. Guerin decides to teach skills that she has noticed the children are missing. Knowing that she needs to break skills down into bite-sized pieces for children this young, she begins by teaching how to sit so as to share the book harmoniously. She decides to use the strategy of Interactive Modeling so that children will get to see what this community-oriented behavior looks like and sounds like.

With the children gathered on the rug, Ms. Guerin demonstrates the correct way to sit so that the children see the skill in action. She sits side by side with Charisse and asks the students what they notice about the way she and Charisse are sitting. "Your knees are touching," says Manuel. "Your shoulders are touching," says Marie. "When your partner reads," says Ms. Guerin, "you'll sit knee to knee, shoulder to shoulder. You may sit on the floor or in chairs but either way you need to be right next to each other."

Over a series of days, the class learns other needed skills such as how to hold the book (spine in the middle between you and your partner) and how to decide who turns the page. The task is broken down to its smallest components so that children will know exactly what to do. Ms. Guerin uses Interactive Modeling for each skill—doing the modeling takes just a few minutes each day but goes a long way toward helping the students get ready for respectful partner work.

Once each skill is taught, Ms. Guerin immediately gives children an opportunity to practice. She assigns reading partners and the children scatter around the room, practicing reading their books. Ms. Guerin circulates and observes, reinforcing the learning by letting children know when she sees them using the newly taught skills. "I notice you reading with the spine in the middle," she comments to Lucia and Janine. "I see you sitting shoulder to shoulder," she says quietly to Pete and Mikey.

Role-play ways to respond to potentially tricky situations

In Interactive Modeling, students learn one way to do something. Through role-playing, students can try a range of positive responses to potentially tricky situations that eventually could lead to bullying. For example, role-playing could be used to help students think through how to share materials fairly, give each group member equal "air time," or integrate a new classmate into an established work group.

The crucial first step in any role-play is to state the problem in a way that engages the students in positive and community-building thought to prepare for discussing solutions. Connecting the challenge to classroom rules that children believe in engages the children in just such a way. You name the ideal when you use statements such as: "Our rules say to be kind to everyone. When a new student joins our class, we need to think together about how to be kind to the new student. We need to bring him into our community in a safe and friendly way." These statements get students thinking about how they can help.

Next, teachers set the stage for the role-play (which some teachers refer to as a "little play") by pretending. "Let's pretend there's a new student in the class and that I'm a student in our class and I'm in a work group for our social studies project. The teacher has told us that the new student will join our work group. Our group has been working together for a couple of weeks. How can I help the new student feel like part of the group?"

The class brainstorms ideas for what the main character—the student—might do. The teacher takes this role in the first round to ensure that things stay positive. Suggestions are made and added to the list: "You could take a few minutes at the beginning of the day to show him the work that the group has already done" or "You could be his partner during his first work session to help him get familiar with the project."

The teacher then picks a partner to play the role of the new student. Again, the teacher plays the main character in the first round of the role-play to ensure that the demonstration stays positive.

"I think I'll pick taking a few minutes at the beginning of the day," the teacher tells the class. "Lights, camera, action," the class says in unison—a favorite way to signal the beginning of role-plays.

The teacher greets the student playing the role of the new addition to their class. "Would you like me to show you what we've been working on in the social studies project?" the teacher asks.

The class debriefs, responding to focusing questions such as: "What did you notice about our play?" "What did the 'greeter' say and do?" "How did the new student respond?" and "How do you think the new student felt?"

Next, students pair up and act out various student-brainstormed ideas with the class watching and discussing how well each idea worked.

Notice that the tone stays positive throughout the role-play. Students aren't acting out the negative, which they know all too well, but rather the positive and prosocial actions that will prevent bullying.

For more information about role-playing, see my book *Solving Thorny Behavior Problems: How Teachers and Students Can Work Together* (Appendix B).

Continually name and reinforce ideal behaviors

In both Interactive Modeling and role-playing, the teacher begins by naming the desired behavior. Naming this ideal repeatedly is one way to keep the expectations of kindness and inclusiveness paramount in the classroom culture. I have found that when we connect that ideal to the rules that students believe in, we engage them in working together with energy and enthusiasm.

Mr. Bean, a second grade teacher, assigns new partners for Word Work every Monday. When they began Word Work in September, he used Interactive Modeling to teach students how to be friendly to new Word Work partners. He began the modeling by naming the ideal. "Our rules say that we'll be kind and friendly to all," he said.

Before the children began to work with their new partners each Monday, he reminded them about the ideal by reflecting with them. "Who can tell us what some friendly behaviors toward your new Word Work partner might be?" he asked. As they worked together he circulated around the room. "I see that you're looking at your new partner and smiling at him in a friendly way," he whispered to Patrick.

On Friday, when the children gathered in a circle at the end of the day to briefly look back on their week and wrap up on a positive note, Mr. Bean asked, "What went well this week?" Tommy said, "We were friendly to our Word Work partners." The children were proud of living up to the ideal.

Use anchor charts to remind students of newly learned skills

Once you've taught a skill, children will need reminders. One way to provide those reminders is to work with them to create an anchor chart, a class-created list of expected behaviors or strategies that students can use as an "anchor" that they can refer to while they work.

Name the ideal when you ask for children's suggestions

Begin creating the chart by asking children what they know about the skill, being sure to specify the ideal behavior you wish to support. For example, to create an anchor chart about what to do if you didn't understand what your partner or group member said, you might begin by saying, "To have a conversation, we need to understand each other's words. Sometimes people say things that their partners or group mates don't understand. What might be a respectful way to tell your partner that you need her to repeat what she said or clarify her ideas?" Notice that the teacher describes the interaction as a "respectful way." Without this clarity, children might suggest inappropriate ways to talk to their partner.

Whenever possible, use children's own words when you record ideas

To build students' investment in the ideas generated, it's important to use their exact words or, if you need to modify or shorten someone's idea, to ask their permission. However, it's equally important to remember that you, the teacher, are the leader of the class. If someone offers an inappropriate idea, be clear that it is inappropriate. Simply state, "That idea isn't respectful. If someone said that, it could hurt the partner's feelings." Be sure when you do this that your own voice tone and body language are respectful rather than judgmental or sarcastic.

When children offer general ideas, ask for specifics

When children offer general ideas, encouraging them to add details can be helpful. Mr. Milner's second grade class was creating an anchor chart about how to work with a writing partner. Jordan offered, "We need to be friendly." Mr. Milner wrote down "Be friendly." He then said, "We need some more details here. What does 'friendly' look like?" Children volunteered such specifics as "smiling face" and "body turned toward your partner."

Post the chart only as long as it's needed

The anchor chart can be hung on the wall, posted on a chart stand with other current anchor charts, or displayed as an electronic chart on a smart board. Before lessons or situations that require the skill, you can post the chart and draw attention to it and ask children to read and share ideas from it. But once the class has firmly mastered the skill, take down the anchor chart. Otherwise your walls may become so cluttered with anchor charts that children can't focus on current, meaningful information.

Use the "fishbowl" strategy to reinforce group skills

When children are working on social skills to facilitate respectful small-group work, they may benefit from a "fishbowl" strategy. In this approach, a few students demonstrate a newly learned skill while the rest of the class observes and notes positive examples of the skill. This strategy builds on children's interest in watching each other and contributing their observations. A fishbowl format is especially effective when you've previously taught the skill through Interactive Modeling and children have had a chance to practice it.

Prepare the children who will be in the fishbowl

Advance preparation gives the students a chance to rehearse and gives you an opportunity to make sure that they will demonstrate appropriate behavior. For example, Mrs. McBride has been teaching math to fifth grade students and has them working in groups of four. She asks one group—Phong, Jesse, Lalo, and Catherine—if they would be willing to model for the class. "You are going to model one person sharing their thinking and the rest of the group asking pertinent questions about how that person solved the problem," she explains. The group huddles for a moment and decides who will be the sharer and what they will share with the class. Then they rehearse. Mrs. McBride watches and notes that the sharing and questions are all on topic and respectful.

Gather everyone into a circle and give instructions to the class

Let students know that a few of their classmates will be coming to the middle of the circle to demonstrate the newly learned strategy. Tell the class specifically what to look for and let them know what they should do when they notice someone using the desired strategy. "You're going to watch a math group," Mrs. McBride says. "One person will share how they solved a problem and the others will ask clarifying questions. As they talk, you'll put your thumb up every time you see one of them ask a question that is on topic—in other words, a question that is about how the person who is sharing solved the problem."

Before you begin, prepare the "observers" to treat the "modelers" with respect

You might say to the class, "The group is taking a risk in showing you their process. What do we all need to do to treat them respectfully and considerately?" Students might respond with ideas about listening carefully and stifling impulses to laugh if one of the modelers asks something that seems unrelated to the topic.

After children have observed, discuss the behaviors they noticed

In the example of the fifth grade math group, Mrs. McBride asks questions such as "What were some of the words that you heard students say when they asked on-topic questions about the sharer's work?" and "What body language did you notice that showed that students were listening to each other?"

Finally, of course, it's important to let students know that you'll be expecting them to use this skill in their small-group work. You could say, for example, "I'll be listening for your on-topic questions as I stop by your math groups" or "As I look around the room I'll be looking for respectful and attentive body language, like the body language that we saw in the fishbowl."

For more information about using the fishbowl strategy, see *The Language of Learning: Teaching Students Core Thinking, Listening, and Speaking Skills* by Margaret Berry Wilson (see Appendix B).

Coach individuals and small groups

The discussion thus far has applied to whole-class work, when you notice that all or most of the students need to learn, review, or practice a particular skill. Sometimes, however, teachers notice that one student or a small group of students are struggling with skills such as using respectful body language, listening to others with interest, or using words that are respectfully related to ideas that others have shared. In cases like these, there is no reason to reengage the whole class in learning and practicing skills that they already possess.

When it's one student or a small group, meet with them separately. Review or practice the missing skill just as you would review or practice a reading skill when you meet with an individual in a reading conference or a few children in a reading group.

Coach an individual student who is struggling with collaborative work skills

Before the coaching session, take some time to reflect on how you're feeling toward the student. If you're feeling annoyed, your annoyance will come out right along with the teaching, blocking the effectiveness of your instruction. If you're not feeling so positive toward the student (it happens to all of us sometimes), step back and note the student's good qualities. Once you feel that you can honestly articulate some positives, set up a time to meet privately with the student.

What follows are steps a teacher might take when coaching an individual student who is having a hard time listening respectfully during peer writing conferences.

1. **State the goal clearly.** Begin with a clear, simple statement of the desired behavior. For example, "We're meeting today to talk about how to have a respectful writing conference with your writing partner."

2. **Be clear about what you've noticed, positive and negative.** Use concrete evidence and examples. Start by describing what is going well and then move to the problem area: "When you share your writing with your writing partner, you read your writing in a way that she can understand. Your voice is loud enough and you say your words clearly. I've also noticed that when it's her turn to read her story you roll on the floor and look away."

3. **State the reasons that the negative behaviors are a problem.** You might go on to say: "Our classroom rules say that we will be friendly and respectful to everyone. To be respectful, it's important that you look at your partner and listen to her read her writing. You need to let her know that you're listening. When you roll on the floor and look away, your behavior is distracting and you seem not to be listening."

4. **Gather input from the student.** You might ask, "What have you noticed about your writing conferences?" This is the point at which the student might say that he is listening, despite the fact that he's rolling on the floor. You can clarify by sharing the information that his partner doesn't know that he's listening unless he's looking at her. At this point the student may also complain about his partner, saying, for example, that she's not his friend. You can clarify by referring to the rules and reminding him, "Our rules say that we will be respectful and friendly to everyone. That's your job."

5. **Once the problem is clarified, articulate the desired skill.** You could say, for example: "When you listen to your partner, it's important that you keep your body still and look at her. You could look at her face or you could plan ways to share her paper so that you can look at her writing. Either way, you need to show her that you're listening to her with friendly interest as she reads her writing piece."

6. **Show the student what the skillful behavior looks like.** You could listen to the student read a few sentences and then ask, "What did you notice that I did while you read?" Sometimes it helps to write down what the student noticed on an index card so that he can keep the list of skills as a reminder.

7. **The next time the student needs to use the skills, remind him privately of what he needs to do.** Right before writing time, you could quietly and privately remind the student by saying, "Remember, turn your body toward your partner and look at her," or by asking, "How are you going to show friendly interest in your partner's writing today?"

8. **Reinforce positive efforts.** As the students are meeting with a partner or in small groups, it's important to circulate, observe, and support. Of course, it's particularly important to take a look at the student whom you met with individually. Privately let him know what he's doing well, either with a nonverbal signal like a thumbs up or a whispered private comment such as "I see you listening to your partner."

Of course, if you suspect that "she's not my friend" is veering into bullying behavior, your most important goal is to protect the child who is targeted by giving her another partner. In addition, be careful not to have the person demonstrating the mean behavior pair up with their best friend—this could give the message that you're "letting them off the hook."

For more extensive information about coaching individuals in social skills and group work skills, see my book *Sammy and His Behavior Problems: Stories and Strategies From a Teacher's Year*. I also recommend that you take a look at Chapter Two, "Problem-Solving Conferences," in my book *Solving Thorny Behavior Problems: How Teachers and Students Can Work Together* (see Appendix B for both resources).

> **Some Language to Try**
>
> *We're meeting today to talk about how to have a respectful writing conference with your writing partner.*
>
> *Our classroom rules say that we will be friendly and respectful to everyone. To be respectful, it's important that you look at your partner and listen to her read her writing.*
>
> *When you roll on the floor and look away, your behavior is distracting and you seem not to be listening.*
>
> *How are you going to show friendly interest in your partner's writing today?*

Coach small groups that aren't working together effectively

Although most of the children in the class are working together smoothly in small groups, perhaps there is one group that is struggling. In this group arguments abound and little work is accomplished. The situation is ripe for meanness and bullying.

Watch the group at work. What positive behaviors are they using? What are the negative behaviors? Are there skills that everyone in the group is missing? If all children in the small group are exhibiting similar negative behaviors such as talking all at once, doing other work while group members speak, snatching materials away from their peers, passively staring out into space, or otherwise showing group-work skill deficits, think about coaching the whole group. Use the same steps and strategies that you used to teach the entire class; for example, name the goal and then model the desired behavior. When a small group of children watch and listen to you teach and then practice the skill under your guidance, their skills should improve.

When coaching individuals and small groups, watch for and intervene in mean behaviors

Sometimes in the course of coaching students, you might notice signs of bullying or those small mean behaviors that can be gateways to bullying. For example, if one child in a group orders a particular group member around while others remain silent, or if one child in a pair lobs nasty remarks at her writing partner rather than giving helpful feedback, you'll need to respectfully take firm, immediate, and nonpunitive action to stop the behavior.

The first step is to make sure everyone is safe. If a child's unkind behavior is persistent or severe enough to put other children at risk of emotional or physical harm, remove the child who is hurting others from the group or partnership. I can't state this strongly enough: The child who is bullying or engaging in pre-bullying behavior is the child who needs to be removed, not the child who is targeted. If you need to end a partnership because of one child's mean behavior, be sure that the child they were targeting has another partner to work with. Because there is a strong connection between social isolation and being targeted for bullying, the student at risk of being targeted needs stronger social connections and not isolation. The child who is hurting others can take a temporary break from peers.

Talk with the child who is engaging in mean behavior. Begin by clearly and concretely stating your observations. For example, you might say, "I heard you tell Micha to 'be quiet' several times today when your group was working." Avoid such general statements as "You're mean to Micha" or vague statements such as "You and Micha don't get along very well."

Next, ask the student what he or she has noticed about the problem. You'll learn a lot by garnering the student's perspective. If the student responds by saying, "Micha kicks me under the table" or even "Micha tells me to be quiet, too," you may suspect that there's more going on than was immediately apparent. On the other hand, a response such as "Micha's just so annoying" may point you toward thinking about this as a situation where one student is targeting another.

It's important not to make assumptions. Find out the facts from both children's points of view. If you suspect that one child is picking on another child in a way that is one-sided and mean, it's important to talk with each child separately. All too often, a child being targeted will say, "That's okay," when expected to state their point of view while sitting next to a child who has been systematically hurting them.

Children who bully often feel that what they're doing is just fine and will blame the child targeted. Stick to the facts. If Troy is telling Micha to be quiet over and over, that's unacceptable behavior. "Micha is annoying" is not a reason to act mean toward her. There is no excuse that makes mean behavior acceptable. Whether or not Troy thinks that Micha uses a loud voice, contributes ideas to the group that don't make sense, or talks too much is not germane, even if Troy keeps bringing up these opinions in the discussion. Keep in mind that the most important goal is to preserve a classroom climate that is emotionally and physically safe for all children.

If you believe that you're dealing with a potential bullying situation, it's important to stop the behavior and give clear consequences. These consequences need to be matter-of-fact, nonpunitive, consistently applied to any child who engages in such behavior, and framed to protect the child who is targeted. You might say, for example, "Telling one group member to be quiet is not respectful behavior. You will miss the next two group meetings and work independently. We'll talk again before you rejoin the group." When the child is ready to rejoin the group, remind him about the expectation for respectful behavior. Then, once the child rejoins the group, watch the group closely. If you see any hint of mean behavior after the child has rejoined the group, permanently remove them from the group and place them in a different one. It's important to protect the child who is being targeted. Often it takes close observation to detect such ongoing behavior.

In addition, follow the protocols that your school may have in place already for responding to bullying or behaviors that are gateways to bullying.

For more detailed information about intervening in gateway behaviors, see Chapter One.

Provide structures for taking turns within a small group

Learning how to listen respectfully and take turns talking in a small group can be especially challenging for children. If you notice that children are having trouble listening and responding respectfully with more than one other student, the first thing to do is to assess developmental readiness for small-group work. Students seven years old and younger will most likely not be successful working in small groups, and partnering with just one classmate may be a better option for them. Even when children are developmentally ready to learn the skill of working in a small group (often around eight years old), listening and responding respectfully in a small group can be difficult. (For more about developmental considerations, see the box on pages 106–107.)

Often children who can listen to one other child become confused and overwhelmed when multiple children are in the group, all hoping to be heard. Children might use mean words and refuse to work with group members who feel troublesome to them. To deal with these challenges, children can benefit from learning structures that keep them firmly rooted in respectful practice. Two such structures are "talking stick" and "question, talk, talk, talk, question."

Although these two learning structures may seem a bit formulaic, they can help children over the bumpy spots in the road on the way to learning respect for all. Once the bumps are navigated, children can grow in more natural ways to be together.

The "talking stick" structure

Many structures can help children take turns speaking when there's more than one other student waiting to be heard. One such structure is to use an object as a "talking stick," where children are instructed to speak only when they have the talking stick in their hand.

I first used this structure the year my classroom was wired with a sound system designed to help Vivian, a deaf child. I found that when the students passed the microphone, a real-life necessity, it brought order to the conversation during whole-class discussions. The children stayed focused on the child speaking with the microphone. When we began working in small groups, the one that needed to use the microphone functioned smoothly while the other groups struggled with taking turns speaking. I then introduced objects to the other groups to mimic the use of the microphone, including a puppet, a carved stick, and even a feather, and watched their discussions become as orderly as the discussions in Vivian's group. After that, I used some form of talking stick whenever groups struggled with learning how to listen to each other.

Carefully teach how to use the talking stick. As with other structures, it's important to carefully teach children how to use a talking stick. Interactive Modeling lends itself to teaching this procedure. To introduce the talking stick, a teacher might begin by naming the ideal: "We all have things to say and we can learn from each other when we take turns speaking." As the teacher and then a student model passing the talking stick and speaking only when holding it, the class forms an image in their minds of what it looks like to use the talking stick, to take turns. As everyone practices using the talking stick, the teacher observes and coaches so she can reinforce when children are using the structure well and guide them when they start to veer off course.

Supervise initial use of the talking stick. When children are ready to use the talking stick, have them do so as a whole group, under your supervision. Whole-class sharing time is a perfect opportunity for this first use of the talking stick. After one student shares some news, others raise their hands to respond with questions and comments. The sharer passes the stick to one of the potential responders. Students wait until they have the talking stick before they speak.

Once the class is comfortably following the rules for using the talking stick as a whole group, they're ready to use the structure for discussions in small groups. Be sure, however, to provide guidance by circulating, listening in, reinforcing, reminding, and redirecting when necessary.

The "question, talk, talk, talk, question" format

Children can also learn to take turns speaking in small groups by using a "question, talk, talk, talk, question" format. I'm naming it this because that's how it would work in a group of four, an ideal group size. (If you have groups of five, for example, it would be "question, talk, talk, talk, talk, question.")

The first student in the small group asks an open-ended question. Then each of the other students responds one at a time with thoughts about the topic of the question. Once each child has responded to the first question, student number two asks a question, and again the others respond one at a time. This continues around the group until each student has had a chance to ask a question and hear group members' responses.

Here's what this format might look like in a third grade book club group. The students are reading *Charlotte's Web*. In preparation for the book club meeting, each student has written questions about the assigned chapter on a small card with the "question, talk, talk, talk, question" steps written on it. Erica asks, "If you were a pig and lost your only friend, how would you feel?" Each participant answers in turn. Suzanne talks about loneliness, Daniel about finding new friends, and Andrew about how he can't imagine being a pig, much less a lonely pig. Then Suzanne asks her question, "Was Charlotte actually eager to be a pig's friend or was she just really patient?" The others reply in turn. Daniel and Andrew will each take their turn as well with their question and listen to the group's responses.

While the children meet in their book clubs using the "question, talk, talk, talk, question" format, their teacher circulates, listening in and reinforcing their use of the structure. She resists the temptation to join in with student literature discussions and instead sits back, observes, notices, and reinforces the children's positive interactions.

Plan a transition toward real conversations

The "talking stick" and "question, talk, talk, talk, question" formats both provide a step toward learning how to have a real conversation. When one person asks a question and each group member answers in turn, the discussion doesn't have the flow of a true conversation. It does, however, give children practice in taking turns and listening to each other's questions. Once the children have learned to take turns and listen to each other, you can plan a transition away from the formulaic conversation into a more nuanced and natural discussion.

Considerations About Child Development

Our goal in working on children's small-group and partnership skills is to foster a classroom atmosphere that feels safe and inclusive and prevents bullying. But if we force children outside their comfort zone, we'll undermine our efforts. Children's readiness to work in partnerships and small groups has a predictable developmental progression. Understanding this progression helps us decide when children are ready to learn a new group work skill and protects us and them from the frustration of reaching for a skill that they're not ready for. The following are some considerations about child development that can help you set up successful partner and group work situations.

These guidelines are very general ones; the students you teach may develop at different rates. I mention grade levels as defined by a "typical" age, which may or may not be true for your own classroom. I offer these guidelines so that you can set goals for students that are realistic, developmentally speaking. I also offer them so that when something isn't working for the students, you can examine the situation through a developmental lens.

Kindergarten: If you teach kindergarten, your students may be happy to partner chat but might have very little recall of what their partner said. Experienced kindergarten teachers often listen in to partners and then make observations to the class about what the children said.

"I heard several partners say that they noticed the rhymes in Mrs. Wishy-Washy," says Mrs. Hauer. "Rhymes help us read the words," she adds.

First grade: First graders, often six years old, will frequently beg to be allowed to work with partners. This is a highly social age. Nonetheless, to ensure success you'll need to teach basics such as how to hold the book, how to take turns speaking, and how to share materials with a partner.

Second grade: Second graders, many of whom are seven years old, tend to be private and self-absorbed. Putting these children in groups of four is often a frustrating experience for all involved, but they usually do well working alone or with just one other person. They thrive with restricted structures such as "talk, listen, talk, listen" when written out for them to follow: First Jenine talks while Mikey listens, then Mikey talks while Jenine listens. Keeping their finger on the step they're doing will help each child remember when it's time to talk and when it's time to listen.

Third grade: Group work is the métier of many eight year olds, the age of the majority of third grade classes. With direct teaching about how to work in a group, eight-year-olds can manage smoothly in a group of four. Any group larger than that will most likely overwhelm them.

Fourth grade: By age nine, children may become more individualistic and self-conscious, so it's particularly important in fourth grade to teach group structures meticulously and follow up with reinforcements and reminders. With careful teaching, fourth graders can work successfully in groups of four or five.

Fifth grade: Fifth graders, in many cases ten-year-olds, are commonly as willing and eager to work in groups as eight year olds. I've found that four is still the ideal group size, but most ten-year-olds can handle a group of up to six members if need be.

By fifth grade, many children are also beginning to define themselves by who their friends are. Left to themselves, they may choose to work only with classmates whom they think of as their friends, but they will work with everyone if you, the teacher, set the expectation that they work with all classmates in respectful and friendly ways. When we explain that they need to be "friendly" rather than "best friends," they will comply because "our teacher makes us." Using this simple excuse, they will learn to be respectful to all while still engaged in the developmentally appropriate task of making choices about friends.

For more on common child developmental characteristics in the classroom and their implications for teaching, see *Yardsticks: Child and Adolescent Development Ages 4–14*, 4th ed., by Chip Wood (see Appendix B).

Communicating With Parents About Cooperative Learning Structures

As with other classroom structures you put in place, it's important to have open and clear communication with parents about how you organize partner and group work, and how you introduce cooperative learning structures. Doing so will help reassure parents that you are making every effort to ensure that this important part of their child's day is safe and productive.

Nonetheless, you may hear from parents about concerns they have, especially if you've worked on establishing good communication with them and they feel comfortable talking with you. For example, concerned about her daughter's reading partner assignment, Laila's mother contacts you and says, "I hear that you partnered Marie with Laila for reading. They can't work together." Sometimes the reason is that Marie and Laila have joined with different cliques in an undersupervised after-school activity. Sometimes it's that the families don't like each other. Often the parent is concerned about their child's safety with a particular partner. You want to preserve your relationship with the parents, make sure that all of the students are safe, and preserve the class's sense of inclusion. What do you do?

Listen

It's important to listen to the adults in students' lives and hear what they have to say. Keep in mind that they have information that you don't have. Once you've listened carefully, it's important to investigate and learn about the situation that parents have described. It's equally important to reassure them that you will keep their child safe.

Investigate the situation

When Mrs. Safar, Laila's mother, explained to Mr. Reston, Laila's teacher, that Marie was calling Laila names at soccer practice, he investigated. He knew that he had to make sure that Marie wasn't bullying Laila. If that were the case, it would be dangerous to pair Laila with Marie as a reading partner.

Mr. Reston watched Marie and Laila work together in class. They listened to each other and made friendly comments. Knowing that children who are targeted are usually not able to assert their needs in front of the child doing the bullying, he had a private talk with Laila to try to understand what was going on. Laila assured him that both girls called each other names at soccer practice and that everyone on the team called everyone else names, too. Although Mr. Reston wasn't pleased to hear about the name-calling that prevailed at soccer practice, he was reassured about Laila and Marie's relationship.

In another classroom, Mrs. McEntyre received a call from Mr. Hall, who explained that his son, Wayne, couldn't work with his classmate Danielle because their families didn't like each other. Mr. Hall was afraid that Danielle might be mean to Wayne. Mrs. McEntyre said that she would watch the two students carefully. She then observed Wayne and Danielle and noticed that they worked together respectfully and even joyfully in school. Based on these observations, she felt that Wayne and Danielle were appropriate work partners.

Intervene if you discover any unkind behaviors

Sometimes, of course, a parents' concerns will alert you to situations that need an intervention. If either teacher described above suspected bullying behavior, the teacher would stop the bullying behavior and make sure the children did not work in the same group. It's important, at all costs, to make sure that the child who is being targeted is not left to work alone due to the separation. Children who are being targeted with bullying behavior need the social support of the classroom community, not isolation.

Respectfully communicate your decision to parents

Once you know that the students are treating each other respectfully, preserve the inclusive atmosphere in the classroom by letting parents know that the children will continue to work together. Explain why you are keeping them together and reassure the children's parents that you will supervise their children closely and that you will make sure their children are safe in the classroom.

Mr. Reston decided that although Laila and Marie might treat each other disrespectfully while with the chaotic-sounding soccer team, in the positive climate of this classroom they read together in a supportive manner. He called Mrs. Safar to explain this to her. Mr. Reston thanked Mrs. Safar for bringing the situation to his attention and assured her that it was important to him that Laila be safe in school. He described his observation of the two reading partners, focusing on specifics such as the way Laila and Marie listened to each other carefully, and laughed and smiled as they read together. He encouraged Mrs. Safar to call him again if Laila reported any unkind treatment in school.

Mr. Reston also told Mrs. Safar that both girls had reported that "everyone calls each other names on the soccer team." He asked Mrs. Safar if she had noticed this and encouraged her to discuss this behavior with the girls' coach. The fact that Mr. Reston seemed concerned about Laila's life outside of school helped to build a bond between him and Mrs. Safar.

Wayne's teacher called Mr. Hall to explain that Wayne and Danielle worked together smoothly in school. She described enough specific details to reassure Mr. Hall that it would be safe for Wayne and Danielle to remain partners for the time being.

Plan opportunities for parents to experience their child's classroom community

Parents may base their mental image of their child's classroom on a less-than-safe classroom from their own childhood, unfriendly interactions they may have seen between children outside of school, or the way classrooms are portrayed in TV shows with sarcastic comments punctuated by a laugh track. Once the classroom community is friendly and inclusive, invite parents in to see and feel the climate of kindness.

Another way to have parents experience their child's class is to invite them to serve as classroom helpers or to join in classroom activities. You could invite parents in for a Morning Meeting, a writing workshop, a math games period, or any other time of day when you can showcase the way students work together respectfully. Parents' anxiety is often assuaged when they have a mental image of the way the classroom actually is.

KEY IDEAS

▸ **Cooperative learning structures** provide an important way for children to get to know each other and learn to treat each other respectfully.

▸ **For cooperative learning structures to be effective,** children need explicit teaching of respectful work skills such as listening carefully, taking turns, and sharing materials.

▸ **The first step is to observe children** at work so that you can identify any deficits in their skills.

▸ **Interactive Modeling, role-playing, and the fishbowl format** are useful strategies for teaching positive group skills.

▸ **Naming the ideal for students** reinforces the importance of behaving in safe and inclusive ways.

▸ **Anchor charts provide useful reminders** of newly learned skills.

▸ **Provide coaching for individuals or small groups** that are struggling with newly learned skills.

▸ **Provide structures to help students** learn how to take turns in small groups. Two such structures are the "talking stick" and the "question, talk, talk, talk, question" formats.

▸ **Pay attention to developmental considerations** as you plan cooperative structures.

▸ **Plan groupings carefully** so that no child is placed in a group that could make the child feel unsafe.

▸ **Remove the child who is doing the bullying** rather than the child who is targeted if you suspect that bullying behavior is occurring in a group.

▸ **Listen carefully to parents' concerns** about children's small-group work arrangements, then investigate and follow up with parents.

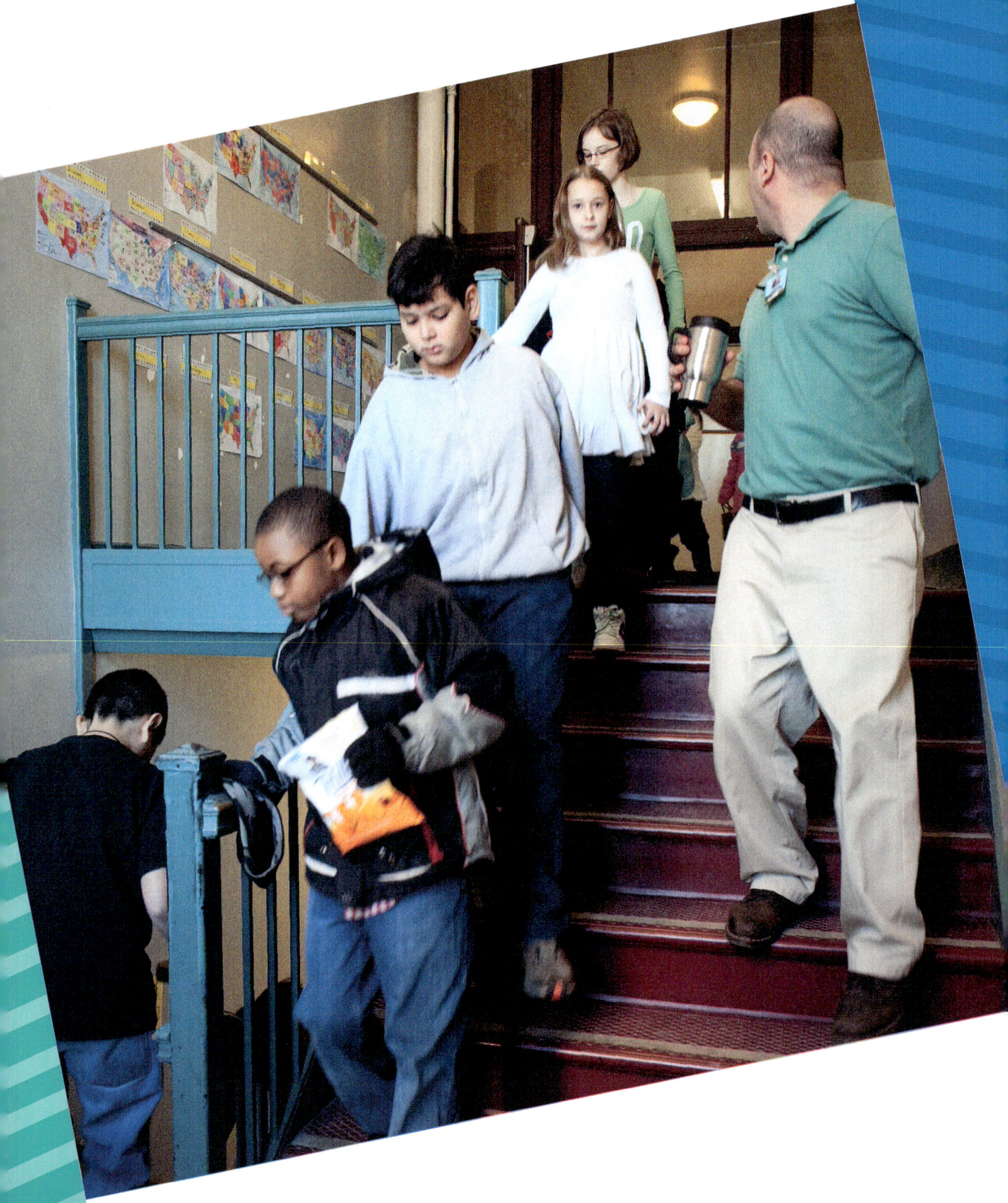

CHAPTER FIVE

Outside of the Classroom

Sandy and Miranda appeared to be close friends. They played together at recess, sat together at lunch, and talked about visits to each other's homes. However, every day at lunch Sandy insisted that Miranda give up her dessert. And every day, Miranda, confused and frightened, turned over her fruit or her cup of pudding to Sandy.

Jake seemed like a solid member of the classroom community. He worked smoothly with other students and was friendly to all. Nonetheless, Jake was alone every day at recess—and not by choice. If he tried to join a team game on the playground, no one picked him. If he tried to join the lineup when kids were shooting baskets, others turned their backs.

Remember Paul from the introduction to this book? From kindergarten well into middle school, he was targeted by children engaging in overt bullying behavior on the school bus. Mean words led to exclusion and physical assaults. But despite the severity and duration of the bullying, his parents and classroom teachers were not aware of what was going on.

Bullying and the mean behavior that leads to bullying often take place in the more lightly supervised areas of school: the halls, the playground, the cafeteria, and the school bus. In addition, children often don't report incidences of mean behavior to adults that occur in those areas. Miranda, Jake, and Paul were each part of a cooperative classroom community that emphasized safety and inclusiveness. However, once they and their classmates moved out of the classroom and away from the supports that kept their communities kind and caring, these students were no longer safe. Their peers tested the limits and discovered that they had free rein to try out mean behaviors. When these behaviors were not stopped, they escalated.

What can classroom teachers do about this problem? The optimal approach is to connect classroom teaching to a comprehensive schoolwide bullying prevention plan. But even if a school or district doesn't have such a plan, there is a lot that classroom teachers can do—on their own, and in collaboration with paraprofessionals, specialist teachers, and grade-level colleagues—to help students use the social skills that they're learning in the classroom as they move into settings that require more independence.

Specifically, in this chapter you'll learn about the following:

- Keeping a close eye on areas outside the classroom
- Taking classroom rules outside the classroom
- Using modeling and role-playing to help students practice safe and inclusive behaviors outside the classroom
- Giving students reminders and reinforcements for outside-the-classroom behaviors
- Providing structures that enhance inclusiveness outside the classroom
- Collaborating with colleagues who supervise outside-the-classroom areas

Collaborating With Grade-Level Colleagues

In many cases, the ideas I present in this chapter can be put into action on your own, but in some cases I would suggest working with a grade-level team. Whether you use a brief portion of team meetings to strategize with colleagues or informal moments such as lunchtime in the teachers' room, it's helpful if you and your teammates can work together in your bullying prevention efforts. When children move out of the classroom, they are often moving into settings that include other children from their grade level, and some percentage of children from that grade level will be involved in any mean behaviors taking place. Having teammates involved will help you monitor the children outside of the classroom.

Keeping a Close Eye on Areas Outside the Classroom

In previous chapters, I've discussed the role of close observation within the classroom. Observing students outside the classroom is equally valuable. Through close observation, you can learn about students' kind behaviors as well as their unkind behaviors. You learn who is "in" and who is "out," and you can notice those small mean behaviors that are gateways to bullying. This knowledge is essential to preventing bullying.

Admittedly, outside-the-classroom observation is sometimes hard to fit into a busy day, especially when you're not scheduled for lunchroom, hall, or recess duty. However, even a few minutes observing these times outside of the classroom can yield a tremendous amount of information. When scheduled for lunchroom, hall, or recess duty, you can use that time effectively to observe students and learn about their lives outside the classroom.

Research supports the need for this increased vigilance. An international meta-analysis of all bullying prevention programs indicated that effective playground supervision is one of the key elements in preventing bullying at school (Ttofi and Farrington 2011). In addition, there is extensive evidence that a great deal of the bullying behavior that happens on the playground is not noticed by the adults in charge. In their classic study, Wendy Craig and Debra Pepler videotaped children's interactions during recess. They observed frequent bullying incidents with minimal adult intervention. However, most of these same adults reported that they "nearly always" intervened in bullying incidents. In one instance, two children march another child with hands held behind her back across the playground before ordering her to "kiss the tree" while a teacher stands nearby, oblivious to what is occurring (Craig and Pepler 1998).

It's easy to see how things like this can happen. I know from my own experience that it's not always clear what role classroom teachers or specialists should be playing during our stint on recess duty. Because of this lack of clarity, it's easy to fall into visiting with colleagues and treating recess duty as a much needed break. But this stance provides space for mean behavior to emerge.

The same thing can happen in the lunchroom. Teachers who are off duty during lunch often only pass briefly through the cafeteria, if at all, dropping off students before hurrying to make copies, return phone calls, and eat their own lunch.

You can play a different role. As you work on bullying prevention strategies with your students, I encourage you to do some detective work—either on your own or with grade-level colleagues—to discover what children's lives are like in areas outside the classroom. What follows are some ideas on how to do this.

When you are on duty

If you are assigned to lunchroom, recess, or hall duty, you can spend some of the time closely observing student interaction. Here are some things to look for:

- **On the playground, who decides on the teams for group games?** Is it the same children consistently? Do they carefully select a "cool" team and a team of "losers"? This can set the stage for bullying behavior.

- **Who plays with whom on the playground or sits with whom in the lunchroom?** Cliques that may remain underground within the structure of the classroom become evident when children choose where to sit in the lunchroom or whom to play with at recess. You may see children running to their lunch seats, saving seats for some and pushing others away. If you listen for it, you may hear name-calling between groups. On the other hand, you may see groups of friends who are inclusive toward others. You may see welcoming expressions and hear friendly words. Exclusive cliques can set the tone for bullying. Inclusive friendships can set a tone of community and caring.

- **Who sits alone in the lunchroom or relies on chatting with the teachers at recess?** When I started to observe students closely during my recess duty, I noticed that Jake, who I had believed to be fully a part of the social life of the class, wandered the playground alone. Without the inclusive structures I had put in place in the classroom, Jake's social isolation during recess became apparent. The same thing can happen in the lunchroom. Social isolation is a serious problem because there is ample evidence that it is connected to a child being targeted (Buhs, Ladd, and Herald-Brown 2010).

- **On the playground, watch children's body language.** Are some children always the chasers or do they switch roles? When the first graders run outside to play, Mark shouts, "Let's chase Jamie." The first grade boys chase Jamie throughout recess, a daily pattern and a not-so-subtle form of picking on Jamie that can quickly escalate to even more aggressive forms of targeting him.

  What is the posture and affect of a child who walks the playground alone? My student Becca walked the perimeter of the playground by herself. Her body was relaxed, her face calm. When I asked her if she'd like someone to play with, she replied, "No, I've been with people all morning; I need to be by myself now." Becca was fine—she simply needed the respite of some time alone.

  Pete, on the other hand, stood outside the basketball game with his head down, feet shuffling, looking as though he longed to be included. When I asked him if he'd tried to join the game he said, "They told me I'm a loser and I can't play." This type of exclusion is a step along the continuum toward bullying.

- **Who is laughing and who looks fearful or unhappy?** Children's facial expressions and body language will often let us know whether one child is teetering on the verge of bullying the other or whether they're just playing together.

  The school day is over, the buses are being called. Ms. Meyer stands in the hallway supervising as children make their way to the buses. Eric and Frankie bump into each other rhythmically as they move down the hall. As Eric bumps Frankie, Frankie laughs uproariously. Frankie then gives Eric a bump and Eric grins. These two are having fun, bonding and releasing tension after an afternoon of too much sitting still.

  Meanwhile, Elena and Kim walk down the hall together. Kim reaches out her hand and tickles Elena. One might think that this is a benign and friendly gesture, but Elena cringes, her mouth turns down slightly, and her eyes turn away from Kim. This unwelcome gesture may be a gateway to bullying, a warning that things are going to heat up on the way home.

Ms. Meyer ignores Frankie and Eric's playful behavior. However, she stops Kim and says, "That doesn't look friendly to me." She also makes a mental note to tell Kim and Elena's teacher, Mr. Richardson, about the behaviors that she saw so that he can follow up with some careful observation of the girls' relationship.

When you aren't on duty

There are lots of ways to learn about children's lives outside of the classroom even if you're not spending an entire recess on the playground or an entire dismissal time in the hall. Brief observations can reveal more information than you might imagine.

Besides keeping children safe everywhere in school, another reason to make the time for these brief observations, even if you're not on duty, is that the mean behaviors that go on outside the classroom have an impact on classroom life. For example, the child who is worried about being targeted on the playground will be preoccupied with thoughts about recess today and what recess will be like tomorrow—and this preoccupation can interfere with the ability to concentrate on academics.

What follows are some ideas for fitting brief outside-the-classroom observations into a busy teaching day.

Accompany children to the cafeteria and the playground

Even if you aren't assigned to cafeteria, recess, or hall duty, an occasional brief observation in these areas can be enlightening. When you walk your class to recess, spend a few extra minutes on the playground, watching the children sort themselves out into play groups. Who plays with whom? Who is accepted? Who is rejected? If you pick up students at the end of recess, plan to arrive a few minutes early once in a while and note some of these same interactions.

If you pick up students in the cafeteria, occasionally arrive early. Or if you drop off students, spend a few minutes watching as they get settled. Who sits with whom? How are they treating each other? Use these and the other observation questions that I suggested in the "When you are on duty" section to assess what you're seeing.

Observe children as they enter the classroom from recess, lunch, or the bus

Listening to children's conversations with each other and paying close attention to what they say to us about the time spent outside the classroom are seemingly obvious yet often neglected tools we can use to gain insight into children's experiences outside their classrooms.

Jessica, Annie, and Gretel ride bus 7 and arrive together. Jessica and Annie have their arms wrapped around each other's shoulders. Gretel follows behind, her head down, eyes on the floor and feet dragging. You can guess that something has gone wrong on bus 7 and make a mental note to keep an eye on how things are going among the three girls.

Listening can also help you identify recurrent problems. As children tumble in from recess, teachers often hear "That wasn't fair" or "They wouldn't play with me." Although these might seem like small complaints that don't warrant intervention, when you hear the same complaint day after day, it's time to investigate. Do children complain about certain games? Perhaps the game that is accompanied by complaints of unfairness needs more supervision.

Notice patterns in children's behavior around outside-the-classroom times

You can also notice patterns in children's behavior: Who's on time to school and who's regularly tardy? Who tries to get to the end of the line when the class lines up to leave the room? These behavior patterns offer hints to follow up on.

When Alexis was consistently late for school, I contacted her mother. "She doesn't want to ride the school bus so she keeps missing it," her mother explained. Upon further investigation, I learned that Alexis was being mistreated by a group of older girls on the school bus. I spoke to the teacher of the children engaging in the mean behavior. Their teacher had a serious talk with them. The mistreatment ended once they knew that their teacher was "on to" their school bus behaviors.

Pay attention to behavior patterns around recess. Would certain children rather stay inside and "help you out" than go to recess? Do some children consistently "forget" their homework and then offer to finish it during recess time? Those children may be targets of bullying behaviors on the playground.

The same pattern can emerge around the lunchroom. Do you have a student who needs to go to the nurse every day right before lunch? Perhaps the lunchroom is feeling unsafe for that child.

Talk with children about their experiences outside the classroom

In addition to listening informally to what children are saying, you can structure ways for them to reflect on their experiences outside the classroom. One area that teachers have little access to is the school bus. Taking the time to reflect with students about life on the bus can yield information that you can act on, despite the fact that you're not physically on the bus.

As the kindergarten students arrive on Monday morning, Mr. Rinaldi has them draw pictures of themselves on the school bus for their morning work. Mr. Wright assigns a journal reflection for his sixth graders about how children are treating each other on the bus. Later on in the day, both groups of students spend a few minutes sharing their reflections. The emphasis here is on the children's thoughts and feelings. "When do you feel welcome on the bus?" asks Mr. Rinaldi. "What might you do to be a leader on your bus and help younger children feel welcome?" asks Mr. Wright.

You can also reflect with children about areas in the school that you have some access to, which can richly complement the information that you glean by observing. "How are things going in the lunchroom? What is friendly about the lunchroom? What feels unfriendly about the lunchroom?" asks a written message from Ms. Taylor on the white board as fourth graders enter their classroom. Later on, as part of the daily Morning Meeting, the children discuss times when they feel included in the lunchroom and times when they feel excluded. Ms. Taylor is gathering information that will help her ensure safety in the lunchroom.

Use a survey with the children to identify safe and unsafe areas

Evidence-based bullying prevention programs often recommend surveying students to discover where they feel safe and where they feel unsafe in school (Luxemberg, Limber, and Olweus 2019; Olweus and Limber 2007). These surveys usually offer a definition of bullying and then ask children if they have experienced or seen behavior that fits the definition happening in a variety of specific spots such as the lunchroom, the playground, the halls, the bathrooms, and the school bus. With the resulting information, schools can increase supervision in areas where children feel unsafe. The Olweus Bullying Prevention Program survey begins with third graders and goes through high school.

You can survey just the children you teach or work with grade-level colleagues to survey all children at your grade level. In Chapter Seven, you'll find information about creating a survey, including sample questions you could include.

Although written or electronic surveys are generally not used with children younger than eight years old, there are ways to gather information from young children. Ms. Pelis has prepared a chart for her first graders to respond to. At the top she has written "Safe" with a smiley face and "Unsafe" with a frowny face. She's created a box on the chart for each of a variety of areas in the school such as playground, lunchroom, school bus, bathroom, and hall. As the students arrive, she carefully guides them to draw smiley faces in the boxes for the areas where they feel safe at school, frowny faces for where they feel unsafe. Many of her students place frowny faces in the "playground" box.

Down the hall in Mr. Oakley's second grade class, the children are working on mapping skills as part of their social studies curriculum. First, the whole class creates a map of the school. Then Mr. Oakley adds a bullying prevention component to the lesson. He asks children if there are places in school where they feel unsafe. If they feel unsafe somewhere, he asks them to place a red adhesive dot on that spot. Mr. Oakley is surprised to see that many children in the class put a red dot on the second grade bathrooms, down the hall from their classroom.

Once you gather information from children, it's important to follow up with investigations and any other steps that may be needed. For example, later in the day students in Ms. Pelis's first grade classroom discuss their chart about playground concerns. The class has just recently completed a bullying prevention lesson where the children have learned to "report to a responsible adult" if they feel that they are being targeted (see primary grades Lesson Three in Chapter Seven). Ms. Pelis realizes during the discussion that the children are not sure who that responsible adult would be on the playground. The class makes a list of who they might report to. Ms. Pelis makes a note to herself to talk with these adults so that they will be ready to take action when the children report to them.

Meanwhile, the second graders in Mr. Oakley's class sit on the rug and discuss the second grade bathrooms. "The fifth graders use our bathroom if they need to go during lunch," declares Maurice. "When they see us in there they call us 'little twerps' and say they're going to stuff us in the toilet." Later on in the day Mr. Oakley discusses the bathroom situation with his principal. His principal will work with the fifth grade team to build kind behaviors toward younger children. He also decides to reconfigure the fifth grade lunchroom arrangement so that fifth graders use a different bathroom during lunch.

Taking Classroom Rules Outside the Classroom

Rules that guide behavior are essential to creating a safe environment not just in the classroom but throughout the school as well. Some schools establish whole-school rules that serve this function; such rules are a key component in a schoolwide bullying prevention effort. But even if you don't have schoolwide rules, you can teach students that "our rules go with us," right down to having a student representative carry a copy of classroom rules and posting these rules in the cafeteria, specials classrooms, and other spaces the class goes to.

However, it's not enough to simply carry the rules from place to place. It's essential to spend time discussing what abiding by the rules will look like and sound like in those places to help children pay attention to the rules in a variety of specific situations.

Classroom rules can help make recess safer

Bullying at school often begins on the playground. A good starting point for teaching safe and kind recess behavior is to reflect with students about how classroom rules apply to recess. Ask questions such as "How does our rule to respect each other apply to games of tag during recess?" or "What would it look like and sound like to be kind to classmates during recess today?" These can help students think more concretely about how to put their in-class rules into action outside of the classroom.

Remember that it's beneficial to collaborate with grade-level colleagues on recess issues. Although individual teachers can have fruitful discussions about specific applications of the rules, coordinating with teachers whose students are on the playground with your students can yield even better results because all the students will then be operating from the same set of expectations.

A third grade team applies classroom rules to the playground

One year the third grade students at my school fell into playing a violent and hierarchical version of football at recess. Football became a way that socially powerful children intimidated the less powerful children. Many of my students returned from recess each day upset, angry, and dejected.

I knew that I needed to address this problem—and that I needed to coordinate my efforts with the other third grade teachers because it wasn't just students from my classroom playing these rough games. We each decided to talk with our students.

In my class, we reflected on how the classroom rules to "be safe" and "be kind" would help us know what to do during football. What would kind behavior look like and sound like as students divided into teams, played football, and congratulated each other at the end of the game? I also invited the PE teacher to attend our grade-level meeting about safety on the playground. We all met, students and educators, to discuss ideas that each class had come up with.

The children devised rules that would support safe and kind behavior during their football games and posted them by the door to the playground. As they lined up for recess, they took turns reading these student-generated rules aloud:

- A teacher must supervise the football game.
- Teams will be chosen by counting off.
- Players will pass to everyone.
- Quarterbacks will rotate.
- Touch only.

When they returned from recess each day, they evaluated themselves, reflecting on how they'd done at following the football rules. I used simple structures for the reflection; for example, saying, "Hold up fingers, one through five, to show how you did at following our football rules today." The vast majority of the children who played football held up four or five fingers. I certainly wasn't expecting perfection at this challenge—four fingers was a huge improvement over their past behavior.

In addition, the teachers and paraprofessionals on recess duty took responsibility for stopping the game if it degenerated, and they made a point of letting the child's classroom teacher know if one child spiraled out of control. Recess safety improved immeasurably.

Talk with children early in the year about how classroom rules apply to lunchroom behavior

Take the time at the beginning of the year to talk about how classroom rules can guide lunchtime behavior. Doing so can save you from spending hours trying to solve the inevitable problems that will crop up.

Early in the year, Mr. Gonzales discusses with students how the classroom rules apply to the cafeteria. "If our rule is to be kind," he says, "how can we be kind in the cafeteria?" Children's responses are as simple as "We can help someone who drops his tray" and as sophisticated as "We can make sure that everyone has someone to sit with."

Mr. Gonzales then checks in with students after lunch to see how they did with being kind. "Think to yourself about how you did at following our rule to be kind during lunch today," he says. He then asks them to think of a goal for the next day: "What's one thing you can do tomorrow to make lunch more friendly?"

Structuring reflections

The discussions that Mr. Gonzales had with the children helped them feel invested in the classroom rules. Discussions such as these are valuable at the beginning of the year, when children are first learning about behavior expectations, and throughout the year, when new and challenging situations arise. Here are some guidelines for structuring and facilitating these discussions.

Help children remember the purpose of rules

First, prompt the children to remember their relationship to the rules. "We created rules to help us keep our classroom safe and friendly" or "Our rules help us to have a safe and friendly classroom" are statements that remind children about the purpose of the rules.

Frame the challenges in positive terms

Second, bring up possible outside-the-classroom challenges while keeping your language positive. Keep the focus on what we do want (safety outside the classroom) rather than what we don't want ("We will not be mean").

To stimulate this discussion, it's helpful to use open-ended questions—questions that have multiple possible answers. Here are some possibilities:

- How can we keep the cafeteria as friendly as our classroom is?
- How can we make sure everyone's feelings are safe on the playground?
- What might you do if you see someone alone on the playground (or in the lunchroom)?
- How can we make sure that everyone who wants to play has the chance to play?

- How can we make the school bus feel safe in the same way our classroom feels safe?
- (For older children) How can you be a leader and take care of the younger children on the school bus?

Gather students' ideas

Next, collect student ideas while keeping the discussion focused on what they do want. Students can be highly invested in their hopes for friendliness and safety, whereas they're not likely to be invested in a list of prohibitions. For example, if a child says, "We shouldn't throw stuff on the school bus," a teacher might say, "If you aren't going to throw things, what will you do?"

It's often helpful to use a T-chart, a two-column chart with "What will it look like?" at the top of one column and "What will it sound like?" at the top of the other. The T-chart can stay up in the classroom for a while or it can be stored in a convenient spot, physical or electronic, and brought out when the challenging time (recess, lunch, independent hall walking) is about to begin.

Young children often enjoy drawing pictures to remind themselves what safe and careful outside-the-classroom behavior will look like and sound like. The act of creating posters and pictures cements the learning for the students, and the visuals can serve as a strong reminder of positive behaviors.

Quick conversations can have a positive impact

In addition to in-depth discussions of rules, you can also have quick, in-the-moment conversations about behavior expectations outside the classroom. Ms. Gilbert's fourth graders are lined up at the door, ready to go to lunch. Today, their lunch period overlaps the first grade lunch period. Ms. Gilbert says, "One of our rules says to respect each other. How can you show respect to others today at lunch?" Several hands go up and children respond: "Be kind to the younger kids," "Say 'Hi' to kids in other classes," "Don't bump people." Mrs. Gilbert then prompts, "If you're not going to bump people, what will you do?" "Watch where you're going and keep your body in your own space," a child replies. "Sounds like you're ready for the cafeteria," Ms. Gilbert says, and the children head out the door.

A quick conversation at the end of the day can help keep expectations of kind and safe behavior alive for children as they ride the bus home. The fourth graders in Ms. Nelson's class are packed up and ready to go home. They sit in a circle. "Our school rule says to be kind," says Ms. Nelson. "How might that rule apply to the bus ride home?" she asks. The children think for a minute and then hands go up. "I could sit with Jenny," offers Sarah. "She just moved into our neighborhood and doesn't know many kids yet." Other children nod in agreement.

Strategy in Action

A Fifth Grade Team Creates Playground Rules

One spring, as part of their bullying prevention efforts, a fifth grade teaching team administered a questionnaire to all of the fifth grade students. Children responded to questions about where in school they felt safe and where in school they had experienced behaviors defined by the questionnaire as "bullying," which included being hit, pushed, kicked, teased, called names, or being purposely excluded. To their teachers' surprise, one quarter of the children surveyed reported experiencing bullying on the playground during the past month. The fifth grade team could see that they needed to improve safety on the playground.

The team gathered information as a first step

Each teacher closely observed their class for a week during their recess duty. The teachers followed students who hid behind trees, really listened to the play under the play structure, and noticed the body language and facial expressions of children chasing each other. The teachers also discussed playground safety with the recess paraprofessionals. As might happen to many of us when we first actively observe outside-the-classroom behavior, what they saw surprised and alarmed them.

- Many of the boys who played on the high-status travel soccer team played soccer every day. They took charge of choosing teams and excluded children who were less skilled at the game.

- Students who weren't playing soccer didn't have much to do. Many girls gathered in small groups and whispered about each other, hiding behind the play structure and jumping out to make mean comments as girls in other groups walked by.

- Four children grabbed the swings each day and monopolized them. This group engaged in lots of unsafe behavior, such as getting the swings going really high and then jumping off or twisting the swings and flinging them at children swinging next to them. When other children tried to get a swing, the four children loudly chanted, "We own the swings."

- One small group of children spent recess throwing rocks at classmates.

The information that the teachers discovered provided a wake-up call. When they sat down to talk and began to list the behaviors that they had seen, they realized they needed to take immediate action.

The team intervened quickly to stop the misbehaviors

Some of the more dangerous misbehaviors needed to be stopped immediately. After discussions with the recess paraprofessionals, the teachers decided to tape off the swing area until they could establish expectations of physical and emotional safety on the swings. As the children lined up for recess, the lead recess teacher explained to them that swings were off-limits until together everyone decided how to make them safe. They also announced that any behavior that hurt children's bodies (or any attempts to hurt children's bodies) would lead to separation from other children at recess for the day. The adults supervised recess behavior closely. The first time a child picked up a rock and started to fling it, they honored their words by following through and quickly separating that child from the other children.

The team then established clear rules

At their next grade-level meeting, the fifth grade teachers looked at their classroom rules, identified which ones related to recess, and consolidated them to make a few simple recess rules:

- We will be safe

- We will be fair

- We will include everyone

They discussed their plan with the fifth grade recess paraprofessionals and explained how they hoped to improve supervision. Needless to say, the paraprofessionals were delighted by the support.

The rules were presented to the students

Back in their own classrooms, the teachers presented the rules to the students. Each teacher explained that they had noticed that recess had become unsafe. They shared the "recess rules," explaining that they were derived from their own classroom rules which the children had helped to create. They brainstormed with their students what the rules might look like and sound like on the playground.

The children had a lot to say. "We'll need to share the swings if we're going to include everyone," said Kevin, who often was the "king of the swings." Jeff said, "I guess the teachers will choose the soccer teams now if we're going to include everyone." And Maxine added, "If recess is going to be safe, some kids are going to have to stop saying mean things."

Reflection with the students continued on how the rules applied to playground behavior

In the following days, each teacher devoted brief periods of time in class each day to reflect with the students about what their recess rules "be safe," "be fair," and "include everyone" would look like and sound like on the playground. As the children lined up for recess, Mr. Roland asked, "What might you do today to include everyone on the playground?"

When the children returned from recess, Ms. Young asked, "Think about how you did today at being safe. Chat with the person next to you in line about something you did to be safe or something safe that you saw a classmate do." Ms. Young listened in while her students chatted with partners. "It sounds like everyone shared the swings," she said.

Each teacher continued their careful observations and interventions in the days that followed. When Mindy clung to Fiona's neck and Fiona, with a distressed expression, said repeatedly, "Stop it, stop it," Ms. Young quickly stepped in. "Mindy, that's not safe. Play over here by yourself for the rest of recess."

The tone of the playground became much more positive. Children laughed, chatted sociably, and enjoyed themselves. The teachers' interventions had made recess safer.

Using Modeling and Role-Playing to Help Students Practice Safe and Inclusive Behaviors

Discussing how the rules apply to all areas of the school is an important first step, but children need opportunities to actually practice safe and inclusive behavior. The *Responsive Classroom* strategies of Interactive Modeling and role-playing help children do this. (See Chapter Four for detailed information about both strategies.)

Use modeling to review and practice specific procedures

The *Responsive Classroom* strategy of Interactive Modeling can be used to help children practice specific procedures that will maintain order and minimize opportunities for mean behavior. For example, you can use modeling to teach them how to listen respectfully to a lunch buddy or how to sit safely—child's back to seat back and child's bottom to seat bottom—on the school bus. Modeling is also a way to teach safe and careful tagging when playing a game of tag at recess, or safe standing or sitting in line while children wait to go home on their school buses.

Early in the year at Kensington Avenue School in Springfield, Massachusetts, teachers use Interactive Modeling to review lunchroom protocols with students, including lining up, getting their lunch, using appropriate voice levels, and sitting at their correct table. When students are asked to demonstrate the appropriate behaviors themselves and notice how their classmates demonstrate these expected behaviors, the behaviors become lodged in their memory and students are more likely to use the behaviors when the time comes. Interactive Modeling is a key reason that the lunchroom behavior at Kensington is safe, orderly, and inclusive.

To model safe sitting on the school bus, first grade teacher Ms. Guerin lines up chairs in the front of the classroom, mimicking the arrangement of school bus seats. "We're going to practice how to sit safely on the bus," she explains to the children. Ms. Guerin sits on one of the chairs. "What do you notice about how I'm sitting?" she asks. "Your feet are on the floor," says Mark. "Your back is against the back of the chair," says Lucy. "Your bottom is on the seat of the chair," says Malik. "To be safe on the school bus, you'll sit back to seat back, bottom to seat bottom," Ms. Guerin explains. Then she asks, "Who else would like to show us what this looks like?" Eager hands go up and Ms. Guerin gives everyone in the class a chance to practice.

As the children line up for the bus, Ms. Guerin reminds them, "Remember, to be safe, back-to-back, bottom-to-bottom." When the children's bodies are in their seats, opportunities to engage in mean behaviors are diminished.

Use role-playing to help children prepare for potentially tricky situations

Role-playing is a strategy to help children explore a range of responses to potentially tricky situations. As you observe a specific group of students in the lunchroom, on the playground, or hear about their struggles on the school bus, you can learn which challenges they're facing as they practice taking care of their own needs as well as the needs of those around them. Challenges that might benefit from role-playing include:

- What to do if you notice a classmate alone on the playground every day
- How to ask to join a game on the playground
- How to share the jump ropes or other equipment on the playground so that it's fair and fun for everyone
- How to invite someone to eat lunch with you
- What to do if two students want to sit next to the same person at lunch
- What you might talk about when you sit with a lunch partner
- What you might do to keep yourself busy on the bus to and from school while allowing the bus driver to do their job safely
- How you might help younger children feel safe on the school bus

Fourth grade teacher Mrs. Jones has noticed that students have been struggling with where to sit at lunch. One girl in particular seems to be a desired lunch partner. As soon as Anna sits down, several other children vie for the spot next to her. Mrs. Jones knows that this situation has the potential for mean and exclusive behavior.

She gathers students in a circle and says, "Today we're going to do a role-play to help us think and practice how to decide who sits where in the lunchroom. Our rules say to include everyone. How can we do that when several people want to sit in the same spot?" The students nod knowingly. They are interested. This is a problem that they're all well aware of.

"Pretend I'm a student," she says. "We're going into the lunchroom and I really want to sit near my friend, Denise. I know that Mary and Paulina want to sit near Denise, too. What might I do to include everyone and take care of my own wishes to be with my friends?" Mrs. Jones has created fictional names to keep the role-play at a slight remove from the actual classroom struggle.

Mrs. Jones collects ideas and writes them on a flip chart:

"You could talk with Denise, Mary, and Paulina and make a plan so that you can all sit together without arguing about the seat next to Denise."

"You could sit in partners, Denise and Mary, you and Paulina, and then switch another day."

"You could try sitting with someone else. We have lots of nice kids in our class."

Mrs. Jones tries out one of the ideas. "Okay, I'm going to try one idea while Suzette, Stacy, and Janet play the roles of Denise, Mary, and Paulina."

She goes up to the other players. "I have an idea," she says. "I think lunch might be more fun for all of us if we sat with some other kids in our class and not only with each other. Let's see if we can get some other kids to join us."

Mrs. Jones says, "Stop," and the class discusses what they noticed. Many students comment that the girls might indeed have more fun if they sit with more people.

The class continues to act out some of the ideas on the chart and debrief about what they noticed.

The next day Mrs. Jones notices that the girls who normally all rushed to one seat have planned ahead about who would sit in the coveted spot. When she picks up the students after lunch she notices a large group of children sitting at the table where Anna is sitting, everyone appearing to enjoy themselves.

Giving Students Reminders and Reinforcements for Outside-the-Classroom Behaviors

Once teachers have introduced strategies for making the areas outside the classroom safe and friendly, and children have had opportunities to practice these strategies under supervision, teachers can use reminding and reinforcing language to help children continue these behaviors.

Reminders prompt children to remember the established behavior expectations. For example, after teaching safe sitting on the bus, remind children as they leave the classroom: "Remember, back-to-back and bottom-to-bottom." You can also ask children to do this reminding. For example, as the children line up to go outside, ask, "Who can remind us which strategies we came up with yesterday for making sure that everyone has someone to play with?"

Reinforcements acknowledge and name children's attempts at positive behavior. For example, as the children arrive in the morning, a teacher might say to the class, "I'm noticing friendly conversation as you walk down the hall" or, to an individual who has been less than inclusive in the past, "I saw that you were friendly with all of the girls who have lockers near yours."

> **Some Language to Try**
>
> *Remember, back to seat back and bottom to seat bottom.*
>
> *Who can remind us . . . ?*
>
> *I hear friendly conversations.*
>
> *You were friendly to everyone in your group.*

Here are some tips for using reinforcing and reminding language effectively:

- Keep your language positive, reminding children of the class's vision of a caring community.

- Remind children about behaviors that you have already taught rather than reminding about behaviors that you assume they should know.

- Use reinforcing language to support children's actual positive behaviors rather than pretending they're doing something that they're not.

- Reinforce individuals privately rather than using your public observations of one child's successes to manipulate other children into behaving well.

For more information about reinforcing and reminding language, see *The Power of Our Words: Teacher Language That Helps Children Learn* 2nd ed., by Paula Denton (see Appendix B).

Providing Structures That Enhance Inclusiveness Outside the Classroom

Sometimes children need specific structures to ensure inclusiveness and safety at recess, in the lunchroom, and on the bus. Depending on the developmental level of the children you teach and the time of year, you may decide to set up a format that minimizes choice and maximizes equitable treatment for all. Assigned seating in the cafeteria, for example, guarantees that everyone will have someone to sit with. What follows are some ideas for providing structure to increase inclusiveness at recess, in the lunchroom, and on the bus.

Provide structures at recess that include everyone

You and your colleagues may have observed rough or excluding behavior on the playground. Perhaps students have reported that the playground is a spot in school where they feel unsafe. If so, you can plan structures that will increase inclusiveness and safety.

Structure selection for team sports

Choosing sides for team sports is an area where exclusion often flourishes. If this is the case in your school or grade level, then you might consider, in collaboration with others who supervise recess, using a structure for forming teams. You could group the children who plan to play a particular game and have them count off by 2s to select teams. You could pass out numbered craft sticks, with those drawing odd numbers on one team and those drawing even numbers on the other.

Whatever method you use, it's important to discuss it first with the children, making sure that they understand how team selection structures connect with classroom rules and support a positive vision for life in school. To avoid arguments about team selection methods, children also need to know which method will be used on a particular day.

Sometimes it's helpful to stop team sports for a period of time (a few days to a week) and then reopen the sports with a new structure, which you've carefully introduced. That way you'll have a fresh start with a fresh way to make sure that everyone is taken care of.

Set an expectation that all children will be inclusive on the playground

When announcing a new expectation of inclusion, teacher and author Vivian Paley (1992) would tell her kindergarten class, "You can't say you can't play." When you say to children "You don't have to be best friends with everyone, but you do need to be friendly to everyone," you're telling them that the expectation is that they will include anyone who wants to play.

You can then remind children that when they line up to shoot hoops on the playground, it's important that they include anyone who wants to join in. When they organize jump rope or Four Square, they need to make sure everyone gets to play.

Once you've clarified your expectations, quick reminders before recess and a quick evaluation after recess can keep the goal of friendly inclusion paramount in everyone's mind.

Provide activities for children who are less interested in sports

Not all children want to engage in sports activities. It's important then to provide activities for these children as well, especially if you observe them wandering around the playground aimlessly. Children who aren't engaged will amuse themselves, and not always in positive ways.

Inexpensive materials can provide opportunities for engagement. I suggest Hula-Hoops, jump ropes, or chalk for drawing on the pavement. You can also create spots for simple games of four square or hopscotch. Some teachers and paraprofessionals arrange a walking club where a group of children walk the perimeter of the playground, counting their laps and trying to improve their personal best on each walk.

Provide noncompetitive games

More game options can bring peace and cooperation to the playground. Classic, noncompetitive children's games such as Red Light Green Light and Fish Gobbler can provide a fun experience for everyone. There are scores of tag games such as Freeze Tag, Blob Tag (where every time someone is tagged they become part of the Blob), and my students' favorite, Toilet Tag (where the person tagged becomes a toilet until he's freed by being "flushed").

Before introducing new games, take the time to teach procedures for safe and cooperative play. One such procedure is "tagger's choice," where the person who does the tagging gets to decide whether or not she actually tagged a person. It's especially important that an adult supervise the game the first time or two it is played to ensure that it is safe, fair, and inclusive for everyone. It's even better if the adult actually plays with the children, setting a tone of fun and fairness.

There are a number of options for teaching and supervising these games. I have taken students outside for a five- to ten-minute midmorning break during which I teach a group game. I then provide a simple direction sheet to recess supervisors to keep them in the know. PE teachers can also teach children age-appropriate, noncompetitive games. And you can divide game supervision among colleagues who supervise recess.

In Appendix B, you'll find resources for noncompetitive games.

Provide structures at lunch that promote a positive, friendly atmosphere

The lunchroom can be a place where cliques flourish, leading directly to bullying behaviors. It can also be a place where children have the opportunity to get to know everyone, leading to friendly inclusion.

Change lunch partners—every day

Early in the year, you can provide structures that will help students sit with a variety of lunch partners.

During the first week of school, fourth grade teacher Mrs. Ryan explains, "In this class we're becoming a community. Part of becoming a community is getting to know everyone. As one way of doing that, you're going to sit with a variety of lunch partners."

She reaches into a cup filled with students' names. "Shamika, you may pick a lunch partner," she says. "Whomever Shamika picks will sit with her at lunch today. Tomorrow, that person will have a chance to pick a different partner." Shamika invites Rachel to eat lunch with her. Mrs. Ryan continues to pick names until every child has a lunch partner. Mrs. Ryan has already taught students how to invite someone to lunch and she has modeled what a friendly acceptance would look and sound like.

Down the hall in Mr. Bissell's third grade, children are matched with a lunch partner through the luck of the draw. They pick a multiplication flash card and find their match by locating the person with either the factors or the product that matches their card. In Mrs. Ruffles' first grade, she simply announces a different partnership each day. "Ricky, you will eat lunch with Marie today." Although children might be embarrassed to choose a partner of a different gender, they willingly sit with a partner that Mrs. Ruffles assigns.

Mrs. Ryan, the fourth grade teacher, arrives a few minutes early to meet the children after lunch. She sees smiling faces and hears happy laughter. She asks Mrs. Zunick, the lunchroom supervisor, how things went. "They got along well," Mrs. Zunick says and notes that even some of the kids who avoided each other the previous year in the lunchroom looked like they were fine. For the next few weeks, students will continue to choose lunch partners until everyone has had a chance to sit with many different classmates.

Teach conversation skills

If children are to get to know one another over lunch, they'll need to know how to talk with each other and what to talk about. Mrs. Ryan teaches children how to have a conversation with someone they don't yet know very well. She asks, "What might you talk about if you want to get to know someone?" Children suggest topics such as family members, favorite after-school activities, or favorite animals.

Even with good topics, children can easily fall into a pattern where each person talks but neither one listens to the other. I suggest using Interactive Modeling to explicitly teach how to listen to a lunch partner and respond appropriately.

You might have already taught these skills as part of helping children learn how to work with partners and small groups (see Chapter Four). Even so, the reality is that children may learn a skill in one setting (such as the classroom) but have no idea how that skill applies to a new setting (such as the lunchroom). It's important for students to see their teacher model any new application of a skill and have a chance to practice it before they're expected to use it in a new situation.

Provide structure throughout the year, if needed

Changing lunch partners can go on for the first six weeks of school, for the entire year, or for any length of time in between. Some children quickly learn how to be inclusive while others continually need structure to protect an atmosphere of kindness and inclusion.

Those quick observations that I described earlier in this chapter can serve you well in deciding how to use lunchroom structures. Notice how your students are doing with partners. How do they do when you loosen the structure a bit? Are they ready for more independence or do they need slightly tighter controls? The goal is to keep the lunchroom safe and friendly for everyone, and to protect against an all-too-common negative atmosphere in which bullying can flourish.

Provide structures to increase safety on the school bus

The school bus is a prime environment for bullying. Supervision is minimal, older and younger children are mixed together, and some children spend long periods of time on the bus. Bullying behaviors that begin on the school bus often continue surreptitiously throughout the school day. Even though we have minimal presence on the bus, we can still provide structures that have an impact on the peace and safety of students' bus rides.

Safe structures

The Peaceful School Bus program is used in many U.S. schools and treats each school bus as an individual community. School staff members lead bus-by-bus meetings to promote safe, kind, and inclusive behavior on each bus (Dillon 2008). A whole-school approach to bus behavior such as this is optimal, but classroom teachers can have a positive impact by using a modified version of these bus meetings. Children can spend a few minutes at the end of the day with the other children in their class who share their bus. With teacher facilitation, they can draw pictures of safe ways to be on the bus, or write about the kind words they'll use on the bus.

Often bus drivers develop structures that promote bus safety, such as assigned seats. Our job as classroom teachers is to support the bus driver in implementing these structures. We can check in with children to make sure that they're using their assigned seats and that they're using other structures the bus driver has set up.

Big buddy/little buddy

In multiple studies, younger children report being bullied by older children and older children report doing the bullying (Olweus and Limber 2007; Smith, Madsen, and Moody 1999). One place that age groups are most likely to mix is on the school bus. The challenge for teachers is to replace the attitude of "I can show that I'm powerful by making a younger child uncomfortable" with "I can show that I'm powerful by being a leader and taking responsibility for younger children." An effective way to do this is to help older children learn to actively take care of younger children.

Mrs. O'Hare, a kindergarten teacher, teams up with the fifth–sixth grade teacher down the hall from her to create cross-age buddy pairings. In the first week of school, the older students meet their kindergarten buddies at the school bus and walk them to their classroom. During the year they work on both academic and nonacademic projects together. They do research on mammals, go on field trips, and create holiday gingerbread houses together. Younger and older children alike look forward to Friday afternoon "buddy time."

The big buddy/little buddy strategy can also work for individual students. When Ray, a student in my third grade classroom, began to bother first grader Jamal on the school bus, the principal and I each discussed the situation with Ray's mother, Mrs. Snyder, who came up with a promising solution to try. "Jamal is in Miss Cooper's class and Miss Cooper was Ray's first grade teacher," said Mrs. Snyder. "Ray loves Miss Cooper. What would happen if Ray went to Miss Cooper's class to help out? He could practice being kind to Jamal in that setting."

Ray went to Miss Cooper's class once a week to help her students with their math. Ray was proud of his role and would start reminding me a day in advance, "Tomorrow I go to Miss Cooper's class." Miss Cooper made sure that Ray's contact with Jamal was indeed kind. Soon Ray was Jamal's special protector on the school bus. Ray discovered that he didn't need to be mean to feel powerful.

Notice that in this situation we didn't force Ray and Jamal together. Ray went to Miss Cooper's class to work with all of the first graders.

It's also critical to understand that this strategy worked well because Ray wasn't actually bullying Jamal, although he was trying out "bugging" Jamal in a way that could have developed into bullying if it had continued unchecked. In addition, Miss Cooper supervised the boys carefully. When there's a potential bullying relationship between two children, forcing them together can be dangerous.

Collaborating With Colleagues Who Supervise Students Outside the Classroom

In every school there are many adults who supervise children outside the classroom. To be successful in preventing bullying behavior outside the classroom, you'll need to collaborate with these adults and support them in the hard work of keeping the lunchroom, the playground, the halls, and the school bus physically and emotionally safe.

Begin by telling the adult supervisors about strategies that you've taught children and listen when they tell you about strategies that they're using in the settings that they supervise. I recommend something as simple as saying to the lunchroom supervisor, "We assigned lunchroom seats today; here's the diagram of where each student will sit" or "We practiced hand games that children can play when they've finished eating their lunch. Could you let me know how the hand games went when I pick up the children?"

You can also check in with outside-the-classroom supervisors about how things are going in their setting. When you ask, "How did my class do today?" you're communicating collegiality and support.

It's also important to collaborate with these colleagues in efforts to stop mean behaviors. It was the end of the lunch period when Suzanne threw food at Michele and called her "Mickey Meat Loaf." Mrs. Murphy, the lunchroom supervisor, reported the incident to the girls' classroom teacher, Mr. Adair. He arranged for Suzanne to give up her Quiet Time that day to help the custodian with cleanup.

Later on, Mr. Adair met with Suzanne. "Michele is part of our classroom community," he said. "I'll be watching to make sure that you treat Michele kindly when you're in our classroom. I'll also be checking in with Mrs. Murphy to make sure that you're treating Michele kindly in the lunchroom."

If Mr. Adair had taken the stance that discipline in the lunchroom was "not my job," the unresolved incident would have surely spilled over into the classroom. It would have most likely escalated into increasingly mean behavior.

To solve the problem of bullying, we need to treat everything that happens to the students we teach as "our job."

In addition, it's important that any bullying prevention training that is available to classroom teachers involves all educators. We feel better able to intervene when we see social cruelty if we've had training that includes possible responses. In a recent study, researchers discovered that paraprofessionals who supervise some of the most behaviorally challenging parts of the day have the least training about how to stop social cruelty and bullying and thus are least likely to intervene (Bradshaw et al. 2013).

Communicating With Parents About Outside-the-Classroom Behaviors

Parents are more likely to know about some of the bus, cafeteria, and playground mean behaviors than teachers are. Parents watch their child get on the school bus and see others move away from their child, leaving him isolated. They see their child get off the bus at the end of the day, in tears, explaining that older children have stolen their hat or lunch or drawn with marker on their coat.

Parents sometimes assume that teachers aren't interested in what goes on in the cafeteria or on the school bus. They aren't sure whom to talk with about outside-the-classroom issues. If you let parents know that you care about events outside the classroom, they'll tell you about them.

For example, if you've discovered that the playground is the place in your school where your students feel least safe, you might communicate with parents about this area of the school. Begin by sharing specific information about steps you've taken to create a safe environment on the playground. Then ask for their help.

You might include a statement like this in your newsletter home:

> We're working to make the playground a safe place for all children. The teachers on our team are taking turns supervising a large group game every day so that all children will have a closely supervised place to go

at recess. Children report that recess is "more fun." However, mean behavior can still happen out of our sight. Please help us by letting us know if your child reports to you that he or she feels unsafe at recess. We all want recess to be fun for everyone.

Once you've made this overture, it's important to listen and respond immediately when parents do report unsafe behavior. Making school safe for all is a team effort.

KEY IDEAS

- **The majority of mean behavior happens** in the often lightly supervised areas of the school, outside the classroom.

- **Teachers can play a key role** in preventing bullying in "hot spots" such as the playground, cafeteria, halls, and school bus.

- **Observe students outside the classroom,** if only briefly. This can yield rich information.

- **Teach students that classroom rules "go with them"** when they move around the building, and model safe and kind behavior outside the classroom.

- **Collaborate with grade-level peers** and outside-the-classroom supervisors to keep the entire school safe and friendly for everyone.

- **Promoting positive relationships** between older and younger students may help prevent bullying.

- **Providing structures that increase inclusiveness** in outside-the-classroom areas can help prevent meanness and bullying.

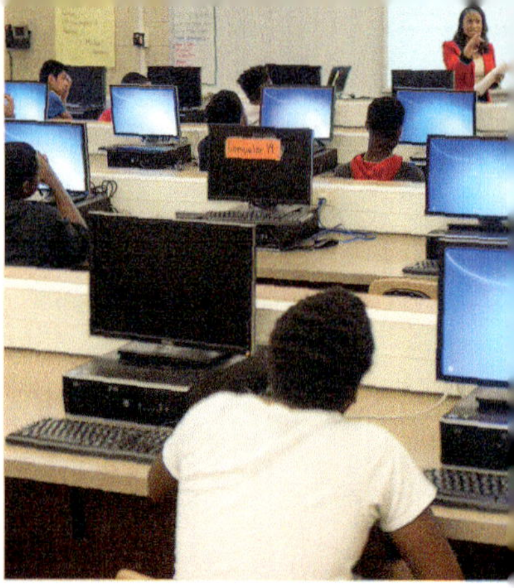

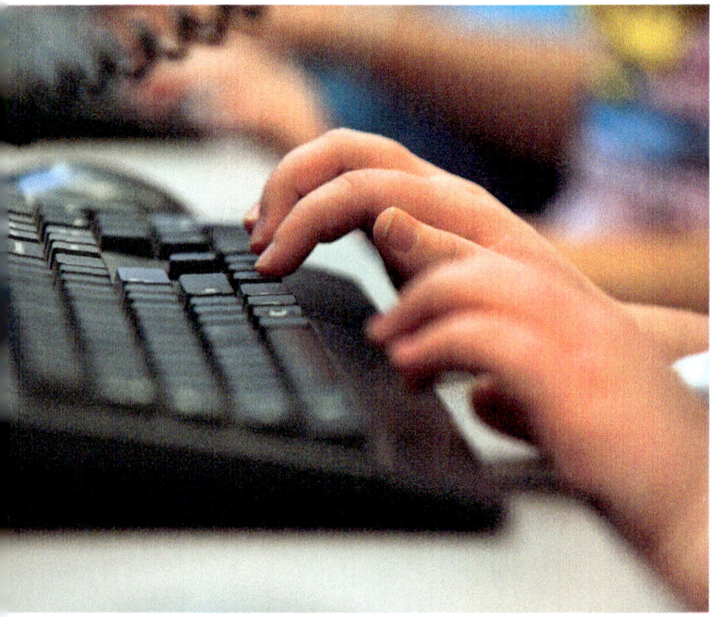

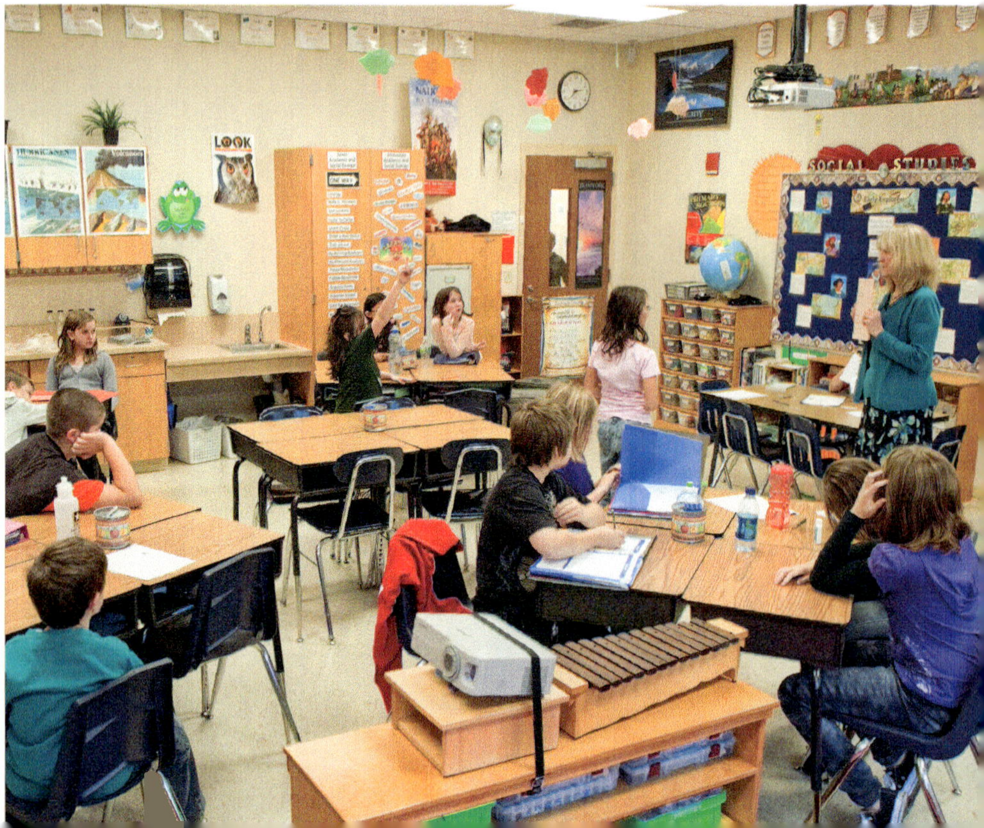
LOOK

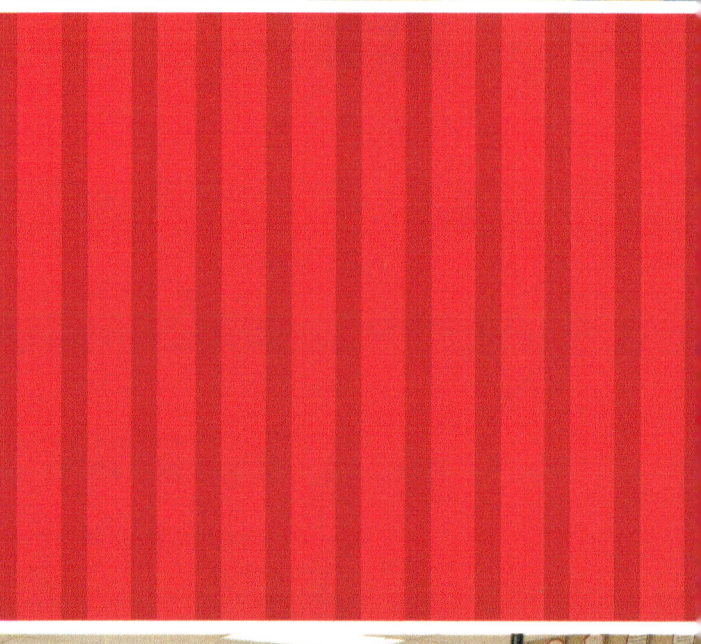

CHAPTER SIX

How to Prevent Cyberbullying

One April day Suzanne was absent from our third grade classroom. Her mother reported that Suzanne was sick. At the end of the day I received a text from Suzanne's mother: "Suzanne wasn't sick at all. When I got home from work I checked her phone account, did some investigating, and discovered that she spent the day sending mean texts to Molly."

Shy and a bit eccentric, Molly lived in the social margins of our classroom. Yet this cyberbullying event surprised me. I had spent the past eight months making sure that Molly was included in every classroom activity. And Suzanne had always appeared ready to include children who might otherwise be left out. What had happened?

I investigated. Social cruelty toward Molly had begun on the school bus. After these incidents, Molly's family had encouraged her to play an online game as a way to connect with the other girls in our class, but classmates excluded Molly from the game. Cruelty escalated. Suzanne knew better than to reveal this dynamic in front of teachers in school, and sending mean texts from home while her mom was at work felt like something she could get away with.

I had a serious talk with Suzanne and then separated her from Molly at school in order to protect Molly. I talked with the bus driver about the situation and then let Suzanne know that if the mean behavior on the bus continued, she would be off the bus. In addition, Suzanne lost the privilege of playing online games at home.

Our class revisited some lessons on cyber safety we covered earlier in the year, and I alerted the parents of other girls in our class that gaming and other phone use needed to be monitored. Our classroom climate soon took a positive turn.

What Is Cyberbullying?

Cyberbullying, like traditional bullying, is a way that a child with social power can abuse a less powerful child (Olweus 2013). It is bullying that takes place over digital devices, and involves sending, posting, or sharing negative, harmful, false, or mean content. Cyberbullying may involve sharing personal or private information that causes embarrassment or humiliation (StopBullying.gov 2020). Dr. Sameer Hinduja and Dr. Justin Patchin (2014), experts on cyberbullying, define it as "willful and repeated harm inflicted through the medium of electronic text." In contrast, Dr. Elizabeth Englander (2013) argues that all electronic mean behavior is by its nature repetitive as comments are forwarded and posted.

Remember that Molly's mistreatment began on the school bus. Cyberbullying nearly always begins with acts of traditional bullying in school or its environs. The Olweus report on bullying in U.S. schools (Luxemberg, Olweus, and Limber 2019), compiled from 245,000 student questionnaires, found that although 16 percent of boys and 17 percent of girls in grades three through five reported that they had been cyberbullied, only one percent of these children reported that they were cyberbullied as a stand-alone, with no additional bullying preceding it in school.

The cyberbullying of Molly followed the incidents on the school bus and began with Suzanne and a group of girls excluding her from an online game. Next, Suzanne sent mean texts to Molly and then forwarded these texts to that same group of girls. If Suzanne's mother had not discovered the texts, they would have been disseminated more widely.

Although I realized that Molly was a child who was at risk, I didn't know that she was actually being bullied, either on the school bus or in the digital world. Cyberbullying is hard to notice (StopBullying.gov 2021a). Unlike bullying that occurs only at school, cyberbullying follows children home and takes away their sense of safety (National Crime Prevention Council 2020). It is sometimes described as a 24/7 extension of cruelty on the playground, and almost impossible to escape (Slonje, Smith, and Frisén 2013).

Paulette, a fifth grader, was the focus of persistent cyberbullying. Her mother confiscated her phone at bedtime, hoping that Paulette would be able to sleep. Instead, Paulette became frantic, wanting to read every word that the others said about her and terrified that she would miss something happening in her social milieu. This response is all too common. Many children feel that their only choices are being the focus of contemptuous cruelty or being isolated and friendless.

Children often know the person who bullies them, as Molly certainly did, but there still is a perception of—and sometimes actual—anonymity on the part of the person doing the bullying (Depaolis and Williford 2015). This anonymity is why many children who cyberbully believe that they can get away with it, just as Suzanne did.

Cyberbullying is primarily indirect. The person who does the bullying does not see the facial expression or hear the tone of voice of the person being bullied. This allows the person who does the bullying to pretend to themselves that their behavior is not actually painful to the person being bullied, and they continue to escalate the bullying. Furthermore, the act of repeatedly writing one's negative feelings and making increasingly contemptuous comments toward someone can escalate those feelings, deepening the damage for both players in the drama.

In summary, people tend to be crueler online than in person. When students are engaging in such cruelty day after day, around the clock, it can be deeply disruptive to classroom communities, whether the cruelty is happening at home, at school, or both. Could this be happening in our elementary school classrooms?

Who Is Involved?

We know that even preschoolers can bully and be bullied. Three-, four-, and five-year-olds can mock, exclude, and hit in a bid to establish their own place in the classroom social order. To cyberbully, however, children need access to the cyber world. How much access to digital devices do elementary school students have?

In a 2016 survey, researchers at the Erikson Institute asked parents of preschoolers how they used technology with their child. The survey found that more than half of children six years old and younger used tablets for online games and communication (Erikson Institute 2016). As children get older, they have increased independent access to the internet. In a 2019 study, Common Sense Media found that 19 percent of eight year olds owned a smartphone. In that same year, 26 percent of nine year olds, 36 percent of ten year olds, and 53 percent of eleven year olds were smartphone owners (Robb 2019).

Common Sense Media has been exploring these trends over time. In data gathered during 2011, they found that 8 percent of children eight years old and younger used a tablet. By 2013, 40 percent of children in this age group used a tablet, and by 2017 it was up to 78 percent of children in this age group (Common Sense Media 2017). It's clear that children are using electronic media at younger and younger ages to communicate, to play games with friends, and to post and watch videos. And this trend is likely to continue.

The pandemic that began in the spring of 2020 created a need for even more online use for children. Toddlers began spending more time with everyone from grandparents to friends via video calling apps. Preschoolers were posting to social media. Elementary school students were distance learning from home via tablets and computers. Everyone was connecting digitally. It's unlikely we will ever go back to a time when children are "too young" to use electronic devices.

How does this information connect with cyberbullying? Research shows that younger children who have less unsupervised access to the internet report less cyberbullying (Monks, Robinson, and Worlidge 2012). However, we also know that access to the internet is increasing at younger and younger ages, and that nearly 20 percent of children in grades three through five report being cyberbullied (Depaolis and Williford 2015; Luxenberg, Olweus, and Limber 2019).

It's likely the trend of younger children having increased access to the internet with less supervision will continue. These cyberbullying experiences almost always begin with precipitating events in the classroom (Juvonen and Gross 2008; Monks, Mahdavi, and Rix 2016) and can be a strong predictor of a child being cyberbullied (Chen, Ho, and Lwin 2016; Guo 2016; Kowalski, Limber, and McCord 2019). With this in mind, educators' may need to increase efforts in their classrooms to prevent bullying and protect against possible cyberbullying.

How Can We Prevent Cyberbullying?

Whether your students engage in cyberbullying on school-owned devices or on devices at home, it will permeate the culture of the classroom and do damage to the positive classroom climate that you have worked so hard to create. There are many proactive strategies that educators can use to prevent cyberbullying both in and out of the classroom. Positive classroom culture, clear rules for respectful behavior in person and on cyber platforms, and social skills training that links the classroom and cyber platforms are all key. It's also important that students know who to report to if cyberbullying occurs and that educators know how to respond to such reports.

We can't start teaching bullying prevention strategies too soon. Early childhood is the ideal time to foster anti-bullying behavior in children. Young children are more likely than older children to seek guidance from parents and teachers. Furthermore, if children learn to engage in casual cruelty as small children, habits will develop that are hard to turn around (Yerger and Gehret 2011). By the same logic, the best time to teach positive digital behaviors is when children first have access to digital devices (Sprung, Froschl, and Gropper 2020).

Positive classroom culture

The foundation of a bully-free classroom or school is a positive classroom culture. High quality instruction, student engagement in learning, classroom and school rules that students believe in, clear routines, and strong positive relationships all contribute to a positive culture. Respectful relationships among all students and supportive relationships between teacher and students are key (American Psychological Association, n.d.; Zych, Baldry, and Farrington 2017; Monks, Mahdavi, and Rix 2016).

How can educators achieve this culture? Our own social skills are important. We need to model positive relationships with our students and our colleagues. Teaching practices that connect students to one another are also vital. The more our students get to know each other, the more they will feel empathy and show kindness toward each other.

Mr. Park has just finished reading R.J. Palacio's *Wonder* to his fourth graders, a book about a boy who has been homeschooled until fifth grade and struggles to be accepted by his new classmates. "You're going to talk with revolving partners about some of your impressions and feelings right now," Mr. Park says. "Think about how you're feeling about the book's ending," he adds. "When you have something to share, put your thumb up. Now look at your feet. Find a classmate who has on shoes that have something in common with yours. Partner up with that person. Make sure that everyone else has a partner, too. Now share some of your thoughts with your partner." Mr. Park makes sure that everyone has a partner, gives the partners a few minutes to talk, and then gives another prompt for discussion. This time students match by shirt color. As the students continue to match with new partners and discuss the book, they are building connections that will protect the classroom community.

Create and reinforce clear rules

Mrs. Bailey's first graders are sitting in a circle, about to start math time. "Yesterday you played a number sentence game on DreamBox," she says. "Today you'll play that same game with a partner. Which of our classroom rules will help you to make this game fun for everyone?"

Students look at the classroom rules, thoughtfully, reflecting on the rules that they worked so hard to create. "Be kind?" suggests Matt.

"What would 'be kind' look like and sound like?" asks Mrs. Bailey.

"If your partner makes a mistake you could say, 'That's okay,'" offers Sam.

"You could make sure that you and your partner can both see the screen," says Fan.

"It sounds like you're ready to go," comments Mrs. Bailey. "Put up your thumb when you're ready to be kind as you play the game. I'll call you to play when I see your thumb up."

When children begin to use digital devices in school, it's important to be clear that all classroom and school rules apply. As children progress to completing school assignments on digital devices at home, we need to reinforce that the rules still apply. From the beginning of school, children need to be respectful, kind, and inclusive toward all classmates. Class- or school-created rules reinforce that expectation.

Mr. Fernandez knows that a major snowstorm is predicted and the school may close for a series of snow days. The fifth graders will be completing lessons on their digital devices from home. "Let's look at our classroom rules," directs Mr. Fernandez. "Which one will help everyone do their best work while they're working from home?"

"Always do your best work," offers Mark.

Mr. Fernandez takes a sentence strip and a marker. "What shall we add to 'Always do your best work' to clarify that it also applies to working from home?"

"Let's add 'at school and at home,'" suggests Mark. Mr. Fernandez writes, "At school and at home," and tapes the sentence strip to the rule.

"While you're working from home I might ask you to go to your breakout groups and have you work in groups of four. Which rule would help you?" asks Mr. Fernandez.

"Take care of everyone," suggests Lonnie.

"Let's add 'at school and at home' to that rule too," suggests Danielle. Mr. Fernandez amends the rule.

"You're going to practice now, as if you were all at home," says Mr. Fernandez.

As students work on their tablets, Mr. Fernandez spends a few minutes to circulate and observe the students' efforts. Then he announces, "Now move to your breakout groups." As the students move, electronically, to pre-selected breakout groups, Mr. Fernandez looks for respectful communication in the virtual environment. He writes down respectful phrases that he hears students use and shares them with the group at the end of the lesson.

"I heard phrases such as, 'Can you help me?' and 'Now you're getting it,'" he says.

A few days later the blizzard arrives, closing down the school building. While students are completing assignments on their tablets from home, Mr. Fernandez sends a message to all parents. He reminds them of the classroom rules and mentions some of the respectful language that he heard students use as they practiced "learning as if you were at home" earlier in the week.

Even if students understand the expectations in one setting, they will still need explicit support to practice these expectations in a new setting. Mrs. Bailey and Mr. Fernandez each connected rules that children have created in the classroom to experiences in a digital environment. Mrs. Bailey's focus is on the simple act of playing a partner game in a virtual setting while the teacher supervises. Mr. Fernandez' fifth graders learn about using a digital device at home while living up to school expectations for respect and care.

(For more information about this topic, see Chapter Three, especially the section "Help Children Connect the Rules to Cyberbullying," and Chapter Five, "Taking Classroom Rules Outside the Classroom.")

Teach social skills of respect, kindness, and inclusion in every setting

Empathy is foundational for bullying prevention. Respect, kindness, and inclusion grow out of empathy. As educators, we can model empathy as we listen respectfully and display caring attitudes toward students, colleagues, and parents. We can also teach empathy through day-to-day inclusive community-building practices. As students share with classmates what they like to do after school, their favorite subject in school, or their favorite recess game, others are listening and learning about them. Learning about others opens a door to empathy (Lambe et al. 2019). (See Chapter Two for more sharing ideas.)

Mrs. Hauer displays a large graph on the smartboard for her kindergartners to complete. The heading directs them to color in the boxes that show how many siblings they each have. Later in the day, the class examines the graph and discusses what they have in common and what are their differences. Mrs. Hauer helps her students celebrate both similarities and differences.

In Mr. Ryan's second grade classroom children listen to him read *You, Me and Empathy* by Jayneen Sanders. As he reads about children and their emotions, he asks the following: "What makes you happy? What makes you sad? What makes you worried? How are you similar to the children in the book? How are you different from them?" Through Mr. Ryan's questions, the children are learning about how others feel.

Susan, a second grader, has struggled with gender identity and has decided to become Saul. Their parents come to school that morning to support Saul as he announces the news to his classmates. As Saul shares in Morning Meeting, his parents worry, "Is this going to be okay?" As Saul finishes, Angel raises his hand and asks, "Can we have a birthday party for you?" Saul's classmates understand his rebirth because his teachers have created an empathetic environment in school.

Keeping social skills instruction culturally relevant enhances student understanding and investment. Children in school on the Lakota reservation in South Dakota sit in a circle, ready to discuss how to be kind as they give others feedback online on their Seesaw writing work. Mr. Spencer says, "One of our important Lakota values is courage. It takes courage to be kind to classmates."

It's important that we teach social skills in a way that is attuned to the children we teach. Mr. Spencer links kindness to Lakota values. Mrs. Hauer teaches kindergartners how they are the same and how they are different in a concrete way. Mr. Ryan's lesson on emotions and empathy adds a level of subtlety for older children. The second graders' response to Saul's gender change is based on years of developmentally appropriate teaching toward understanding. (For more information about child development, see *Yardsticks: Child and Adolescent Development Ages 4–14*, 4th edition, by Chip Wood [see Appendix B.])

According to a 2015 study, most third through fifth graders who reported being cyberbullied had been excluded while gaming online (DePaolis and Williford 2015). Teaching the social skill of inclusion can be a first step toward preventing being cyberbullied by exclusion.

Early in the school year, Ms. Pratt tells her fifth grade students, "We are one community here." She expands on this by saying, "To keep our community safe, you need to be friendly to everyone—not necessarily best friends, but friendly." As the class discusses their upcoming recess, Ms. Pratt explains, "When you play group games outside, you need to include everyone. If you're going to play soccer, everyone who wants to needs to be part of the game."

When recess is over, Ms. Pratt asks, "Who can tell us what made recess fun?" Several children mention, "No one was alone."

The next step is to create a bridge from inclusion on the playground to inclusion in an electronic environment. The following week, the class has indoor recess due to bad weather. Ms. Pratt explains to her students, "The computers and tablets will be open for game time as long as anyone who wants to play is included." The fifth graders immediately begin to organize groups for Minecraft.

Between 2015 and 2019 children ages eight through twelve substantially increased their use of online videos, especially YouTube (Common Sense Media 2019). Without teaching and supervision, this development might lead children to post embarrassing videos of classmates.

Educators of third, fourth, and fifth graders can meet this need with some explicit teaching about using kind words, respecting classmates' privacy, and checking in with friends before they post pictures of those friends or use their name. Without such skill training, children might develop long-term negative habits.

The fourth graders in Mr. Shenk's class have started to bring their phones to school and snap photos of each other at recess time. Mr. Shenk isn't sure what happens with these photos and thinks this might be a good time to do a class role-play about safe and careful use of each other's photos.

The students form a circle of chairs on the rug and the "audience" takes their places. Mr. Shenk begins by taking the point of view of a student.

"Pretend I'm a student and I have a new phone. I'm excited about taking my phone to recess because I'd like to take pictures of my friends and post the pictures on Snapchat. I also know that sometimes kids don't want their pictures posted. What can I do so that I can enjoy my phone and not upset my friends?"

Students offer ideas and Mr. Shenk writes them down.

"You could ask first, 'Could I take your picture?'"

"You could show your friends the pictures and ask if you can post them."

"You could secretly take pictures and post them."

When that idea is suggested, Mr. Shenk says, "How would that idea fit in with our classroom rules?"

The student who suggested the secret pictures said, "I guess it doesn't fit with 'Be respectful to all.'" Mr. Shenk doesn't write the suggestion to secretly take pictures on the list.

Next, students take turns acting out the suggestions. Mr. Shenk goes first and chooses "Show your friends the pictures."

Sarah goes next and chooses "Ask first."

The class discusses the results of the dramatizations. Most students decide that it will work best if you show friends the picture after you've taken it, just to make sure that the friend likes the picture.

When it's time for recess, Mr. Shenk pairs up students through the magic of the random sort—"Find someone with a shirt the same color as yours"—and has them discuss what they learned from today's role-play. The role-play has been a start toward making respectful choices about posting friends' pictures. (For more information on role-play, see Chapter Four.)

As the fourth graders line up to go into the building after recess, Mr. Shenk says, "Think privately as you walk in, 'Was your picture taking and posting at recess respectful and caring?'"

The vignettes in this segment are brief glimpses of teachers including social skills instruction in their day. You may decide to try some of the strategies that are embedded in day-to-day classroom life, such as Mrs. Hauer's kindergarten math lesson, or you may try an explicit social skills lesson, such as Mr. Shenk's lesson about posting others' pictures. Either way, the topics in these lessons need to be discussed frequently, woven through the teaching day and modeled in the way we relate to students. Our students are watching.

Enhance Internet Safety by Teaching Developmentally Appropriate Skills

Children's Approximate Age	Characteristic	Specific Skill Instruction
5	Respond to simple, clear instructions and rules	How to share the blue crayon, how to share the computer screen with your partner
6	Competitive, sometimes poor sports	How to treat each other respectfully, class rules to reinforce this
7	Sensitive to their own and each other's feelings, strong sense of right and wrong	How might your classmate feel if not included in a game, if you use mean words
8	Like to socialize and work in groups of four	The importance of and how to work in frequently changing groups
9	The age of self-definition, cliques can be a problem	It's OK to have good friends but it's important to be friendly to and work with every classmate
10	Friendly, strong sense of right and wrong, love to work together	Classroom rules apply in a virtual school environment

Adapted from *Yardsticks: Child and Adolescent Development Ages 4–14*, 4th ed. by Chip Wood (Center for Responsive Schools 2017).

Aspects of Cyberbullying That Are Specific to the Electronic World

Many aspects of cyberbullying are similar to traditional bullying. Whether it's in school or in the electronic world, children use mean words, tease to the point of humiliation, exclude others, engage groups of children in the abuse, and escalate their cruel behavior rapidly. But there are also some aspects of cyberbullying that are unique to the electronic world.

In the electronic world, bullying, by its nature, is indirect. Without the clues of facial expression, body language, or tone of voice, the child doing the bullying can justify and make light of the abuse they are perpetrating. Disinhibited from norms against cruelty, the child who is doing the bullying continues. Suzanne appeared to be inclusive toward others in our classroom. She let go of these norms as she cyberbullied Molly from a digital distance. We can let students know that if you find yourself making mean comments from a distance, step back and think about how that person might feel. We can teach children that if they find themselves the target of such behavior, they can take a screenshot, cut off contact with a child who is mistreating them in this way, and report the incident to a responsible adult.

When children—or adults, for that matter—have a difference of opinion, a face-to-face discussion can lead to resolution. In contrast, sending repeated texts complaining about a person one cannot see can prime the pump of anger, building up feelings that are hard to let go of (Englander 2013). We can teach children to address such serious differences in person.

In the cyber world, posts can be spread widely and quickly. An embarrassing picture, even of a complete stranger, can seem funny. One post of a compromising picture can go viral and soon spread worldwide. Many other people can get involved and it's hard to turn back (StopBullying.gov 2018a). We can teach children that before they post an image, they need to make sure that it's okay with the person depicted.

Embarrassing posts don't just spread widely. They can also be permanent, lasting after the person in the picture has grown and matured into quite a different person (Kowalski, Limber, and McCord 2019). We can remind children of the fact that posts could be permanent.

It's also important for children to know how to guard their passwords in order to protect their identity and their reputation. If they don't, they can find themselves communicating with strangers who pretend to be their friends. Cyber safety programs for children teach them to share their passwords with only their parents and no one else.

Kindergartners and first graders will easily understand connections between classroom rules ("we will be kind" or "we will take care of materials") and safe and careful use of computers or tablets. It works best to devise some concrete experiences to help young children understand some of the more technical expectations of cyber safety, such as "passwords are private." One teacher passes out "messages" to her students in sealed envelopes. The "messages" can be simple phrases for readers or pictures for nonreaders. She explains that the messages are only for the student or their parents. After everyone has read their messages, she explains, "These are private, just the way your password for your tablet is private" (Sprung, Froschl, and Gropper 2020).

The Olweus Bullying Prevention Program suggests using stories to help older children make connections to what might go wrong if they share their passwords with others. For example, the teacher tells the class: "Felicia shared her password with her older sister. Her sister used Felicia's tablet to go on the classroom website and say mean things about Felicia's classmates."

Another tool for teaching internet safety is children's picture books. In Patricia Polacco's *Bully*, sixth grader Lyla earns the highest score on the state test. Her erstwhile "friends" use the internet to accuse her of cheating on the test. Reading *Bully* aloud provides an opportunity to discuss how quickly rumors and accusations can spread in an internet environment.

How do you know if cyberbullying is going on among your students?

No matter how proactively you teach cyber safety, cyberbullying can emerge in the most surprising ways.

Before Suzanne was found to be cyberbullying Molly, I knew that Molly was a vulnerable child. Nevertheless, I had no idea that she was being bullied by other girls in our third grade class. How can you make sure that you notice those cyberbullying behaviors?

Do you see signs of traditional bullying or social cruelty? For example, does one student appear to be isolated on the playground, in the lunchroom, or even in the classroom? Do you hear "funny" but cruel comments followed by laughter? Are those comments frequently directed at the same child? These are a few clues to watch for that may indicate bullying, which could then easily lead to cyberbullying.

There are clues that a student may be cyberbullying in school. Does a student quickly shield their screen as you walk by? Do they immediately close the application? Is there a small group gathered around a tablet, laughing harder than usual?

Watch for clues that a student may be being cyberbullied. Does the student seem upset as they open or shut down their electronic device? Do they appear upset or depressed after using their device? Or maybe the student seems to be avoiding using their device altogether (Hinduja and Patchin 2014).

If you do see signs that may indicate cyberbullying taking place, it's time to observe more closely. Sit in as a group gathers, laughing, around a tablet. The signs mentioned above may be perfectly innocent, or they may lead down a more serious path.

Are Children Engaged in Cyberbullying? Clues to Look For.

Could there be traditional bullying going on?

- Is one child isolated from the others?
- Do you hear cruel comments?
- Do small groups gather, laugh, and then suddenly stop as you walk by?
- Do you see secretive screen behavior?

As you walk around the room, do you see:

- A child who shields their screen or quickly closes their application?
- A child who seems upset or sad as they close their computer or tablet?

What can a teacher do to react to cyberbullying?

If you believe that there is cyberbullying going on among your students, it's important to act on it quickly. Even if your school is not ready to take formal disciplinary action, there are many proactive steps that you can take.

The first step is to have one or more serious private discussions with each student involved. Let the student who is bullying know that you are aware of their behavior. Remind the student of classroom rules about kindness, and review the expected behaviors with the student. Let the student who is being bullied know that it is your intention to protect them.

The student who is being cyberbullied needs a safety and comfort plan (Englander, n.d.). This always starts with removing the person who is doing the bullying from the environs of the person who is being bullied. You also need to identify a safe place where the person who is being bullied can go if the abuse starts again, whether it's the counselor's office, the library, or another place where they will feel safe.

It's essential to notify parents, preferably before they notify you. It is best to avoid the word "bully" when you notify parents. Instead, describe the behavior explicitly. For example, you might say, "Sophie has admitted to changing Cathy's Facebook name to Cheating Cathy and replacing her profile picture with one altered to make it look like she is copying from Simon's test paper." It is also important to tell parents what actions you plan to take. For example, "We have set up a safety plan for Cathy so that she will be able to eat lunch with friends who are kind to her." Remember that federal law prohibits explaining the consequences that will be applied to other people's children (i.e., the one doing the bullying). (For more information on this topic, see the "Communicating With Parents About Misbehavior" section in Chapter One.)

At this writing, not all states have laws against cyberbullying. (For an overview of each state's laws, see www.stopbullying.gov/resources/laws.) Regardless of whether your state has cyberbullying prevention laws, if the cyberbullying causes a "substantial disruption" at school, your administrators may take disciplinary action—even if the cyberbullying has taken place entirely off school grounds (Starks 2010).

Strategies in Action

Responding to a Clique's Cyberbullying

Lori, Chrissie, Devon, and Jen had been best friends since kindergarten, and referred to themselves as the Cool Girls. They sat together at lunch and played together on the playground during recess. If another student asked to join them, they would respond with, "Well, you can play with us if we can bury you in the sandbox. Don't worry, we'll leave your face out." When a student attempted to sit next to one of them on the school bus, they would push them away, and if a classmate tried to sit with them in the lunchroom, they would quickly block the seat.

Their group had been carefully divided up during placement meetings in kindergarten, and first and second grade. However, the third grade teachers were unaware of their alliance and the Cool Girls ended up being placed in the same fourth grade class. The group sat together at Morning Meeting and always tried to pick each other as partners.

Their teacher, Ms. Smith, created a safe and trusting classroom environment. When the class worked together to prepare rules, Ms. Smith encouraged reflection on how to include everyone and how to treat all classmates kindly. When dividing the class into small groups or partnerships, she used random sorts to keep the clique separated.

One day Lori was assigned to work on a PowerPoint project with Crystal, a shy but kind girl and not part of the Cool Girls. When Crystal signed in to her computer account, Lori took note and remembered Crystal's password.

The next day it poured rain and the administrators decided that recess would need to take place in individual classrooms. In contrast to the usual teaching and learning environment, indoor recess provided limited activities and casual supervision.

The Cool Girls gathered around a computer during this recess. "I have an idea," said Lori. "Let's send emails from Crystal's account. I have her password." The girls were focused. Mean words flew from their fingers. Messages were sent from Crystal's account to nearly all of the other girls in their class.

The school's IT department had student accounts set up so that inappropriate language would be flagged, and by the middle of that afternoon, Ms. Smith was notified that Crystal had sent cruel messages to all of the other girls in her class—except the Cool Girls. Ms. Smith had a pretty good idea of what had happened.

Ms. Smith first met with Crystal and told her that nasty messages had been sent from her account. Crystal was shocked. Ms. Smith said that there would be an investigation. She then spoke with the school dean, who followed up with individual meetings with Lori, Chrissie, Devon, and Jen. The dean told each girl that she knew that nasty messages had been sent from another student's account and that she had reason to believe that the girl she was meeting with was involved. Lori assured the dean that she knew nothing about the incident, but Chrissie, Devon, and Jen each confessed their involvement immediately and revealed the details of what they had done.

The school's policy for cyberbullying behavior was a warning for the first infraction and for the second infraction the loss of privilege to have an internet account. All four girls received a warning.

The Cool Girls incident was discovered by the IT administrator within moments of the behavior. Because of the way the school's internet is set up, the IT staff is alerted to cyberbully events almost immediately and then able to respond quickly and efficiently. In addition, because of the safe and positive atmosphere in the school, the IT department finds that 40 percent of such incidents similar to the Cool Girls one are reported to IT by students who know about the events.

In the case of the Cool Girls, further steps were taken. Lori, Chrissie, Devon, and Jen were separated on the playground and on the school bus. This step would protect Crystal and contribute to breaking up the Cool Girls clique and end the bullying behaviors occurring in the classroom. The teachers also created a safety plan for Crystal. She chose an adult to go to if the bullying behavior began again. Lori, who had refused to take responsibility for her role, was removed to the safe room for a day, supervised by a paraprofessional. The Cool Girls' foray into cyberbullying ended up being a onetime incident.

Ms. Smith held a class meeting about cyberbullying with the school principal and the IT administrator also in attendance. The class discussed classroom rules about kindness and inclusion, and then connected these rules to the electronic environment and decided what being kind and inclusive would look like and sound like when sending emails. The school principal let everyone know that Crystal had not sent the mean messages that so many students had received. The look of relief on Crystal's face was clear for all students to see.

Everyone felt safer after that discussion. Expectations were clear. The class created posters to remind everyone of expectations for internet kindness, and Ms. Smith kept expectations clear by reminding the students how to take care of the class rules for inclusion and kindness whenever they engaged the electronic environment.

The positive environment in the classroom was restored. All students felt that their classroom was a place of safety and trust.

Tools for children to use to cope with cyberbullying

Best practice is to do everything we can to prevent bullying and cyberbullying. However, in all likelihood, it will happen at least occasionally and thus we need to give children some tools to cope in the moment.

- Talk with students about what cyberbullying is, how to guard against it, and how to cope with it if it happens.
- Help each child choose an adult in school (a "safety person") who they would feel comfortable reporting to about a cyberbullying incident. Talk through how they would contact that adult and what they would say.
- Let your students know that you will support them and let the chosen adult know that one of your students would like them to be their safety person.
- Encourage children to take a screenshot of the abusive message or picture to share with this adult.
- Make sure that the children know that it's best not to respond in kind to the cyberbullying, and that the most effective approach is not to respond at all (Notar, Padgett, and Roden 2013).

Students will often fail to report cyberbullying because they assume that adults at school do not care or will not act on it. You can let children know that you do care. You can also let parents know in your back-to-school letters and meetings that you want to know if they are aware of any cyberbullying, even if it's going on outside of the school campus.

Sometimes students are right about whether adults at the school care. Research on traditional bullying shows that adults at school sometimes fail to take action because they don't know how. Schools need a cadre of well-trained adults who can be safe contacts for children and address any cyberbullying that takes place at home or in school (Hoff and Mitchell 2009).

There are also technical tools that a child, teacher, "safe" person, or parent can use to stop or mitigate cyberbullying. These include switching passwords, changing telephone numbers, or deleting unread messages received from an unknown address (Slonje, Smith, and Frisén 2013). In addition, some phones allow you to block incoming phone numbers and there are blocking apps such as Bully Block for Android phones. There are also blocking services provided by websites to stop abuse perpetrated on their sites.

> **Teaching Skills to Help Children Cope With Online Challenges**
>
> *If you find yourself making mean comments in the electronic world, step back and think about how the other person might feel.*
>
> *When we are annoyed, sending repeated texts can prime the pump of anger. If you have a serious disagreement with someone, talk with them about it.*
>
> *If you want to post a picture of someone or a comment about them, ask them first if it's OK to do so.*
>
> *Keep your passwords private. Share them only with your parents.*

Parents' Role in Preventing Cyberbullying

Children need teaching and supervision as they learn to engage with digital devices. Our "digital native" children may be comfortable and competent with pointing, swiping, and clicking, but there are many things that they don't understand about the cyber world. Without our guidance, they may encounter dangers.

Parents should to talk with their children about safe, responsible, and respectful use of the internet. In 2015, between 84 percent and 87 percent of children between the ages of eight and twelve reported that their parents spoke with them about safe, responsible, and respectful use of digital devices (Common Sense Media 2015). You will not be alone as you take on this challenge.

Parents should make sure that they know what their child is doing online. In 2019, 50 percent of eight- to twelve-year-olds reported that their parents regularly track their digital devices (Common Sense Media 2019). You may remember how I learned that Suzanne was cyberbullying Molly: her mother was tracking her phone use.

It's best to keep digital devices in common family areas so that you, the responsible adult, can keep an eye on what your children are doing. If your child plays digital games, play the games with them once in a while so you better understand what they're doing. Notice, listen, and engage with your children in their digital life.

Just as schools create rules to follow when using digital devices in the classroom, parents can create family rules and expectations. For example, you might ask your child: "How can we make using devices in our family safe, respectful, and fun?" Get your child's ideas about what that would look like and sound like. Rules can be as general as "Keep your device safe," or they might be as specific as "Only share your password with your parents." Of course, an important expectation would be, "If something feels unsafe, then discuss it with your parents."

Four-year-old Paul started using his mother's iPad without much discussion of expectations. One day he dropped it in the bathtub. At that point, his parents wished that they had started out by creating expectations first.

Many families create an "internet use contract" or a "mobile phone use contract" that parents and children sign as a condition for using devices. A contract will provide a clear understanding of acceptable use (Notar, Padgett, and Roden 2013).

Be aware of how your children are interacting with each other online. Older children can provide negative models for younger siblings. As in other areas of life, teach your older children to be positive family leaders. It's not unknown for older children to cyberbully younger siblings. Notice and act.

A child experiencing cyberbullying needs your support. Rather than taking your

Tips for Parents

Create a positive home climate for your children's digital life.

- Cocreate family rules for digital safety.
- Teach older children to be family leaders.
- Be a positive digital role model yourself.
- Keep computers in common family areas.
- Monitor settings on tablets and phones.
- Track your child's online use.
- Play digital games with your child.
- Communicate fully with your child's teacher.

Could your child be engaged in cyberbullying?

- Are relationships with friends changing?
- Is your child suddenly unable to let go of their device?
- Does your child suddenly close or cover up their screen when you walk into the room?

child's phone away (an all-too-common but punitive reaction), make an effort to share online games and experiences with them. Help your child find new friends and acquaintances to text with. Be sure to let your child know that the cyberbullying is not their fault.

Don't forget to model appropriate internet use yourself. If you're using insults and negative language in your own social media life, sharing it with your family as you go, your child will learn how to behave this way.

To solve the problem of cyberbullying, educators, parents, and community members need to work as a team. With common goals of inclusion and kindness, we can together lead children along a more positive path.

KEY IDEAS

- **Traditional classroom bullying is linked to cyberbullying.** Cyberbullying is seldom a stand-alone practice.
- **Cyberbullying prevention should begin at an early age** as digital devices are available to younger children. Discussion and supervision are vital.
- **Positive classroom culture,** classroom rules that children believe in, and social skills instruction are protective against all bullying, including cyberbullying.
- **Educators need to make a bridge** between positive behavior in the classroom and positive behavior in an electronic environment.
- **Educators need to teach skills** that will help children cope with specific internet challenges.
- **Cyberbullying is easy to miss.** Keep your eyes and ears open for clues.
- **Provide support** for children who are being cyberbullied.
- **Teach children to respond** to cyberbullying by taking a screenshot, cutting off contact with the person bullying, and reporting the cyberbullying to a trusted adult.
- **Parents need to supervise children** as they begin to engage in the cyber world.
- **It takes a team** to support our children: educators, family members, and children.

February 3, 2020
Dear Rule Keepers,
Keep in your own bubble.
Be kind and use respectful words.
Use manners and follow directions.

CHAPTER SEVEN

Sample Lessons for Teaching Children About Gateway and Bullying Behaviors

Second graders sit in a circle on the rug. Their bodies are still, their faces serious and intent as their teacher, Mr. Monardi, reads aloud from *Nobody Knew What to Do: A Story About Bullying* by Becky Ray McCain. The vivid illustrations make the story real for each child in the class.

"Sometimes kids pick on me," blurts out Maya, a child with an autism spectrum disorder diagnosis. "I'd like to talk with you about that after the lesson is over," Mr. Monardi replies to her.

Mr. Monardi is pleased to see that Saul, Nico, and Frankie look deeply engaged with the story. Just last week he had discovered these three boys in the hall teasing another student, Len, about his lisp.

Immediately after the incident, all three boys lost the privilege of walking in the hall without an adult escort. Mr. Monardi knows, however, that to put a stop to future mean behaviors, he'll need to establish a class understanding about just how unacceptable such mean teasing is. The read-aloud is a good place to start.

In teaching this and other lessons about bullying behaviors, Mr. Monardi is establishing a vocabulary with the class. He is naming mean behaviors and establishing a common expectation that they are not acceptable.

It's important to teach children directly about bullying as part of prevention efforts. Through this direct teaching, we can reinforce the idea that cruel behavior of any kind—whether physical or relational—is unacceptable. We can also teach students what to do when they see bullying behavior or any kind of meanness occurs.

Notice that I put the focus here on the witnesses rather than on the person who is bullied. It's common to think that the solution to bullying is in the hands of the child who is bullied. This is not true. Although the child targeted for bullying behavior may sometimes be able to speak up for themselves or leave the situation, this is often not a realistic—or safe—option.

Bullying behavior often loses its power without an audience to support it. Classmates can learn to befriend, or at least be friendly to, the person being bullied. Classmates can also learn to report cruel behavior to adults. Once a sympathetic adult knows about the bullying, the adult can protect the bullied child.

In this chapter, you'll find lesson plans for primary and upper elementary students that are designed to help children identify bullying behaviors, learn ways they can help the child who is bullied, and learn how and when to report bullying and pre-bullying mean behaviors. These lessons have been used extensively in classrooms and are developmentally appropriate and engaging.

What Is in the Lessons?

Each of the five lessons takes between 20 and 30 minutes to teach. Each lesson has a version for primary grades (K–2) and one for upper elementary grades (3–5). If you teach third grade, I suggest you read through the lessons at both levels and decide which will best fit the needs of the students in your class.

Lessons for kindergarten through second grade

Bullying and behaviors that are gateways to bullying can begin in kindergarten and before. It's important that right away, as children begin school, teachers make clear that school is to be a place where they can feel safe and be safe. The first two lessons focus on helping children identify what is safe and unsafe behavior. I don't use the term "bullying" until the end of Lesson Two. This term might be a bit abstract for young children, who are still quite literal-minded. They can, however, relate easily to descriptive terms such as "safe," "included," or "kind words." Conversely, they can understand concepts such as being "teased in an unfriendly way" or being "left out." Of course, they know what it means to get hurt.

Once these basics are established, I introduce the concept of bullying at the end of Lesson Two and then Lessons Three through Five address the issue of "bullying" directly, using that word. These lessons focus on the role of classmates in preventing bullying by letting adults know about unkind behaviors and by befriending or being friendly to the child who is targeted. These are both research-supported practices in bullying prevention (Davis & Nixon, 2010; Olweus & Limber 2010). Since the majority of bullying takes place outside the classroom, there is a lesson about what to do if children experience bullying in "hot spots" such as the cafeteria or the playground.

> **Use of the Word "Report"**
>
> Throughout the lessons I use the word "report" rather than "tell an adult." I do this because I want to avoid the negative associations that many children and adults have with "tattling" and "telling." I'm not suggesting that children need to "report" in an official way.
>
> In addition, the definition of bullying I use in these lessons does not necessarily describe behavior that is a reportable offense in your state. To understand when and how to officially report bullying, you will need to become familiar with your state's guidelines.

Lessons for third through fifth grade

The lessons for older children begin by defining "bullying." The class then sorts through scenarios to identify whether or not a situation is bullying. This activity will help students identify whether behavior they see in real life is acceptable. They also learn some basic strategies for preventing bullying, which will help them know what to do when they observe or find themselves participating in real-life mean behaviors.

As children reach the age of nine, ten, and eleven, they begin to define themselves by who their friends are. Children sometimes are reluctant to support a child who is targeted for mean behavior because they are afraid that then they'll have to be the person's close friend. For this reason, I have drawn a clear distinction between being friendly and being friends. It's important that everyone in the classroom be friendly and community-minded. However, just because a child is friendly to someone and supports them when they are teased or excluded doesn't mean that they need to be best friends.

Older children, left to themselves, are often reluctant to let an adult know about bullying. Many bullying prevention programs, however, have shown success in encouraging third graders to report to an adult. International research has shown that even fourth and fifth graders can feel comfortable reporting if the adults handle the information with sensitivity, allowing the child who is targeted maximum privacy (Olweus & Limber 2010).

Structure of the lessons

At both levels, each lesson begins with information to help you plan and teach the lesson. I give lesson objectives, key phrases and concepts to keep in mind, and a list of any materials you'll need. Each lesson also includes follow-up activities designed to build student investment in creating a kind and respectful classroom and school climate.

Teaching the Lessons

Scheduling

These lessons will be effective only if you've begun to build a kind and empathetic community in the classroom. All of the strategies that I discussed in previous chapters will set the tone so that children will be ready to receive the information that you'll be teaching.

In my classrooms I taught bullying prevention lessons in October, November, and December. By mid-October the classroom community was strong enough that children wanted to learn how to keep our community safe and friendly, yet it was early enough that children learned skills that they could then use for the rest of the year.

You may want to repeat the lessons in the spring or simply use more of the follow-up ideas in the early spring.

I recommend scheduling one lesson a week for five weeks. If you teach the lessons once a week, you'll have time to use some of the follow-up ideas in between. If you let more time elapse between the lessons, you may find that the continuity is broken.

Developmental considerations

At the beginning of the set of lessons for each grade range, you'll find a list of developmental characteristics for the span of ages that you might have in your classroom. I focus on characteristics that might affect how children respond to the content of the lessons or structures and give suggestions for how to use this information in your planning.

As you think about the developmental information, keep in mind the following:

- **All children go through developmental stages as they grow up.** Just as children's physical characteristics change, so do their social-emotional and cognitive characteristics.

- **Children go through the stages at different rates.** Although children in any given culture share some general characteristics at each stage of development, how quickly a child proceeds through the stages depends on many things, including the child's personality and environment. Some children achieve developmental milestones earlier than others. In addition, each child might mature more quickly in one area, such as physical development, but more slowly in another area, such as language skills. The developmental characteristics I list in the lessons are ones that have been commonly observed in students in U.S. schools. You may see variations among your students.

- **Children don't change suddenly on their birthdays.** For example, a child who just turned six years old might still display a lot of five-year-old behavior. By the same token, a child who is eight years old might display some nine-year-old traits.

For more information about child development, see *Yardsticks: Child and Adolescent Development Ages 4–14*, 4th ed., by Chip Wood (see Appendix B).

Use of picture books

Many of the lessons are based on picture books. I've found that children can easily relate to the concepts at this slight remove. "What might DJ do next?" is an easier step than "What might you do in such a situation?" After you've taught and practiced what the book character might do, students may feel safe moving on to what they might do.

As part of preparing each lesson, I suggest you read each picture book all the way through for yourself. In the lessons, I give ideas for good places to stop and discuss, along with suggested discussion questions. You might consider marking the book by placing small sticky notes on the pages where you plan to stop and discuss. When I used these lessons in classrooms, I often wrote the question that I planned to ask on the sticky note, thus preserving the flow of the lesson.

As with most literature-based lessons, students will benefit from many re-readings and discussions of these books. You may wish to begin by reading the book through with the students just for enjoyment. Many of the books have discussion questions listed in the back that you could use when you reread the book on another day. In addition, some of the authors have websites with suggested classroom activities. You also can do these lessons early in the year and repeat them later on as a reminder and to take advantage of your students' increased maturity. The possibilities are endless.

In Appendix A, you'll find an annotated list of children's books that are especially useful for helping children talk about bullying. You may want to replace some of the books used in the lessons with books recommended in Appendix A. Choose the books that are right for your students.

The importance of classroom rules

The lessons are predicated on your having established classroom rules that students believe in and care about. When students have rules that they believe in—either because they created them collaboratively or because they have reflected deeply on how the rules will help make school a safe and fun learning environment for everyone—they have a shared vision of how school should be. This vision is the necessary foundation for learning to prevent and respond to bullying.

If you do not yet have rules that students care about, I suggest that before using these lessons, you spend some time creating rules that embody a shared positive community vision. Then you will have a basis for teaching specific positive behaviors that can prevent bullying. For more information about creating such rules, see Chapter Three.

Keeping things calm and respectful

Bullying and its prevention is a hot-button topic. It's stressful to talk about hurting and being hurt. However, all of us—adults and children alike—think most deeply and clearly when we're calm and feel that our ideas are heard and respected. Furthermore, students mirror adults' emotions and actions.

For these reasons, it's important to lead discussions about such a potentially emotionally fraught topic in a calm, matter-of-fact manner that communicates respect. A calm tone will help students look at the topic thoughtfully. A respectful tone will help them feel comfortable sharing their true thoughts and feelings.

Model respectful listening

When you model respectful listening, children will follow your lead and listen respectfully to each other. Specifically, it's important to look right at children who are speaking, maintain a calm and nonjudgmental expression on your face, and acknowledge all of their ideas.

Expect children to treat each other with respect

It's important to expect children to treat each other with seriousness and respect when addressing this very important topic. Use immediate reminders or simple logical consequences such as time away from the group if students start to joke about what a classmate says or use disrespectful words or tone.

Partner chats and group work

For these lessons to be effective, it is vitally important that the children are engaged. This is most likely to happen if they have plenty of chances to talk rather than only sitting quietly and listening. For this reason, I recommend using lots of partner chats and small-group work.

Even kindergartners can turn and talk with a partner about topics such as "How do you think Ray is feeling?" or "What could you do to be kind to Chrysanthemum?" Because children this age may not yet be capable of then sharing with the class what their partner said, many experienced kindergarten teachers circulate, listening to children's ideas and then sharing them with the class: "I heard Juan say that he thinks Ray is scared" or "I heard Julia say that she would ask Chrysanthemum to play."

Children in first grade and up can usually turn and talk with a partner and then share with the whole group what they heard their partner say. With first and second graders, I suggest that you ask the whole group a question, have the children turn and talk to an assigned partner (so as to head off any exclusionary behaviors), and then have the children share out to the whole group.

For students in grades three, four, and five, you may want to pass out scenarios to partners or small groups, listen in while they work independently, and then have each partnership or small group share out. As they share out, you can lead a discussion about each scenario.

Investigating: Where do children feel safe and unsafe in school?

To teach Lesson Five about "hot spots" in school, you'll need to do some investigating. Most bullying prevention programs use some form of computerized questionnaire to learn about children's experiences with bullying. These questionnaires are designed for children in grades three and up. Many are based on the Olweus Online Survey, which has been in use in one form or another since the early 1990s. Various other questionnaires can be obtained at no cost on the internet.

You can also design your own questionnaire based on what you hope to learn and set it up on a free or low-cost internet site.

Here are some sample questions that you might ask:

- During this school year, has anyone kicked you, hit you, or pushed you on purpose in order to hurt you?
- During this school year, has anyone spread rumors about you to try to hurt your feelings?
- During this school year, has anyone spread rumors about you by texting, sending an email, posting on a social networking page, or using another electronic device?
- During this school year, has anyone called you hurtful names or teased you when you didn't want them to?
- During this school year, if you have seen mean or bullying behavior happen (such as the behaviors described above) check off the places you have seen it happen:
    - ☐ Walking to or from school
    - ☐ At breakfast
    - ☐ In the before-school program
    - ☐ In your classroom, the hall, or the bathrooms
    - ☐ During lunch, recess, PE, music, or art
    - ☐ On a tablet or cell phone

☐ On the school bus

☐ During the after-school program

To determine frequency, you could ask children how often the behaviors that they reported have happened: never, once or twice, at least once a month, or more than once a month.

A word about timing of the questionnaire

It's best to administer a questionnaire such as this one a couple of months into the school year so that children will be able to remember what has happened since school started. With end-of-the-year questionnaires, children might have difficulty sorting out what has happened recently and what happened a long time ago.

Younger children

Bullying prevention programs don't usually use such computerized questionnaires for children younger than third grade. As an alternative, some programs use individual interviews for these children. Another approach is to create a large map of the school and have the children mark the areas where they feel unsafe.

I suggest using a morning message that includes tally boxes (see primary grade Lesson Five for an example). You can ask "Where do you feel unsafe in school?" and include boxes labeled "recess, school bus, school bathrooms, hall, cafeteria." Children put a tally mark in every box naming a place where they feel unsafe. Using this method, you can obtain data that will spark lively discussion about how to make some areas safer.

Specific Strategies Used in the Lessons

These lessons incorporate three strategies that will help children think more deeply about the difficult topic of kind and unkind behaviors: role-play, open-ended questions, and card sorting.

Role-play

Role-play is a strategy for helping children think through a range of responses to potentially tricky situations. The teacher describes a situation that might present challenges and asks children to brainstorm positive ways to behave in the situation. The teacher and students act out some of the suggestions while the other students observe and comment on what they noticed. Role-play is used in the primary grade lessons in Lesson Four, when children think about how to befriend someone who is being bullied. Role-play is used in the upper elementary lessons in Lesson Three, when children think about how to be an ally.

I give a detailed description of role-play in Chapter Four.

Open-ended questions

Children are more likely to become invested in preventing bullying if their own thoughts and feelings are expressed, listened to, and respected. To help children express their thoughts and feelings, it's important to ask open-ended questions—questions for which there are many possible, acceptable answers. These questions encourage children to think deeply.

To help children believe that we do care about their ideas, it's important to then accept all answers that are even partially connected to the question. For example, when we ask, "How do you think Velvet felt?" children might answer "Sad" or "Lonely" or "Happy that she had such a pretty name." Any of these answers are perfectly acceptable. If a child answers in a way that seems off-base to you, you might encourage the child with follow-up questions such as "Tell us more" or "What makes you think that?"

For more information about open-ended questions, see *The Power of Our Words: Teacher Language That Helps Children Learn*, 2nd ed., by Paula Denton (see Appendix B).

It's also important to let children know when you're asking a question that has one right answer, which might happen with some of the more clear-cut sort-card scenarios, and to think about how you'll respond if a child gives the wrong answer. For example, if you ask, "Is it bullying or not bullying for an older kid to tease a kindergartner in a mean way on the school bus?" you might alert children that this is a one-right-answer question by saying, "We've learned enough about bullying so we can figure out that there's one correct answer to this question." If a child responds, "When the kindergartner is teased by the older kid he must have deserved it," it's important to respond in a matter-of-fact way. In a friendly, calm, respectful way, you might say, "It's the job of older kids to take care of younger kids. Mean teasing of younger kids is nearly always bullying."

Card sorting

Several of the lessons are based on having children sort scenarios into categories such as bullying, not bullying, or need more information. Whenever I teach these lessons on bullying I find that the discussions about "Is it bullying or not?" are rich and nuanced, with lots of gray areas. Those gray areas lead to deep thinking on the part of the group. I learn something every time I teach one of these lessons. With that said, I want to caution you to remain calm, not let unexpected comments fluster you, and honor all contributions while clarifying obvious misunderstandings. If you maintain an attitude of true curiosity, then students will, too.

Facts to Keep in Mind as You Teach the Lessons

What follows is a list of important facts about bullying and elementary-age children. All of this information is covered in depth in previous chapters of this book. I provide this list as a quick reference for you to review before you teach the lessons.

- Even very young children tease and exclude (Alsaker 2004; Pellegrini et al. 2007).

- If allowed to continue, these behaviors may become habitual (Espelage, Polanin, and Low 2014; Wessler 2003; Yerger and Gehret 2011).

- Bully prevention, started at an early age, has long lasting results (Bradshaw et al. 2009).

- Stopping the smaller mean behaviors can keep them from escalating into full-blown bullying (Englander 2013; Wessler 2003).
- All children have the potential to tease and exclude, and even to bully. For that reason, it's important to focus on "bullying behaviors," not "the bully" (Swearer, Espelage, and Napolitano 2009).
- Teachers are often unaware of bullying and hurtful gateway behaviors going on among students (Craig and Pepler 1998; Ostrander et al. 2018; Zych, Baldry, and Farrington 2017).
- Educators will continue to be unaware of bullying and gateway behaviors unless we teach students to share this information with us. To stop bullying, we need to teach children to report (Davis 2007a; Olweus and Limber 2007).
- Increased supervision and increased use of consequences for bullying and gateway behaviors can significantly reduce bullying and support a climate of kindness (Davis 2007a; Ttofi and Farrington 2011).
- Using the word "reporting" or "talking with the teacher" can encourage children to let adults know about mean behaviors. "Tell the teacher" has negative connotations for children and sounds like "tattling," which can also have negative connotations for children (Davis 2007b).
- If adults respond effectively to children's reports, then children will trust that we care about their safety and continue to report (Bradshaw et al. 2009; Olweus and Limber 2007).
- Children who are bullied are usually unable to protect themselves and need adult intervention (Pepler, Craig, and O'Connell 2010).
- Telling children who are bullied to "ignore it," "stand up to the bully," or "fight back" is not helpful. These strategies have been shown to make the situation worse (Davis and Nixon 2010).
- Doing assertiveness training for children who are bullied or expecting them to talk out their differences with children who are bullying them is not helpful (Davis and Nixon 2010; Ttofi and Farrington 2011).
- Bullying is a social act. When bystanders laugh, cheer, or even just watch, it encourages the behavior (Craig and Pepler 1998; Olweus and Limber 2007; Padgett and Notar 2013).

- Having at least one friend is protective against being bullied (Hodges, Malone, and Perry 1997).

- It can be risky for bystanders to step in and confront the person who is bullying. It's more realistic and safer for children to befriend the child who is bullied (Davis 2007a).

- Most hurtful behaviors (gateway behaviors and outright bullying) take place outside the classroom (Astor, Meyer, and Pitner 2001).

Primary Grade Lessons

Developmental Information

LESSON ONE:
Teasing in Unfriendly Ways Is Not OK

LESSON TWO:
It's Not OK to Leave Someone Out On Purpose

LESSON THREE:
It's Important to Let an Adult Know

LESSON FOUR:
Befriend Classmates Who Are Teased or Left Out

LESSON FIVE:
Hot Spots at School

(For upper elementary grade lessons, go to page 213.)

Developmental Information to Think About as You Plan and Deliver the Lessons

Five-year-olds typically:

- **Are the center of their own universe**
  They seldom see things from another's viewpoint but can be surprisingly empathetic if someone is hurt (and they're not the one who caused the hurt). Although kindergartners will most likely not become empathetic as a result of these lessons, they can still learn that it's not OK to tease.

- **Respond well to "that's the rule"**
  Therefore, as you read *The New Girl . . . and Me* in Lesson One, if kindergarten students don't make the connection that Shakeeta is feeling bad because she's being teased, move on and simply clarify that "it's the rule" that we don't tease.

- **Need adult approval**
  Five-year-olds are often eager to report mean behavior. If they take the information from Lesson Three and use it as a reason to overreport (and they probably will), be careful to encourage them in their reporting rather than shutting them down by saying "Don't tattle." (See Chapter Three for more information about the importance of moving away from the "no tattling" rule.)

- **Have a hard time distinguishing between real and pretend**
  With five-year-olds, it's sometimes helpful to use puppets when doing role-plays (thus making it clear to them that the situation you're acting out is pretend).

Six-year-olds typically:

- **May be bossy, teasing, or critical of others**
  When you read *The New Girl . . . and Me* in Lesson One, sixes might not think it's a problem for classmates to tease Shakeeta. It's important to be clear that this kind of teasing is not OK.

- **Take teacher direction seriously**
  When you talk about excluding in Lesson Two, you'll need to state directly that excluding behavior is not OK.

- **Often report hurtful incidents to the teacher**
  Six-year-olds will take Lesson Three to heart. The teacher's challenge is to distinguish between serious and less serious incidents while erring on the side of taking children's reports seriously.

- **Are eager to make new friends**
  Six-year-olds will especially like the role-plays in Lesson Four, which focus on befriending bullied a child.

- **Are active**
  A characteristic that bursts out in lightly supervised areas of the school. The challenge for adults working with six-year-olds is to be very clear about which behaviors are mean as distinguished from behaviors that are simply rambunctious or impulsive.

Seven-year-olds typically:

- **May find teasing to be particularly painful**
  A good discussion focus for this age group is the difference between laughing with someone and laughing at someone.

- **May find excluding to be particularly painful**
  Yet this is an age when leaving others out is not uncommon. In Lesson Two, it's important to help seven-year-olds think about how the book's characters (Velvet or Julisa) are feeling.

- **Try out friendships and frequently change friends**
  This may lead to many opportunities for hurt feelings. It may feel as though seven-year-olds are constantly complaining that a friend hurt their feelings. Nevertheless, it's important to take their reports seriously so that you don't discourage them from reporting.

- **Often work and play best with one friend**
  Lesson Four, in which children role-play how to befriend a bullied child, might feel challenging for sevens.

- **Need clear rules and expectations**
  Seven-year-olds are particularly helped when adults can work together to establish and maintain these expectations.

LESSON ONE:

Teasing in Unfriendly Ways Is Not OK

Grades K–2

Preparation

Objectives

Children will understand:

- It's important that everyone feel safe and be safe at school

- It's not OK to hurt someone's feelings on purpose (also referred to as "mean teasing")

Materials needed

- Choose one of the following children's books (see Appendix A for more information about the books):

  - *Chrysanthemum* by Kevin Henkes (grades K–2) (Greenwillow Books, 1991)

  - *The New Girl . . . and Me* by Jacqui Robbins (grades K–2) (Atheneum/Richard Jackson Books, 2006)

- Chart paper or other material to display simple drawing of a heart (heart icon) and simple line drawings of a flower (if you use *Chrysanthemum*), fresh and wilted.

Key words and phrases

- It's important for everyone to feel safe in school

- To keep everyone feeling safe, it's important to take care of each other's feelings (it's not OK to hurt each other's feelings or bodies)

- Mean teasing (is not OK)

- Safe and friendly

Procedure

Opening

1. Gather children in a circle. Have a flip chart set up next to you.

2. Begin by saying: *It's important for everyone to feel safe in school. To keep everyone feeling safe, it's not OK to hurt each other's feelings or bodies.*

3. Draw an image of a heart on the flip chart and say: *To keep everyone's hearts safe, we need to take care of each other's feelings and follow our classroom rule that says _____* [choose a rule that conveys the idea of being kind or friendly].

Body

1. Introduce the read-aloud: *We're going to read a book that will help us think about taking care of each other's feelings.*

2. Read aloud from the picture book you've chosen, with the following suggested pauses and discussion questions:

The New Girl . . . and Me

Read to the middle of page 6 (DJ calls Shakeeta "Shakeeta Mosquita").

> Ask: *How do you think Shakeeta is feeling? Why might Shakeeta say "I'll punch you in the head"?*
>
> Clarify that Shakeeta is probably scared.

Read to the middle of page 10 (DJ tells Shakeeta she looks like an iguana).

> Ask: *How do you think Shakeeta is feeling?*

Read to the bottom of page 13 (Mia understands what helps Shakeeta feel at home).

> Ask: *What might Mia do to take care of Shakeeta?*

Read to the bottom of page 18 (when the girls laugh together).

> Ask: *What is the difference between laughing at someone and laughing with someone?*

Additional questions you might ask:

> *How might you feel if this were happening to you?*
>
> *How do you think Mia feels when she's laughing with Shakeeta?*
>
> *How do you think DJ feels when he tells Shakeeta that she looks like an iguana?*
>
> *How might Shakeeta feel?*

Chrysanthemum

Stop periodically (when everyone giggles at Chrysanthemum's name).

>Ask: *How do you think Chrysanthemum is feeling?*

When Victoria says, "You're named after a flower," and Chrysanthemum wilts, explain the meaning of "wilt."

Draw a picture of a fresh flower and a wilting one.

Whenever Chrysanthemum wilts, have the children wilt with their bodies: *Let's make our bodies wilt.*

Closing

1. Say: *Sometimes people hurt other people's feelings or hearts [point to heart icon] with mean teasing, just the way _____ [DJ, Victoria] hurt _____'s [Shakeeta's, Chrysanthemum's] feelings. This is not OK here at our school.*

2. Connect to classroom or school rules:

   Which of our class rules would let _____ [DJ, Victoria] know that teasing _____ [Shakeeta, Chrysanthemum] is not OK?

   For first and second graders:
   If _____ [DJ, Victoria] were in our class, which rule would you remind them of?

3. Additional questions you might ask, as appropriate:

   Our school rule says _____. How does this help us know not to hurt others?

   What can we do to keep our classroom safe and friendly?

   How can we use friendly words?

   What can you do on the playground [in the cafeteria, in our classroom] to make sure that everyone feels safe in school?

Take some ideas and then say: *The next time we meet we'll talk about some things that people have done to keep our classroom safe and friendly.*

Follow-up ideas

- Follow up frequently during the day by asking *How are you helping people feel safe in school?* Do this especially before the children leave the classroom for areas that require more independence, such as the cafeteria or the playground.

- Partner chat, morning message, or question of the day: *How have you seen people keeping our school safe and friendly? On the playground? On the school bus? In the cafeteria?*

- Plan greetings in which children practice the language of inclusion: *Good morning, [classmate's name]; I'm glad you're my friend* or *Hello, [classmate's name]; I'm glad you're here today.* These greetings are especially effective when children are sitting in random order rather than with a best friend.

- Sing a song that celebrates inclusion, such as "All My Friends Are Here Today," "The More We Get Together," or "We're All Back Together Again."

- For second graders: Learn and practice how to give compliments.

Additional children's literature to read

For all ages: Read or reread the picture books in the lesson.

LESSON TWO:

It's Not OK to Leave Someone Out On Purpose

Grades K–2

Preparation

Objectives

Children will understand:

- It's important that everyone be safe at school

- Include others (it's not OK to leave someone out on purpose)

Materials needed

- Choose one of the following children's books (see Appendix A for more information about the books):

  - *Odd Velvet* by Mary Whitcomb (grades K–2) (Chronicle Books, 1998)

  - *Two of a Kind* by Jacqui Robbins (grades K–2) (Atheneum Books for Young Readers, 2009)

  - *The Invisible Boy* by Trudy Ludwig (grades 1–3) (Knopf, 2013)

- Chart paper with icons drawn under the heading "Safe"

  - Heart icon from Lesson One
  - Stick figures holding hands icon (for including people)
  - Puffy oval figure icon (for keeping people's bodies safe)

- Examples of kind behaviors that you've seen since the last lesson.

- Some possible examples of exclusion either written or prepared to share orally. (For example: You can't go to my birthday party, you can't be in our club, you can't play the game with us, you can't sit here, I'm saving the seat for [classmate's name], you can't be my friend.)

Key words and phrases

- Important to be safe in school

- Keep the classroom safe and friendly

- Help everyone feel welcome

- Keep everyone's feelings safe

- Left out on purpose

- Hurting someone

- Say kind things

- Include everyone

Procedure

Opening

1. Gather children in a circle. Have a flip chart set up next to you with the icons visible.

2. Begin by saying: *[Last week/A few days ago/Yesterday] we talked about the fact that it's important that everyone be safe in school—we need to keep everyone's feelings as well as their bodies safe.*

3. Help children focus on ways they've kept each other safe:

    What have you noticed classmates doing since [last week/a few days ago/yesterday] to keep our classroom safe and friendly so that everyone will feel welcome?

Did someone do something friendly for you or someone else?

These are things I've noticed you doing to keep classmates feeling safe...

4. Say: *Today we're going to learn more about how to keep each other safe and feeling welcome in school.*

Body

1. Read aloud from the picture book you've chosen, with the following suggested pauses and discussion questions:

Odd Velvet

Read first few pages. Stop after the line "No one was silly enough to pick Velvet for a play partner."

> Clarify the meaning of "odd"—that children thought Velvet was different. Keep the tone sympathetic to Velvet. Say: *That's what some children thought, that she was different, and they didn't want to play with her.*

> Ask: *How do you think Velvet felt when no one picked her to play?*

Two of a Kind

Read to the bottom of page 4 (Julisa and Anna sit under the slide together).

> Draw attention to the difference between "no one is invited up" and "anybody is invited."

Read page 5 (Melanie and Kayla make fun of Anna and Julisa).

> Point out that Melanie is teasing the way the child in the story you read in Lesson One was teased.

> Ask: *How is Julisa feeling?*

Read to the bottom of page 14 (Kayla and Melanie run off with Anna).

> Ask: *How is Julisa feeling?*

Read to the bottom of page 18 (Julisa sits and stares at her book).

> Ask: *How is Julisa feeling now?*

2. Say: *Sometimes children tell other children that they can't play. They leave them out on purpose.*

3. Give specific examples (either on cards or orally): *Sometimes people say, "You can't come to my birthday party" or "You can't be my friend."*

4. Say the following, depending on grade level.

    For kindergarten: *How might you feel if kids left you out or told you that you couldn't play?*

    People feel sad when they're left out.

    For grades one and two: *Thumbs-up* [or whichever signal you usually use] *if you've ever seen someone left out.*

    We're going to talk about how to make sure that doesn't happen.

5. Say: *It's not OK to leave someone out on purpose at school.*

6. Ask: *If [Velvet/Julisa] came to our classroom, what would you do? How would you include her?*

7. Finish the read-aloud. Then ask these summarizing questions:

Odd Velvet

Ask: *How did classmates include Velvet?*

Two of a Kind

Ask: *What did Julisa do to take care of Anna? What did Anna do to take care of Julisa?*

The Invisible Boy

Read until the students have finished picking teams.

> Ask: *Why do the students say that they have enough players?*

Read the next two pages.

> Ask: *Why do you think Brian wasn't invited to the birthday party?*
>
> *Why does the author call Brian "invisible?"*
>
> *How does Brian feel when no one picks him for baseball?*
>
> *How does Brian feel when he isn't invited to the birthday party?*

Read to the page when Mrs. Carlotti introduces Justin.

> Ask: *What do you think it means when the author says that kids are trying to figure out whether or not Justin is cool enough to be their friend?*

Read through the next two pages about lunch.

> Ask: *How does Justin feel when the kids laugh at his lunch and call it names? Does this remind you of the way the kids laughed at Chrysanthemum?*

Read the next two pages about the note.

> Say: *Brian is being kind to Justin. He wants to help him feel better.*

Read the next two pages about the playground and the next two pages about the classroom.

> Say: *Justin is being kind to Brian too.*

Closing

1. Return to the class rules. Say: *Our rule says that we will [take care of classmates, be kind, etc.]. That means that we won't leave people out on purpose. Remember from our read-aloud [last week/a few days ago/yesterday] that we won't tease people on purpose either.*

2. Point to the heart icon: *It's important to take care of people's hearts.* Point to the inclusion icon: *It's important to include people.*

3. If students seem confused by "leave out on purpose," clarify:

   If your parent says that you can have only one friend over and you invite one person, you're not leaving anyone out on purpose. If you tell someone they can't play with the others at recess, you're leaving them out on purpose.

4. Be explicit that leaving out on purpose, mean teasing, and hurting someone's body on purpose are bullying and are not OK:

   When kids leave other kids out on purpose, when they tease someone in a mean way or hurt their bodies on purpose [refer to body icon], *we call that bullying.*

5. Ask: *What might we do to include everyone at recess? What can you do today at recess to include someone?*

Follow-up ideas

- Partner chat, morning message, or question of the day: *How have you seen people including others? On the playground? On the school bus? In the cafeteria?*

- Children will need more practice in sorting out behaviors that are not OK.

- Use specific examples: *If you tell some kids that you're having a birthday party and they're not included, that is not kind.*

- Before children go out to recess, ask: *How will you make sure that everyone has someone to play with?*

- After recess, say: *Give yourself a score with your fingers (one to five). How did you do at including people today?*

Additional children's literature to read

Read or reread the picture books in the lesson.

Eggbert, the Slightly Cracked Egg by Tom Ross and Rex Barron (Puffin Books, 1997). A story about accepting differences in oneself or others.

The Pebble, a Story about Belonging by Susan Milford (HarperCollins, 2007). A story about acceptance and belonging—a boy finds a pebble and takes it home.

Each Kindness by Jacqueline Woodson (Nancy Paulsen Books, 2012). Maya is excluded in school. After Maya moves away, her class is taught about ripples of kindness by the teacher.

Crow Boy by Taro Yashima (Puffin Books, 1976). A Caldecott Honor book and a classic, set in Japan. A student is left alone and called "stupid" by his classmates for six years until one day the other students discover how much he has to offer.

LESSON THREE:

It's Important to Let an Adult Know
Grades K–2

Preparation

Objectives

Children will understand:

- When we see someone being hurt it's important to take care of them by letting an adult know

Children will learn:

- How to report

- Whom to report to

Materials needed

- *Nobody Knew What to Do* by Becky Rae McCain (grades K–2) (Albert Whitman & Company, 2001). See Appendix A for more information.

- Chart with icons from Lessons One and Two

For first and second graders:

- Column headings for sorting ("Report to keep everyone safe" / "Let it go since everyone is safe")

- Cards with potential incidents described. For example:
  Someone cuts in front of you in line.
  Someone sharpens their pencil at quiet reading time.

Someone reads a comic book at math time.

Three children tell another child that they can't play unless they're the baby.

One student secretly pulls another student's hair on purpose.

A student uses markers when the teacher said to use a pencil.

Someone talks in the hallway, which is supposed to be silent.

A student pushes another student into a puddle and laughs.

Key words and phrases

- Hurting people

- What do you do if you see something unsafe going on?

- Whom might you report to if you see someone being hurt in their bodies or their feelings?

- To keep ourselves and our classmates safe, it's important to report times when you see someone hurt

- Report to keep people safe

- Let it go since everyone is safe

- We don't need to report everything that we see happening; we can let it go, if no one is being hurt

Procedure

Opening

1. Gather children in a circle. Have a flip chart set up next to you with the icons visible.

2. Begin by saying: *When we met [yesterday/a few days ago/last week], we talked about how important it is that everyone be safe and feel safe in school. Our rules say we should [take care of each other, be kind, etc.]. That means if we see something unsafe happening we need to take care of the person being hurt. Remember when we talked about Velvet being left out [point to wilted flower icon]? Remember when the children teased [Chrysanthemum/Shakeeta]?*

3. Ask: *Have you ever seen someone being hurt in their feelings or their body and not known what to do?*

4. Hold up the book. Say: *Let's look at the cover of this book. It's called* Nobody Knew What to Do. *This story will give you an idea of what to do if you see someone being hurt.*

Body

1. Read aloud *Nobody Knew What to Do*. When the text refers to "bullies," substitute "The kids who bullied."

   - Stop after pages 5 and 6 and discuss: *What might they do?*

   - When Ray doesn't come to school, comment that he didn't feel safe in school.

   - Read to the end of the story. Ask: *How did Ray's classmates help him? How might you help someone who's being hurt as Ray was?*

     Teacher Tip
     Some children will think that they should help Ray by telling him how to stand up to the children who were bullying. This is a good time to make it clear that it's the classmates' job and the adults' job to take care of Ray. It's appropriate to teach children to use the skill of assertion when they are learning to deal with conflicts among children of equal power. When dealing with bullying, however, it is neither realistic nor safe to expect them to assert themselves.

     Teacher Tip
     Young children often hit, kick, or push impulsively. This is not bullying (although it's also, of course, not OK). Often young children need direct instruction and practice in

how to use words to express their needs, how to take turns, and other ways to take care of themselves without hurting someone. The boys in *Nobody Knew What to Do* were purposely (versus impulsively) hurting Ray. Thus the school responded by increasing supervision and contacting parents.

2. Draw attention to the fact that the narrator reported the incident and that the next day the classmates included Ray in their play. The teacher, the principal, and the parents all got involved and worked together to make sure that everyone was safe in school.

> **Teacher Tip**
> It's helpful to use the word "reporting" or the phrase "talking with the teacher" rather than the word "telling" in teaching children to let adults know about mean behaviors because "telling" has such negative connotations for children. It also sounds a bit like "tattling," which can also have negative connotations for children. See Chapter Three for more information.

3. For kindergartners:

    Remind students of Chrysanthemum, whose feelings were hurt (refer to heart icon), like the boy in today's story, whose body was hurt (refer to body icon).

    Ask: *Whom might you report to if you see someone being hurt in their bodies or their feelings?* Gather some ideas.

    Ask: *What might you say?* Model one possibility and then take ideas.

    > **Teacher Tip**
    > If kindergartners seem confused, connect Ray's situation to incidents that they do know how to handle. *What would you do if you saw someone fall down and get hurt? What would you do if you couldn't turn off the faucet?* These are other situations where it's important to report to an adult.

4. For first and second graders:

    Say: *To keep yourselves and your classmates safe, it's important to report times when you see someone being hurt. You don't need to tell the teacher everything that happens; sometimes you can let it go, if you're sure no one is being hurt. And if you're ever not sure whether someone is being hurt, talk with the teacher and they can decide.*

Have cards describing incidents prepared and, as a class, sort them into categories (see Materials list for suggested topics): "Report to keep people safe" / "Let it go since everyone is safe."

For each incident, refer back to the icons and ask: *Was his body safe? Were his feelings safe? Was he included?*

Closing

1. Return to class rules. Ask: *How does reporting if we see someone being hurt connect to our rules? Which class rule will help us with this?*

2. For first and second graders:

    Say: *Today we sorted through situations and talked about which ones are most important to report. If you're not sure, it's important to report since it's so important for everyone in our class to be safe.*

    > **Teacher Tip**
    > If children do report unkind behaviors to you, it's important that you make it clear to them that they need to continue to report to you if the behavior continues—children need to report every time; otherwise you won't know whether the problem is solved.

3. This is a pretty serious lesson. You might lighten things up with a song or finger play about inclusion—for example, Red Grammer's "Kindness" or "We're All in This Together."

Follow-up ideas

- Partner chat, morning message, or question of the day: *How are we doing at keeping each other safe?*

- Continue card sort with more incidents. Children will need a lot of practice with this. If students are experienced at working as partners or in small groups, you might have them work with a partner to sort incidents and then place the cards in Hula-Hoops or a pocket chart.

- During writers' workshop, have children do "quick writes" that describe incidents that might or might not be important to report. Let students know that you might use some of the scenarios in class, with no names attached. Also let them know that you'll check in with them if you want to use their scenario.

Screen the scenarios and choose a few to type up (without names or key identifying information). Sort these scenarios with your students. Doing this provides an opportunity to discuss real-life incidents at a safe remove.

- If you have a book that you're reading as a class, you might refer to incidents in the book. Ask: *Is a character feeling safe? Is he included? Is his body safe?*

LESSON FOUR:

Befriend Classmates Who Are Teased or Left Out

Grades K–2

Preparation

Objectives

Children will understand:

- By being a friend, we can help classmates who are teased or left out

Children will learn:

- How to approach and include someone who is isolated

Materials needed

- Chart stand, chart paper, and markers

Key words and phrases

- Take care of classmates who are being teased or left out

- Being friendly

- Feeling included

> **Teacher Tip**
>
> In this lesson, children will do a role-play about inclusion, using the characters from *Chrysanthemum* (or *Odd Velvet* or *The New Girl . . . and Me*). Here are a few tips to help this go more smoothly:
>
> - Assign roles rather than asking for volunteers.

- Take the lead yourself the first time you do the role-play. After that, think about assigning the role of the "inviter" to someone who needs practice with this skill, assuming that the child is willing.

- For kindergartners: Use puppets rather than actual human actors.

- For kindergartners: In step 2 below, have the children partner chat before gathering ideas. Get some initial ideas on the chart by saying, "Here are some things I heard people saying to their partners."

(See Chapter Four for more on role-play.)

Procedure

Opening

1. Gather children in a circle. Have a flip chart set up next to you and have the icons from the earlier lessons visible.

2. Begin by saying: *Last time we met, we talked about ways to keep people safe in school. We talked about making sure that everyone is safe, in their bodies and their feelings, by reporting to a teacher. We talked about making sure that everyone is included. We can take care of classmates who are being teased or left out by including them and being friendly to them.* (Refer to the three icons as you talk.)

Body

1. Set up the role-play:

   Remember when we read about Chrysanthemum [Velvet, Shakeeta, Brian]? I'm going to pretend that I'm one of Chrysanthemum's [Velvet's, Shakeeta's, Brian's] classmates. I can see that Chrysanthemum [Velvet, Shakeeta, Brian] is so sad because kids are teasing [her/him] about [her/his] name [because she's different, because she's new in school]. I'd like to help [her/him] but I'm not sure how. What might I say to show that I'd like to be friendly to [her/him] and include [her/him]?

2. Take ideas from children and list them on the chart.

3. Assign roles and describe what you will do:

   Now I'm going to pretend that I'm one of Chrysanthemum's [Velvet's/Shakeeta's/Brian's] classmates. Max, would you like to pretend to be Chrysanthemum [Velvet/Shakeeta/Brian]?

   I'm going to pick one of our ideas. I think I'll pick going up to Chrysanthemum [Velvet/Shakeeta/Brian] and asking her if she wants to play.

4. Begin the role-play:

   You and your student partner stand in front of the circle of children.

   You say: *Ready, start* or *Lights, camera, action* to indicate the beginning of the role-play.

   You say: *Chrysanthemum [Velvet/Shakeeta/Brian], would you like to play?*

   The student responds: *I'd like that.*

   You say: *Cut.*

   You ask: *What did you notice about our play?*

5. Children contribute ideas. If children have a hard time coming up with ideas, prompt them with questions:

   What did I do?

   What did my face look like?

   What did my hands do?

   Max, when I asked you to play, how did you feel?

6. The class continues to act out various ideas from the chart, this time with students playing both roles.

Closing

Point to the chart with the list of ideas. Say: *Look at all of the ideas we have for ways to be friendly and include people.*

Follow-up ideas

- Partner chat, morning message, or question of the day. Ask: *Have you offered to include someone? Or ask: How might you include someone on the playground? In the cafeteria?*

- For further role-plays:

    What if you try to include someone and they don't want to play with you?

    What if you try to include someone and they want to play a game that's different from the one you want to play?

Additional children's literature to read

For first and second graders:

Bird Child by Nan Forler (Tundra Books, 2009). A girl is bullied and "bird child" steps in. This book provides a helpful springboard to discuss intervening when someone is being mean.

The Brand New Kid by Katie Couric (Doubleday, 2000). Lazlo is new in school. Classmates tease and exclude him, but Ellie befriends him. This book is helpful for initiating discussions of befriending the person being bullied.

LESSON FIVE:

Hot Spots at School
Grades K–2

Preparation

Objective
- How to report if students are hurting each other outside of the classroom

Materials needed
- Chart with student responses about "hot spots" in the school

- (Optional) Morning message that asks children where in school they feel safe and where they feel unsafe. Under the questions, include lines or boxes for school bus, cafeteria, playground, halls, bathrooms, and other areas that might be "hot spots" in your school.

Key words and phrases
- Where do you feel welcome?

- Where do you feel unwelcome?

- Where do you feel safe?

- Where do you feel unsafe?

> Dear Friendly First Graders,
>
> We are working together to make school safe for everyone. Put a check in the box if you do not feel safe in:
>
> | School bus | Cafeteria |
> |---|---|
> | Halls | Bathrooms |
> | Playground | Someplace else |
>
> Your teacher

CHAPTER SEVEN | Sample Lessons   209

Teacher Tip

Before the lesson, gather information from students about "hot spots" in the school. There are many ways to do this. You could:

- Interview children individually.
- Create a map of the school and have students put a blue sticker on places where they feel safe and a red sticker on places where they feel less safe.
- Create a graph or chart and have children fill in boxes showing where they feel most safe and least safe, with choices such as halls, bathrooms, school bus, cafeteria, playground.

It's also important to gather information about adults to whom children can safely report.

- Before you teach this lesson, think about whom children should report to about outside-the-classroom behaviors. Who would handle reporting with sensitivity and tact? Speak privately with those people about how they might handle reports.
- Think about the lines of communication in your school. If you are going to encourage children to report to someone other than yourself, think about what that person will do with that information. How will you find out about the incident?
- Alternatively, decide to simply have the children report outside-the-classroom unsafe behaviors to you.

Procedure

Opening

1. Gather children in a circle. Have a graphic indicating safe and unsafe areas set up next to you.

2. Begin by saying: *Let's look at our graph [map, chart] together. What do you notice? Where do students feel safe? Where do they feel unsafe?*

Body

1. Say: *If something is happening [on the playground, in the cafeteria, in the hall—depending on what children have shared] that makes you feel unsafe or unwelcome, what might you do?*

2. Prompt children's thinking by referring to the previous reading: *Remember when we read* Nobody Knew What to Do? *What did they do?* (In the story the children report to their classroom teacher.)

3. Ask: *Whom else might you report to [on the playground, in the cafeteria or hall—depending on area discussed]?*

4. Write the names of the people the children suggest around the borders of your graph or map so that children can see that the adults at school surround them and keep them safe.

Closing

1. Point to the graphic and say: *Look at all of the adults who can keep you safe! Think about which adult you, personally, feel comfortable going to if something unsafe is happening.*

2. Say: *Hold out your fist. Put out your pointer finger and think about one adult you could go to.* Take note of any children who don't do this and check in with them later about whether there are any adults they feel comfortable reporting to. If not, encourage them to report to you.

Follow-up ideas

- Children draw a picture of someone doing something kind for them on the playground (or on the school bus or in the cafeteria, bathroom, hall).

- Children draw a picture of themselves at lunch, at recess, or on the school bus and chat about how things are going in that setting.

- Check in after lunch and recess. Ask children to hold up fingers (one through five) showing how safe and welcome they each felt in the cafeteria and at recess. Ask children to hold up fingers to show how well each did at welcoming others.

- Have children write stories about a time when someone was kind to them on the playground, in the cafeteria, on the school bus, or in the hall. Pick some of the stories for the class to act out in small groups.

Additional children's literature to read

Yoko by Rosemary Wells (Little, Brown Books for Young Readers, 2009). When Yoko's classmates tease her because she has sushi for lunch, her teacher Mrs. Jenkins plans an international food festival. Only one student takes the challenge of tasting some of Yoko's sushi, but this is enough for Yoko to feel supported.

Upper Elementary Lessons

Developmental Information

LESSON ONE:
What Is Bullying Behavior? (Part One)

LESSON TWO:
What Is Bullying Behavior? (Part Two)

LESSON THREE:
The Courage to Be an Ally

LESSON FOUR:
Deciding When and What to Report

LESSON FIVE:
Hot Spots at School

Developmental Information to Think About as You Plan and Deliver the Lessons

Eight-year-olds typically:

- **Love to take on big projects but sometimes overestimate their own capacity**
  For these reasons, eight-year-olds will often be very interested in the information presented in these lessons and may get excited about figuring out how to take care of everyone.

- **Are forming larger friendship groups and making new friends**
  Eight-year-olds will be open to ideas about being more inclusive.

- **Have a growing sense of moral responsibility and are interested in fairness**
  Lesson Three will be especially interesting to eight-year-olds.

- **May exaggerate**
  Since the heart of Lessons Four and Five is building trust so that when children report we will do something about it, it's important for us to listen carefully to eight-year-olds and take their reports seriously, despite their tendency to exaggerate.

Nine-year-olds typically:

- **Like to work with partners of their own choosing**
  They especially prefer same-gender partners (which can lead to gender-role-based teasing). Discuss some of the examples from *Just Kidding* (in Lesson One) that are gender-role-based, such as Vince calling DJ a "Girlie." Nines need guidance to see that gender-role-based teasing is not OK.

- **May begin to form cliques**
  This tendency could lead to mean or exclusionary behaviors. Offer clear guidelines—you don't need to be best friends with everyone but you do need to be friendly and respectful to everyone.

- **Are concerned about fairness**
  Emphasize the fairness aspect of treating everyone respectfully.

- **Are concerned about who's "in" and who's "out"**
  We need to let them know that we will protect their privacy when they report.

Ten-year-olds typically:

- **Work well with classmates**
  Ten-year-olds will be open to thinking about how to avoid gender-role-based teasing.

- **Are concerned with friendship and social interaction**
  It's important, however, not to put anyone on the spot or lead any of the students to feel that the lessons are calling their friendships into question. Be sure to emphasize "friendly" rather than "best friends."

- **Are highly sensitive to and able to resolve questions of fairness and justice**
  Ten-year-old students will likely show lots of interest in these lessons and be concerned about how to make school safe for everyone. This is a good time for teaching expectations such as "be an ally."

Eleven-year-olds typically:

- **Put lots of focus on cliques, who's "in" and who's "out"**
  Carefully explain the importance of "being friendly" rather than "being friends" with everyone. Also be on the lookout for cliques.

- **Feel that saving face is important**
  It's important to use examples for the sort-card activity that are similar to what might happen in your classroom but not the same as what's going on in your classroom. Ten-year-olds need to be able to examine issues of bullying without losing face.

- **Feel it's important to choose their friends on the basis of common interests**
  It's therefore important to maintain a tone that says that it's important to keep everyone safe and behave respectfully to everyone, but that doesn't mean you need to be friends with everyone.

- **Are less willing to let adults have a role in handling bullying problems**
  Although they may be willing to report to adults, they will be more interested in student-centered solutions such as "befriend the person targeted."

LESSON ONE:

What Is Bullying Behavior? (Part One)

Grades 3–5

Preparation

Objectives

- To engage children in conversations about the difference between bullying behaviors and nonbullying behaviors—conversations that will help them understand that bullying involves an imbalance of power and an intention to harm.

- To raise children's awareness of the fact that we often don't know another person's motivations: an act may appear to be purposeful and actually be accidental, and something that seems accidental may be purposeful.

Materials needed

- *Just Kidding* by Trudy Ludwig (Tricycle Press, 2006) (see Appendix A for more information)

- Definition of bullying written on a chart:
  - Bullying is when someone is mean to someone else on purpose
  - Bullying might be using mean words or leaving someone out or poking and pinching someone
  - Bullying might be to someone's face or it might be behind their back (for example, on a social networking site or by sending a text)

- Chart with icons:
  - Safe in:
    - Feelings (heart icon)
    - Being included (stick figures holding hands)
    - Body (puffy stick figure)
- Cards with examples ("bullying"/"not bullying") on them

Key words and phrases

- You have a right to be safe in school: in your feelings, in your friendships, in your body

- Keep yourself and your classmates safe

- When someone is mean to someone else

- When they are mean to show that they are stronger, more popular, or more important than the person targeted

- Using mean words or leaving someone out on purpose or hitting, kicking, poking, or pinching someone

- Which class rule might help keep people in this class safe from bullying?

- How might we make sure that people in this class/school are included? That they are treated kindly?

Procedure

Opening

1. Gather children in a circle. Have a flip chart set up next to you.

2. Say: *You have the right to be safe in school. You have a right to be safe in your feelings, in your friendships, in your body. Which of our rules might help you be safe in this way?*

3. Introduce what you will do today: *Today we're going to read a book to learn more about how to keep yourself and your classmates safe, how to make sure that people in this class don't get bullied.*

4. Post definition of bullying:
   - Bullying is when someone is mean to someone else on purpose
   - Bullying might be using mean words, leaving someone out, or poking and pinching someone (use icons to demonstrate that following class rules would entail taking care of someone's feelings, including someone, and taking care of their body)
   - Bullying might be to someone's face or behind their back

5. Clarify that bullying doesn't need to be ongoing: *When people pick on others in this way, they often do it over and over, but even a mean behavior that happens once and could easily continue can be bullying.*

6. For fifth graders, help them understand that bullying behaviors involve an imbalance of power between children. Say: *When someone bullies, they are being mean to show that they are stronger, more popular, or more important than the person they are targeting.*

Body

1. Introduce the read-aloud.

2. Read *Just Kidding*, pausing periodically to ask open-ended questions.

Read to page 2 (rock, paper, scissors).

    Ask: *What does DJ mean when he says "I am the joke"?*

    Make the point that when DJ says "I am the joke" he's saying that it just doesn't feel right to him.

Stop at page 3 (tree house), page 4 (playing field), and page 5 (on the school bus).

    Ask: *How is DJ feeling?*

    Ask: *What are some of the ways that Vince was mean to DJ on purpose? (Telling him that you lose if he's on the team, calling him a "girlie," telling him he's wearing PJs, poking him and pinching him)*

Stop reading after the scene on the bus when Vince says, "I was just kidding."

    Ask: *How could you tell that DJ didn't like the teasing?*

3. Ask: *When is kidding fun? When is it mean?* Refer to the definition of bullying: "mean on purpose."

4. Use some examples to clarify "mean on purpose." Say: *How do we know when something is "mean"? It's tricky. Sometimes we wonder whether people are trying to be friendly or just being mean. Remember when DJ said, "I was the joke"? What clues did he have that Vince was being mean?*

5. Give an example of fun teasing: *Paul and Joey are good friends. They call one another by silly private nicknames and both smile or laugh about it. Do you think this is bullying or not bullying?* Ask the class to discuss and reach agreement.

6. Give an example of mean teasing: *Joey is new in school. The other students start calling him "Joey Baloney." They whisper this name to him when he's walking down the hall. Do you think this is bullying or not bullying?* Discuss with the class.

7. Introduce the sort-card activity. Children will look at an index card with a situation written on it and decide whether it fits in the category of bullying,

not bullying, or needs more information. (Note: The situations that children will likely put in "needs more information" are mostly situations where intent is unclear. That's OK—in life we often don't know another person's intent.)

8. Begin as a whole group. Then, with older children, you could continue the activity as partners or in small groups. If students do work as partners or in small groups, it's important that you have them share out at the end. Doing so will let all students hear a variety of examples and give you an opportunity to clarify any misunderstandings.

> **Teacher Tip**
> If fourth or fifth graders haven't had experience working as partners or in small groups, this is a time to first practice what partner work or group work would look like. How will you decide who will hold the card? How will you make sure that everyone gets to talk? What if you don't agree about whether or not your example is bullying?

9. As an example of how to sort, refer back to the situations mentioned in steps 5 and 6.

    Paul and Joey are good friends. They call each other by silly private nicknames and both smile or laugh about it. (Not bullying)

    Joey is new in school. The other students start calling him "Joey Baloney." They whisper this name to him when he's walking down the hall. (Bullying)

10. Do the activity. The following scenarios are just examples, so choose the ones that will be relevant for students in your class. Have the children do the sorting as partners or in small groups, and then share and probe. Ask: *How do you know it's mean? What clues might you have if you were _____ [from each character's point of view]?*

    - A student tells a friend he'd rather not hang out today—he has to do something with his family.
    - Your parents tell you that you may have one friend over. You invite Sammy. Your other friend Mo's feelings are hurt.
    - You're going to have a birthday party. You hand out invitations in school to all but one person.

- A group of students are shooting baskets on the playground. They tell another student that she can't play with them.

- A student accidentally trips in the cafeteria and spills food all over another student.

- A student purposely sticks out his foot and trips another student.

- Mike and Saul are friends. Mike has chocolate chip cookies for dessert. Saul wishes he had one and snatches a cookie away from Mike.

- Elise says to May, "You have to give me your lunch every day." May is afraid that Elise won't be her friend if she doesn't hand over her lunch, so she does it.

Closing

1. Ask: *Which class rule might help keep people in this class safe from bullying?*

2. Say: *Bullying is against our school rules.*

3. Ask: *How might we make sure that people in this class/school are included? That they are treated kindly?*

Follow-up ideas

- Finish reading *Just Kidding* later in the day.

- Either in a class discussion or other reflection format (journal writing, partner chats), ask: *When is teasing and joking fun? When is it mean and hurtful?*

- For a journal writing assignment, tell about:

    A time when I experienced bullying . . .

    A time I was left out . . .

    A time when someone teased me when I didn't want them to . . .

- Do a quick sort of a few more teacher-prepared examples (add them to the chart):

- All the students in the class decide to make up silly nicknames. Together, they make up a nickname for everyone.

- A group of students decides to make up silly nicknames. They call Sam "Sammy silly-face." Sam does not look happy about it.

Teacher Tip
Children (and teachers, too!) will need lots of practice and reflection to figure out which situations are bullying and which ones are not. Teachers who have used these lessons have found that continuing to practice sorting and discussing possible scenarios has been helpful in figuring out when a particular behavior meets the definition of bullying.

LESSON TWO:
What Is Bullying Behavior? (Part Two)
Grades 3–5

Preparation

Objectives

- To teach children that using mean words, leaving someone out on purpose, or purposely kicking, hitting, or pinching are all bullying.

- To engage children in discussions about the difference between bullying and nonbullying behaviors.

- To help children understand that we don't always know another person's motivations. An act may appear to be purposeful but may actually be accidental. Something that seems accidental may be purposeful.

- To tell children that bullying is not OK in this class or school.

Materials needed

- Choose one of the following books. As you choose, think about issues the students in your class will find meaningful (see Appendix A for more information).
  - *My Secret Bully* by Trudy Ludwig (Tricycle Press, 2005). Katie bullies her close friend Monica and calls her names behind her back.
  - *Trouble Talk* by Trudy Ludwig (Tricycle Press, 2008). Bailey says mean things, teases in public and in humiliating ways, and spreads embarrassing rumors.

- Definition of bullying written on a chart (from Lesson One):
    - Bullying is when someone is mean to someone else on purpose
    - Bullying might be using mean words, leaving someone out, or poking and pinching someone
    - Bullying might be to someone's face or it might be behind their back (for example, on a social networking site or by sending a text)

- Chart with icons (from Lesson One)
    - Safe in:

        Feelings (heart icon)

        Being included (stick figures holding hands)

        Body (puffy stick figure)

- Cards with examples ("bullying"/"not bullying") on them

Key words and phrases

- You have a right to be safe in school: in your feelings, in your friendships, in your body

- Keep yourself and your classmates safe

- When someone is mean to someone else

- When they are mean to show that they are stronger, more popular, or more important than the person targeted

- Using mean words, leaving someone out on purpose, or hitting, kicking, poking, or pinching someone

- Which class rule might help keep people in this class safe from bullying?

- How might we make sure that people in this class/school are included? That they are treated kindly?

Procedure

Opening

1. Gather children in a circle. Have a flip chart set up next to you.

2. Say: *Yesterday [two days ago, last week, etc.] we talked about bullying.*

3. Refer back to the book you read in Lesson One. Review some ways that Vince bullied DJ.

4. Say: *Today we're going to learn more about bullying. Bullying might be to a person's face or it might be behind their back.*

Body

1. Introduce the read-aloud.

2. Read aloud from the picture book you've chosen.

My Secret Bully

Pause periodically to ask: *How is Monica feeling?*

Pause when you come to the part where Katie calls Monica "Mon-ick-a" and ask: *Does this remind you of Vince and DJ?*

Finish the story. Ask: *How was Katie mean? What did she do behind Monica's back?*

Trouble Talk

Pause periodically to ask: *How is Maya feeling?*

Stop after Bailey tells Brian that Hua likes him and Hua tells Bailey that she has a "big mouth."

Ask: *What does the phrase "No offense" mean?*

Is it OK to say something cruel if you follow it up with "No offense"?

Have you ever had someone say "No offense" to you?

How did it feel? Did it feel safe?

Discuss the fact that asserting your feelings is not necessarily being mean. Ask: *When Hua tells Bailey that she has a "big mouth" is she being mean?*

Ask: *How was Bailey mean?*

Make sure that the children understand the following: When Bailey tells Keisha "No offense but your shirt is too small," this is overt mean behavior. When Bailey tells kids at school that Maya's parents are getting a divorce, she may not have overtly meant to hurt Maya. Instead, she thoughtlessly spread a juicy rumor.

3. Sort more scenarios (bullying/not bullying/more information needed). Choose scenarios that seem relevant to your students:

   - Pete tells Mark a secret. Mark tells the secret to many other students at school.

   - Kelly tells her classmates not to play with Addie at recess.

   - Two students post pictures of a third student on a Facebook page without the third student's knowledge or permission. (Be clear with students that this behavior is not OK even if it's not considered bullying—always ask someone's permission if you want to post their picture.)

   - A student posts pictures of their birthday party on a social networking site.

   - James locks all of the bathroom stalls and crawls out underneath. Paul sees him do this and reports it, privately, to their teacher.

   - Marty tells other students that Markeith was the one who locked all the bathroom stalls even though he knows it isn't true.

- Melissa, a fourth grader, tells Suzanne, a kindergartner, "You're just a little squirt and you can't sit here" on the school bus. (Be clear with students that picking on younger children is not OK. It's OK to tell a younger child that someone else is going to sit there, but politely and not in a mean way.)

- Lamar tells Jacob that he can't play with him today at recess but that he'll play with him tomorrow.

- Latisha likes to play basketball at recess. None of the other girls in her class play basketball. Marcy tells Latisha, "Only boys play basketball."

- Several students send a text to another student telling her that everyone hates her.

- A group of students sends a text saying unkind things about another student. (Be clear with students that texts can be a source of mean behavior. Kids don't see facial expressions, body language, or hear innuendoes in text messages. When the text is forwarded to others who have even less information, the meanness can grow.)

- Two students tell a third student, "We'll be your friend if you agree not to be friendly with [classmate's name]."

- Suzanne plans a surprise party for her friend Jenine.

- Jill acts as if she wants to be friends with Chrissy. Then she writes on Chrissy's new notebook.

- Maeve trips and spills some paint on Javonne's new shirt.

Closing

1. Let students know that they have a right to be safe in school. Say: *You have a right to be safe in school. You have a right to feel safe in school. You have a right to be included in school.* (Use the icons—safe in body, safe in feelings, and being included).

2. Clarify that it's sometimes hard to tell when someone is being mean. Say: *Sometimes it's hard to tell whether or not a person is being mean* (refer to those scenarios that provoked a lot of discussion during the scenario sort). *Whether it's on purpose or not, it's not OK to hurt someone at school. If we're accidentally hurtful to someone, we need to figure out how to fix it.*

3. Say: *The next time we meet to talk about this topic we are going to focus on ways to help when you see someone being treated meanly or bullied. In the meantime, pay attention to the ways that people in this class follow our rules and help everyone feel included and safe in their feelings and their bodies.*

Follow-up ideas

- For written or oral reflection, ask:
    - *How do you know that someone is a true friend? What might you do to be a good friend?*
    - *When have you noticed everyone being included? How do people in this class take care of each other?*

- Practice inclusion with your students. Mix up seating arrangements so that sitting with a clique is not an option. Do activities that require students to work with many different classmates.

- If you read *Trouble Talk*:

    Finish *Trouble Talk* later in the day or on another day. This story has many rich examples that you may want to discuss at length. You may choose to read the story over a few sessions. One topic you may want to reflect on with students is "When is news yours to share and when is it private news?"

Additional children's literature to read

Bully by Patricia Polacco (G.P. Putnam's Sons Books for Young Readers 2012). This book's main characters are seventh graders and the story is focused on cyberbullying.

LESSON THREE:
The Courage to Be an Ally
Grades 3–5

Preparation

Objectives

- To help children begin to think about ways to move from being a person who joins in the bullying or acts as an encouraging bystander, to being an ally or supporter of the person targeted

- To help children learn and practice strategies for becoming an ally through role-play

Materials needed

Say Something by Peggy Moss (Tilbury House, 2013) (see Appendix A for more information)

- Chart paper and markers

- Chart with stick figures and labels:
    Person who bullies
    People who join in
    Bystanders
    Allies or those who support the person who is bullied
    Person bullied

- Cut-out paper figure

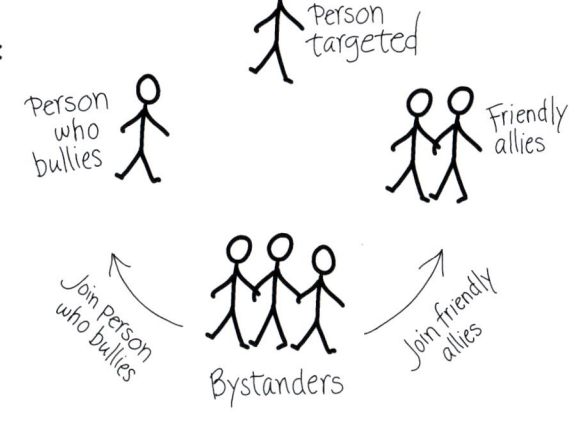

Key words and phrases

- Friends/friendly (the way you act toward someone)

- Person who joins in the bullying, bystander, ally, supporter

Procedure

Opening

1. Gather children in a circle. Have a flip chart set up next to you.

2. Say: *In school, it's important to be friendly to everyone. That doesn't mean that you have to be best friends with everyone, but you do need to be friendly and respectful. What does it mean to be friendly?* (If children have a hard time coming up with a list of friendly behaviors, prompt them to think of a time when someone was friendly to them.)

    For third and fourth grades:

    List what it means to be friendly.

    For fifth grade:

    Create a T-chart and list on the left side what it means to be friendly and on the right side what it means to be friends.

3. Read aloud *Say Something*.

    Ask: *What does the main character do that is friendly?*

    Why does she sit with the girl who's alone on the bus?

Body

1. Introduce the role-play you'll do today.

    Say: *We're going to do some plays about how a person might reach out to help a person who's being targeted for bullying.*

2. Set up the role-play (see Chapter Four for information about role-plays).

    Pretend there's a person whom everyone teases, like the boy in the book. I'd like to help him but I'm not sure how. I want to make sure I'm safe and I also want to take care of him. What might I do?

3. Take student ideas for what a person might do and write the ideas on the chart paper. (Note: In fifth grade classes, students can do the charting. Set up two chart stands and have two students alternate charting the ideas so one child won't get overwhelmed trying to keep up with writing things down.)

    > **Teacher Tip**
    > Have some ideas prepared if you think coming up with realistic ones will be hard for students. For example:
    >
    > Walk over to him at recess and say, "Would you like to shoot some baskets?"
    >
    > Ask him, "Would you like to sit with us at lunch?"
    >
    > Remind students about the way that the student in the book sat down next to the person who was alone on the school bus.

    > **Teacher Tip**
    > When you choose a student to take the role of the person being excluded or left out, make sure that the child you choose is not someone who struggles with that issue in real life. Be sure to coach the child how to respond positively.

4. Choose an idea from the list: *I'm going to pick one of our ideas. I think I'll pick going up to the boy and asking him how he's doing.*

5. Indicate the beginning of the role-play by saying something like *Ready, start* or *Lights, camera, action!*

6. Begin the role-play. Turn to the "excluded student" and act out the chosen idea: *Hi, how are you doing?*

    The student responds: *Better now that someone's spoken to me.*

7. Stop the role-play (*Cut!*). Ask students what they noticed: *What did you notice about our play?*

8. Students respond with their observations.

9. Act out other ideas from the chart, this time with students playing both roles.

Closing

1. Share bullying chart. Let students know that in most bullying situations, several people are involved:
   - Person who bullies
   - Person who is targeted
   - Bystanders: Can be a person who joins in, passive bystanders (who encourage bullying through their lack of action), or allies (like the main character in *Say Something*). Be explicit: for example, the person who laughs at the bullying is someone who is joining in on the bullying.

2. Use a cut-out figure.

   Say: *It's each person's choice which role they want to play.*

   Moving the figure around, ask: *Will you choose to help the person bullying? Will you be a passive bystander like the people in the story who didn't do anything? Will you have the courage to support the person who is being targeted?*

Follow-up ideas

- For reflection (writing prompt, morning message, etc.), ask:

   When have you invited someone to sit with you or join a game that you're playing, or otherwise acted friendly to someone who was alone?

   When has someone invited you to sit with them or join their game, or otherwise included you?

   Ask students to write in a journal:

   If I saw [pick one of the situations from Say Something] what would I do? What might happen if I did that?

A time when I was a person who joined in the bullying: I laughed at the person being targeted.

A time when I was a passive bystander: I watched but I didn't do something.

A time when I was an ally: I befriended the person being targeted or helped the person in some other way.

- Make a connection to social studies: Learn about bystanders in history. Learn about people who had the courage to take a stand.

Additional children's literature to read

Reread *Just Kidding* and talk about how DJ stands up for the boy on the school bus.

LESSON FOUR:

Deciding When and What to Report

Grades 3–5

Preparation

Objectives

- To encourage children to report dangerous behaviors to responsible adults

- To distinguish between dangerous behaviors and those that students can handle themselves

  Teacher Tip
  In this lesson, children will consider scenarios and discuss which scenarios require reporting to an adult. What follows are suggestions for how to group children for the discussion:

  Third grade: Teach the lesson to the whole group.

  Fourth grade: Divide the group into pairs and assign one scenario to each pair. Pairs will then report out to the whole group.

  Fifth grade: Divide the class into groups of four. Small groups consider the scenarios and then will report out to the whole class.

Materials needed

- Chart showing difference between situations students can resolve and situations they need to report

Situations you can resolve yourself	Situations you need to report
"He cut in line."	Help keep someone safe; for example, people are telling a child he can't play at recess.

- Cards with situations on them (see the suggested situations below, but you may want to write up your own scenarios based on events that have happened in your classroom)

- *Just Kidding* by Tracy Ludwig

- The following books to hold up and refer to if it's been some time since students have heard either story:

    My Secret Bully by Trudy Ludwig

    Trouble Talk by Trudy Ludwig

Key words and phrases

- Reporting the behavior to keep someone safe

- It's important to report if someone is being hurt (physically, with words, or with actions, such as excluding)

- When you report, I will keep your information confidential

- All of us have the job of keeping everyone safe

Procedure

Opening

1. Read from *Just Kidding*, starting where it says, "I'd like to say that Vince stopped bugging me after that, but he didn't." Read the next two and a half pages.

2. Ask: *In* Just Kidding, *when DJ tells his dad about the ways that Vince is treating him, what do he and his dad do?*

3. One of the strategies that they use is reporting the behavior to DJ's teacher. Ask: *How does DJ's teacher help?* (She talks to the guidance counselor about helping DJ make new friends. She also watches out to make sure that everyone's safe in the class.)

   (In *My Secret Bully*, Monica reports to her mother. In *Trouble Talk*, Maya reports to the school counselor.)

4. Say: *When you're younger, people sometimes say "don't tattle," and so young children sometimes get the idea that telling an adult when someone is being hurt is not a good idea. In this classroom, I want to know about any hurtful behavior. When you tell me about this kind of behavior, we'll call it reporting. Reporting is about letting responsible adults know when someone is being hurt, when someone is the target of mean behavior that they can't protect themselves from. Reporting can be about something that you see done to someone else or something that's happening to you. It's to help someone who is in trouble.*

Body

Consider scenarios and for each one talk about whether children should report to an adult or take care of the situation on their own. Acknowledge that some situations may fall in a gray area. Suggested scenarios:

- Molly gets on the school bus. Sarah, Becky, and Maeve all quickly rearrange their backpacks so that there's no room for Molly.

- You're about to sit next to your friend on the school bus. Sam quickly sits right where you were going to sit.

- You're in the bathroom. Someone in your grade does something mean to a younger child. They say to you, "Don't tell."

- Paul, a first grader, gets on the bus wearing a new hat. Finn and Gabe, who are in your grade, snatch Paul's hat, throwing it around the bus and laughing.

- It's writing time and Finn doesn't have a pencil. He takes Gabe's pencil without asking.

- Allen has just started in a new school. In the halls and lunchroom, when the teacher isn't listening, kids have begun to call him "Fat Albert" and laugh in a mean way.

- Kate and Anna are friends. Anna is good at sports and schoolwork. Kate has difficulty learning. The kids call Kate "dumb" and tell Anna that they won't hang out with her unless she drops Kate.

- Paulina is hoping to spend time at recess with Beth. Beth tells her that she needs to have a private conversation with Lavonne today but she'll spend time with Paulina tomorrow.

- It's recess time and a group of students are playing Dodge Ball. Some other students gather around and start cheering for the players to get a specific player "out."

Closing

Say:

If you're unsure about whether or not to report something, report it. It's always better to err on the side of keeping everyone safe.

If you report and the problem persists, report it again. The adults around you may believe that the problem is solved unless you let them know.

It's important to report if someone is being hurt (physically or emotionally, with words or with actions). When you report I will keep your information confidential to keep you safe.

> **Teacher Tip**
> To ensure confidentiality, communicate with other adults in school ahead of time to make sure that they understand the need for confidentiality. If in doubt, tell children to report only to you.

Follow-up ideas

- In partner chat, group discussion, or journal writing, ask:

    Why are students reluctant to report?

    What's the worst thing that could happen if you report? The best thing that could happen?

    What can adults do to help make reporting safe?

- In journal writing, tell about:

    A time when I thought about reporting.

    A time when I did report.

- For older children, in journal writing or a discussion ask:

    What could the adults in school do to make it feel safe to report? What do you hope that the adult does? Doesn't do?

    Is it easier to report about other students being left out or about being left out yourself?

LESSON FIVE:

Hot Spots at School
Grades 3–5

Note: Before teaching this lesson, you'll need to have gathered data about where children feel safest and least safe in the school.

Preparation

Objectives
- To help students think about how to keep themselves and their classmates safe in the lunchroom and on the playground and school bus

- To use information gained through questionnaires (*Where do you feel safe or unsafe in school?*) to help children think specifically about keeping themselves and classmates safe in identified "hot spot" areas

Materials needed
- Chart with results of questionnaire (numbers covered)

Key words and phrases
- Felt unsafe

- What might we do

- Make the [name of "hot spot"] safer for everyone

Procedure

Opening

1. Gather children in a circle. Have a flip chart with questionnaire data set up next to you.

2. Say: *Recently, you answered some questions about where you feel safe or unsafe in school.*

3. Ask: *Where do you imagine people felt unsafe? Cafeteria? Bathrooms? Halls? Playground?*

4. Students chat with a partner and then share out their ideas.

5. Reveal the data on the chart, sharing the number of students who felt unsafe in the places in school that stood out as the "hot spots."

Body

1. Ask: *What have you noticed in the [name of "hot spot"] that makes it feel unsafe? Why do you think those behaviors happen there?*

2. Go around the circle with students reporting what they've noticed or why they think these behaviors happen in the "hot spot." Remind students not to mention people's names.

3. Say: *We've learned that it helps when students report mean behaviors to an adult at school or an adult at home. It helps when other students include the student being targeted.*

4. Ask: *What might you do to make the [name of "hot spot"] safer and take care of each other?*

5. Go around the circle again, brainstorming. Say: *Remember, when we brainstorm, everyone's ideas count. We'll accept all ideas and leave out our comments for now.*

6. Record student ideas on a chart (for fifth graders, have two students record ideas).

Closing

1. Sort the listed ideas, using questions such as:

    Might this idea be effective in making the [name of "hot spot"] safer for everyone?

    Is this idea realistic? Would it make a difference?

    Which idea might you feel safe/comfortable trying?

    We know that reporting to adults helps. What might the adults do to help you feel safe reporting?

2. As a class, choose an idea or two to try.

Follow-up ideas

- Upon their return from an identified "hot spot," ask children how their idea for feeling safer in that place worked. Did it help make the area feel safer for everyone?

- If students report that the strategy that they picked isn't helping, revisit the issue and choose another strategy to try.

- For Morning Meeting question of the day, ask:

    What can you do today in the cafeteria to make sure that everyone has someone to sit with? At recess to make sure everyone has someone to play with?

    What would you do if you saw someone else being picked on? Being left out?

Additional children's literature to read

Reread *Say Something,* with particular attention to the cafeteria scenes.

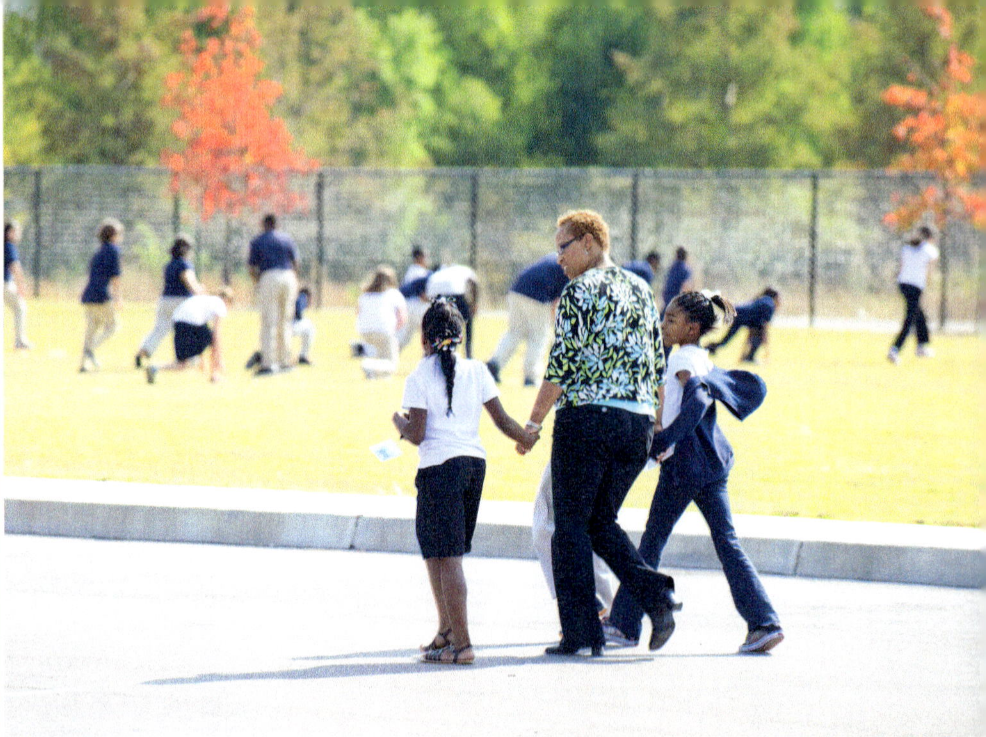

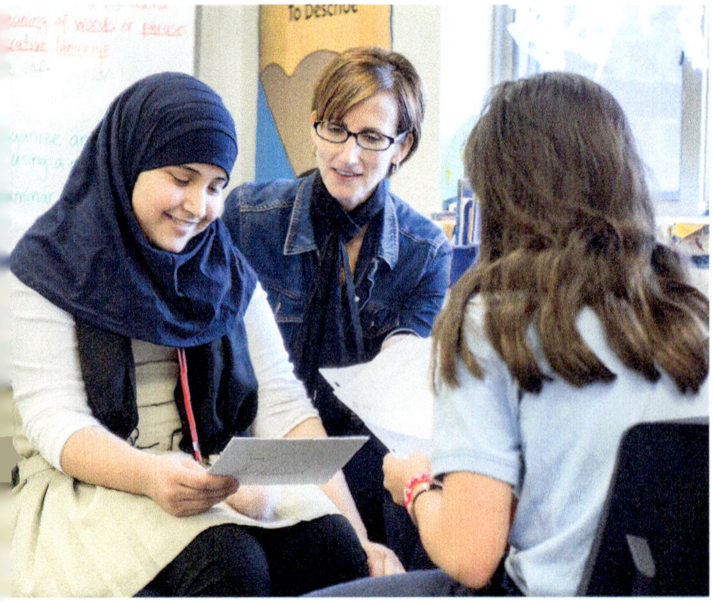
To Describe

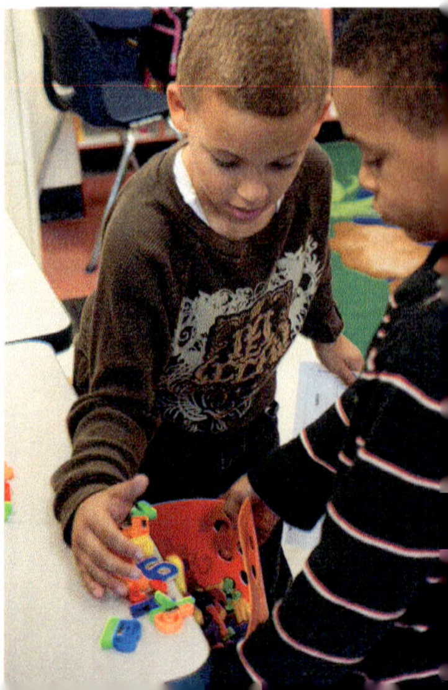

EPILOGUE
The Challenge of Kindness

We serve as powerful models for students—they will behave as they see us behave. When we speak kindly to students and colleagues, students will be much more likely to speak kindly to each other. When we work collaboratively and equitably with colleagues, students will notice us and will be more willing to work collaboratively and equitably with classmates.

In this book I've described many strategies that you can use to create a culture of kindness in the classroom. These strategies include creating classroom rules that children believe in, teaching and reinforcing kind behaviors, and responding quickly and nonpunitively to mean behaviors. But we need to go further. To be effective in bullyproofing our classrooms, it's essential that we model, day in and day out, the kind and respectful behavior we want the children to embrace.

This is not always easy to do. Respectful work with our colleagues means speaking kindly and respectfully to them even when we disagree with them. Respectful work with students means speaking kindly and respectfully to them even when we're setting limits or responding to their mean behaviors. Respectful behaviors toward students' parents means listening carefully and trying to see things from their point of view, even when we're having a difficult conversation about a child's behavior (or even when we see things differently—or view a child's behavior differently). We as educators need to be the change we want to see in the world.

The problem of bullying is actually the challenge of kindness. Our media surround children with a culture of meanness—this is what they learn, over and over, about how to behave and be successful in the world. But you can change things. Using the strategies in this book, you can create a safe, kind, and joyful climate in your classroom and your school and model kind and respectful behavior in all your social interactions, whether in person or electronic. You can create a climate where children gain social recognition for their courage and their kindness, rather than their cruelty and misuse of power. Only a climate of courage and kindness can truly solve the problem of bullying.

APPENDIX A

Children's Literature to Use in Bullying Prevention Work

Reading fine children's literature together, whether a picture book or a chapter book, is an effective community builder no matter what grade you teach. I can still remember the books that my fifth grade teacher read aloud to our class. Many of us had tears trickling down our faces during the last chapter of *A Tale of Two Cities*. Over my more than thirty years of teaching, I read aloud to my students every day.

Books can help children envision an ideal of friendliness and caring. They can show children how they might handle a tricky ethical situation. They can become a powerful shared class experience to revisit and discuss.

Sharing and discussing a piece of literature can also be a safe way to begin a conversation about bullying. Sometimes starting off by addressing the issue directly can lead children, especially older children, to feel defensive. Some children may feel that the class is discussing mean behaviors because they themselves have done something bad, which could serve to close down discussion. In contrast, the indirect approach of discussing the actions of characters in books can open up the issue in a way that feels safe to everyone.

Because of the power of a shared literature experience, it's important to carefully select the books that you plan to read as part of your bullying prevention program.

Choose books that represent everyone. Representation matters. Your students need to see children from a range of nationalities, races, and lifestyle choices. This will help children learn to be kind and inclusive toward everyone.

Choose books that focus on children's interactions rather than an analysis of why children might bully. We know that many people have the potential to engage in bullying behavior. Children jockey for power in this way for all sorts of reasons. It really doesn't help the child who is bullied or their classmates to read an analysis of why the child who is doing the bullying is engaging in that hurtful behavior.

Choose books that encourage children to report mean behavior. Avoid books that make fun of children who "tattle." We want to encourage children to report rather than filling their heads with fears of being like the child whose tongue grew right out of his mouth from too much tattling.

Choose books that paint a realistic picture of how to respond to a bullying situation, with an emphasis on children taking care of each other and adults responding effectively. Books where the child who bullies magically discovers that the child who is bullied is actually "cool" build an unrealistic image of how to solve the problem of bullying. The very best books show children learning about and taking care of each other. They also show the adults at school responding sympathetically and effectively when they learn about bullying.

Being a Bystander

Bird Child **by Nan Forler, illustrated by François Thisdale**
Tundra Books 2009
Picture book, grades 1–5

Eliza's mother teaches her to "fly," to "look down and see what is, look up and see what can be." When a new girl is bullied at school, Eliza protects her and teaches her to fly.

The Brand New Kid **by Katie Couric, illustrated by Marjorie Priceman**
Doubleday 2000
Picture book, grades 1–5

Lazlo is new in school. The other students taunt him and exclude him. When Ellie plays with him after school, she discovers that he's fun to be with.

Come With Me **by Holly M. McGhee, illustrated by Pascal Lemaître**
G.P. Putman's Sons Books for Young Readers 2017
Picture book, K–3

    A child's parents show her the diversity and friendliness in the world.

I Walk with Vanessa: A Story About a Simple Act of Kindness **by Kerascoët**
Schwartz & Wade 2018
Wordless picture book, grades K–3

    Vanessa is new in school. Other students ignore her and one child teases her. A classmate thinks about Vanessa in the night and decides to walk Vanessa to school in the morning. Most suitable to read with an individual or small group as the pictures are small.

Say Something **by Peggy Moss, illustrated by Lea Lyon**
Tilbury House 2004
Picture book, grades 3–9

    The book is set in a middle school where some children are pushed, teased, and excluded. The main character would never engage in those behaviors, but she remains silent. Then one day she is teased and wishes that those around her had said something. This book includes an afterword for students with additional information about bullying prevention.

Children Taking Care of Each Other

***Alfie Gives a Hand* written and illustrated by Shirley Hughes**
Red Fox 2009
Picture book, grades Pre-K–K

Reluctant to go to the birthday party without his mom, Alfie brings his blanket along. He puts down his blanket, though, to take care of Min, who is crying.

***Be Kind* by Pat Zietlow Miller, illustrated by Jen Hill**
Roaring Brook Press 2018
Picture book, grades 1–3

Tanisha spills grape juice on their clothes and their friend puzzles out some of the complexities of how to be kind. *New York Times* bestseller.

***Ordinary Mary's Extraordinary Deed* by Emily Pearson, illustrated by Fumi Kosaka**
Gibbs Smith 2002
Picture book, grades 2–3

Mary picks blueberries for a neighbor. The neighbor then does favors for five people, each of those people do a favor for five people, and the good deeds expand exponentially.

***Those Shoes* by Maribeth Boelts, illustrated by Noah Z. Jones**
Candlewick 2009
Picture book, grades K–5

Just about everyone at school has a certain brand of shoes, but Jeremy's grandmother can't afford to buy them for him. They find a pair at a thrift store, but they're really too small for Jeremy. He gives them to his friend, who also longs for "those shoes." This book also builds empathy for children whose families have limited financial resources.

Excluding and Including

Each Kindness **by Jacqueline Woodson, illustrated by E.B. Lewis**
Nancy Paulsen Books 2012
Picture book, grades 2–5

    Maya is new in school. Her classmates exclude her. When Maya moves away, her teacher does a lesson on kind acts that ripple out across the water and affect our world, a powerful analogy. There is no happy ending to this story.

The Invisible Boy **by Trudy Ludwig, Illustrated by Patrice Barton**
El niño invisible (Spanish Edition)
Knopf Books for Young Readers 2013
Picture book, grades 1–3

    Brian is "invisible" to classmates and to his overworked teacher. He is left out on the playground and during after-school activities. When Justin joins the class, he is teased for his Korean food. Brian reaches out to Justin and begins to connect with classmates. Brian's not so invisible anymore.

My Secret Bully **by Trudy Ludwig, illustrated by Abigail Marble**
Tricycle Press 2005
Picture book, grades 2–6

    Katie and Monica have been friends since kindergarten. Lately Katie has been excluding Monica and calling her names. Monica discusses the problem with her mom and realizes that it's not her fault. She tells Katie that "friends don't do that to friends," and finds other girls to spend her time with.

The New Girl . . . and Me **by Jacqui Robbins, illustrated by Matt Phelan**
Atheneum/Richard Jackson Books 2006
Picture book, grades K–2

    When a new girl joins the class, children exclude her—except for Mia, who decides to befriend her.

Two of a Kind **by Jacqui Robbins, illustrated by Matt Phelan**
Atheneum Books for Young Readers 2009
Picture book, grades K–3

When Kayla and Melanie play together, they don't invite anyone else to join them. When Julisa and Anna play together, everyone's invited. Then Kayla and Melanie include Anna but exclude Julisa.

Respecting and Appreciating Differences

All Are Welcome **by Alexandra Penfold, illustrated by Suzanne Kaufman**
Knopf Books for Young Readers 2018
Picture book, Pre-K–grade 2

A celebration of a multicultural and diverse school, upbeat and joyous.

Crow Boy **by Taro Yashima**
Puffin Books 1976
Picture book, grades K–1

Set in Japan, a student is left alone and called "stupid" by his classmates for six years until one day the other students discover how much he has to offer. A Caldecott Honor book.

The Day You Begin **by Jacqueline Woodson, illustrated by Rafael López**
El día en que descubres quién eres (Spanish Edition)
Nancy Paulsen Books 2018
Picture book, grades K–3

"There will be times when you walk into a room and no one else is quite like you." Rigoberto is from Venezuela, new in the country, new in school. So much bullying is focused on the new child in school. This book builds empathy for the student who is new.

Eggbert the Slightly Cracked Egg **by Tom Ross, illustrated by Rex Barron**
Puffin Books 1997
Picture book, Pre-K–grade 3

A story about accepting differences in oneself or others.

***Fry Bread: A Native American Family Story* by Kevin Noble Maillard, illustrated by Juana Martinez-Neal**
Roaring Brook Press 2019
Picture book, grades K–3

A warm and accurate picture of contemporary Native American culture. Mr. Noble Maillard is an enrolled citizen of the Seminole nation. Winner of multiple awards, including *Publisher's Weekly* Best Picture Book of 2019 and the American Indian Library Association's American Indian Youth Picture Book Honor.

***I'm New Here* by Anne Sibley O'Brien**
Soy nuevo aquí (Spanish Edition)
Charlesbridge 2015
Picture book, grades 1–4

Three students new to the United States from Guatemala, Korea, and Somalia learn to communicate and make friends in their elementary schools. The author has also written a companion book, *Someone New*, told from their classmates' point of view. Both are honest and positive looks at diversity, inclusion, and friendship.

***The Junkyard Wonders* written and illustrated by Patricia Polacco**
Philomel 2010
Picture book, grades 1–4

Based on her own experiences as a student with special needs, Polacco has written a book that builds appreciation of children who learn differently. Caution: This story mentions the death of a student.

***Lovely* written and illustrated by Jess Hong**
Encantador **(Spanish Edition)**
Creston Books 2017
Picture book, preschool–grade 3

Lovely is different; she has one blue eye and one brown eye. The book proceeds with a simple message: we are all different and that is lovely. Bank Street College of Education Best Children's Book of the Year, 2018.

***Odd Velvet* by Mary Whitcomb, illustrated by Tara Calahan King**
Chronicle Books 1998
Picture book, grades K–3

Velvet is different from the other children. Although they are polite to her, the children don't ask her to play. Then, with some help from the teacher, they discover Velvet's special qualities. This is a good story relating to issues arising from income differences.

***One Green Apple* by Eve Bunting, illustrated by Ted Lewin**
Clarion Books 2006
Picture book, grades 2–6

Farah is new in her school and in the United States. She doesn't speak English. Told from the point of view of an immigrant child, this story builds empathy for recently arrived immigrants.

***Pebble: A Story About Belonging,* written and illustrated by Susan Milford**
HarperCollins Children's Books 2007
Picture book, grades K–5

The pebble wanted a special role in the world; it "longed for more." A boy finds the pebble on the beach and takes it home. It says, "I have found what I was looking for."

***The Sandwich Swap* by Her Majesty Queen Rania Al Abdullah of Jordan, with Kelly DiPucchio, illustrated by Tricia Tusa**
Little, Brown Books for Young Readers 2010
Picture book, grades 2–4

Salma and Lily are best friends but the food that they eat divides them. Can they bridge this difference? Based on a true story from Queen Rania's childhood.

***Thank You, Mr. Falker* written and illustrated by Patricia Polacco**
Philomel Books 1998
Picture book, grades 1–4

Mr. Falker sees the potential in a student and helps her learn. Based on Patricia Polacco's own experiences, this book builds empathy for students with special needs.

***Two Speckled Eggs* written and illustrated by Jennifer K. Mann**
Candlewick Press 2014
Picture Book, grades 1–3

Ginger's mother tells her that she has to invite all of the girls in her class to her birthday party. Ginger doesn't want to invite Lyla and yet Lyla turns out to be the kindest and most creative child at the party. Ginger discovers that being different isn't such a bad thing.

***The Ugly Duckling* by Hans Christian Andersen, adapted and illustrated by Jerry Pinkney**
Morrow Junior Books 1999
All ages

In this classic tale, an ugly duckling is teased by his siblings. He grows up to be not a duck at all but a graceful swan.

***We All Sing With the Same Voice* by J. Philip Miller and Sheppard M. Greene, illustrated by Paul Meisel**
HarperCollins 2005
Picture book and song, grades Pre-K–grade 2

First featured as a song on Sesame Street, this picture book is lively, upbeat, and inclusive.

***We're All Wonders* written and illustrated by R.J. Palacio**
Somos todos extraordinários **(Portuguese/Brazilian Edition)**
Todos somos únicos **(Spanish Edition)**
Knopf Books for Young Readers 2017
Picture book grades K–2

The picture book version of *Wonder*. Augie looks different from others but he has the same feelings as all the rest of us do. *Wonder* was the first book in the series but many books have followed.

Weslandia **by Paul Fleischman, illustrated by Kevin Hawkes**
Candlewick 2002
Picture book, grades 3–5

    Wesley marches to his own drummer. He has "no friends but plenty of tormentors." Over the summer, he founds his own civilization in his backyard. His schoolmates are curious and slowly he allows them to join in. This is a book about getting to know and like yourself and the power of following your dreams.

Wings **written and illustrated by Christopher Meyers**
Scholastic Press 2000
Picture book, grades 3–6

    Icarus Jackson has wings. Children tease him. With the help of a friend, he regains his sense of pride and allows himself to soar.

Wonder **by R.J. Palacio**
Knopf Books for Young Readers 2012
Chapter book, grades 3–6

    Augie was born with facial differences and has been homeschooled. He goes to school for the first time in fifth grade and struggles to be accepted. *Wonder* is a mesmerizing whole-class read-aloud with lots of deep learning about empathy, kindness, and being appreciated for who we really are. *New York Times* bestseller.

You, Me and Empathy **by Jayneen Sanders, illustrated by Sofia Cardoso**
Tú, yo y empatía **(Spanish Edition)**
Educate2Empower Publishing 2017

    Teaching children about empathy, feelings, kindness, compassion, tolerance, respect, and recognizing bullying behaviors.

Someone Is Bullied

***Blubber* by Judy Blume**
Yearling 1974
Chapter book, grades 4–6

Caroline and Wendy tease Linda about her weight. Jill joins in. During the course of the book, the tables turn, and Jill is targeted. She gains new understanding about her mean behavior toward Linda.

***Bully* written and illustrated by Patricia Polacco**
G. P. Putnam's Sons Books for Young Readers 2012
Picture book, grades 3-7

Lyla is new in school. She makes a friend, Jamie, on the first day of school. When she wins the competition to get on the cheerleading squad, the "popular" girls invite her into their clique. They cyberbully other kids in school, including Jamie. Then Lyla makes the highest grade in the school on the state test and her "friends" mount a cyberbullying campaign against her. A great book to use as the focus of digital citizenship lessons.

***The Hundred Dresses* by Eleanor Estes, illustrated by Louis Slobodkin**
***Los cien vestidos* (Spanish Edition)**
Harcourt 1944
Chapter book, grades 3–6

Peggy enjoys "having fun with" Wanda—in other words, teasing her. Maddie goes along because she's afraid that if she doesn't, she might be targeted next. Despite the fact that this book was first published in 1944, its message still rings true.

***Just Kidding* by Trudy Ludwig, illustrated by Adam Gustavson**
Tricycle Press 2006
Picture book, grades 3–6

DJ's schoolmate Vince makes fun of him, pokes him, and sticks chewed gum on his chair. Vince brushes it off by saying, "Just kidding." With support from his dad and his teacher, DJ makes new friends who "have fun—without making fun of each other." This book includes information for adults about bullying and discussion questions for teachers to use with their class.

***My Friend Maggie* written and illustrated by Hannah E. Harrison**
Dial Books for Young Readers 2016
Picture book, grades K–2

Paula and Maggie, two animals, are best friends. When Veronica starts to bully Maggie, she lures Paula into the bullying behavior. When Veronica starts to bully Paula, Maggie stands by her friend.

***La mujer que brillaba aún más que el sol/The Woman Who Outshone the Sun* by Alejandro Cruz Martinez, illustrated by Fernando Oliver, translated by Rosalma Zubizarreta**
Children's Book Press 1991
Picture book, all ages

Based on a Zapotec legend. Lucia Zenteno brought powerful gifts to the village. Some people were afraid of her and drove her away. When the village becomes desolate, the villagers retrieve her. In Spanish and English.

***Nobody Knew What to Do* by Becky Ray McCain, illustrated by Todd Leonardo**
Albert Whitman and Company 2001
Picture book, grades 1–3

A group of boys bully Ray, who's new in school. Ray reports to his teacher. The teacher, principal, and the children's parents help stop the bullying behavior. This book includes information for adults about bullying prevention.

***Real Friends* by Shanon Hale, illustrated by Leuyen Pham**
First Second 2017
Graphic novel, grades 3–5

A vivid and heartfelt story of growing up in Los Angeles with cliques, bullying, and true accepting friendship. *New York Times* bestseller.

***Save Me a Seat* by Sarah Weeks and Gita Varadarajan**
Scholastic 2016
Chapter book, grades 5 and up

    Ravi and his family have just moved from India to New Jersey. Ravi wants a friend and picks out Joe, the sparkling boy who is second generation Indian. At first they don't seem to have anything in common but soon realize they are both being bullied by the same person. By the end of the book, Ravi has realized that his true friend is Joe, the boy who receives special education services and who has "more to him than meets the eye."

***Trouble Talk* by Trudy Ludwig, illustrated by Mikela Prevost**
Tricycle Press 2008
Picture book, grades 1–4

    Bailey loves to spread rumors and say unkind things, prefaced by "no offense." When Bailey spreads an untrue rumor about Maya, Maya talks with Mrs. Bloom, the school psychologist. She says that she'll work with Bailey and talk with the whole class about sharing information that's not theirs to share. In the meantime, she tells Maya, "Spend time with people who make you feel safe." This book includes information for adults about bullying and discussion questions for you to use with your class.

***Wolf Hollow* by Lauren Wolk**
Dutton Books for Young Readers 2016
Historical novel, grades five and up

    "The year I turned twelve I learned to lie." It is 1943 and Betty, a girl who bullies, joins Annabelle's one-room country school. Annabelle manages her relationship with Betty in a way that is caring and ethical while keeping the events private until finally she needs to share these events with her family. Betty is a child who bullies physically, and injury and death result.

Teasing

***Chrysanthemum* written and illustrated by Kevin Henkes**
***Crisantemo* (Spanish Edition)**
Greenwillow Books 1991
Picture book, grades K–3

The children tease Chrysanthemum about her name. Mrs. Twinkle, whose first name is Delphinium, saves the day.

***Yoko* written and illustrated by Rosemary Wells**
Little, Brown Books for Young Readers 2009
Picture book, grades K–3

Yoko's classmates tease her because she has sushi for lunch. To increase the children's appreciation of different foods, Mrs. Jenkins, her teacher, plans an international food festival. Only one student takes the challenge of tasting some of Yoko's sushi but this is enough for Yoko to feel supported. This book is good for issues about nationality and the power of friendship.

APPENDIX B

Resources

Bullying and Bullying Prevention

Books

Becoming Nicole by Amy Ellis Nutt. Random Trade Paperbacks, 2015.

Many children who are gender nonconforming are bullied. Amy Ellis Nutt has written a book that helps the reader understand why a child might choose to change his gender. The Maines family adopts a pair of identical twins. One twin wishes to be a girl from the earliest childhood. This is the story of their family journey to acceptance. Pulitzer Prize winner and *New York Times* bestseller.

The Bully, the Bullied, and the Not-So-Innocent Bystander: From Preschool to High School and Beyond: Breaking the Cycle of Violence and Creating More Deeply Caring Communities by Barbara Coloroso. Updated edition, William Morrow Paperbacks, 2016.

Barbara Coloroso is a consultant and lecturer on parenting, teaching, and positive school climate. This book, first published in 2003 and updated in 2016, is clear, thoughtful, and carefully researched. The scope is broad and for that reason the specific information about how to prevent bullying in school is limited to one chapter.

Bullying and Cyberbullying: What Every Educator Needs to Know by Elizabeth Kandel Englander. Harvard Education Press, 2013.

Elizabeth Englander is a college professor, researcher, and parent. She is the founder and director of the Massachusetts Aggression Reduction Center where she supervises college students who present anti-bullying workshops and has run a long-term study about high school students' experiences with bullying and cyberbullying.

Confronting Bullying: Literacy as a Tool for Character Education by Roxanne Henkin. Heinemann, 2005.

    Roxanne Henkin is professor emeritus of literacy education at the University of Texas and director emeritus of the San Antonio Writing Project. In this book she describes how to use reader response and reflective writing to build children's awareness of the importance of a safe and inclusive climate for all. Included are lesson plans and a detailed bibliography.

Cybersafe Young Children: Teaching Internet Safety and Responsibility, K–3 by Barbara Sprung, Merle Froschl, and Nancy Gropper. Teachers College Press, 2020.

    The authors make a strong case for starting digital citizenship education in preschool. This book includes information on child development, young children's use of digital devices, anti-bullying lessons, and materials about cyberbullying prevention.

Dear Bully: Seventy Authors Tell Their Stories, edited by Carrie Jones and Megan Kelley Hall. HarperTeen, 2011.

    Young adult authors tell about their own experiences with bullying. Some of their experiences are relevant to bullying in elementary school.

Empowering Bystanders in Bullying Prevention: Grades K–8 by Stan Davis with Julia Davis. Research Press, 2007.

    Stan Davis has many years' experience as a school guidance counselor and consultant to schools on bullying prevention. This book offers research-based, practical strategies that student bystanders can use in response to bullying.

The Respectful School: How Educators and Students Can Conquer Hate and Harassment by Stephen Wessler, with contributions by William Preble. Association for Supervision and Curriculum Development, 2003.

    Based on the author's experiences as an attorney and prosecutor for the state of Maine, this is a passionate and well-documented book about turning bias, prejudice, harassment, and violence among students into respectful interactions. The emphasis is on middle school and high school.

Schools Where Everyone Belongs: Practical Strategies for Reducing Bullying, 2nd edition, by Stan Davis with Julia Davis. Research Press, 2007.

Stan Davis draws on theory and research to offer practical guidelines for implementing a whole-school approach to reducing bullying.

They Don't Like Me: Lessons on Bullying and Teasing from a Preschool Classroom by Jane Katch. Beacon Press, 2003.

Jane Katch has taught young children for many years. In this book, she reflects on a year of teaching four- and five-year-olds, with a particular focus on the children's social relations and power dynamics.

You Can't Say You Can't Play by Vivian Gussin Paley. Harvard University Press, 1992.

Author and teacher Vivian Paley spent a year investigating ways to help the kindergarten students she taught be more inclusive. She recorded her strategies, reflections, and results.

Websites

glsen.org
Educators and students work together to create positive learning environments for LGBTQ students.

olweus.sites.clemson.edu
The website for the Olweus Bullying Prevention Program (a program used by many schools in the United States) includes resources, research information, and information about services. The Peaceful School Bus is an Olweus program. The Olweus Online Survey is available for purchase at https://www.hazelden.org/store/item/14432.

schoolclimate.org/services/bullybust/
The National School Climate Center at Ramapo for Children is an organization that works with schools to create positive climate and prevent bullying.

secondstep.org/bullying-prevention
The website for Second Step, developed by the Committee for Children, includes information about bullying, research, and services for schools.

stopbullying.gov
This federal government website is packed full of information for teachers, parents, and children.

Child Development

Yardsticks: Child and Adolescent Development Ages 4–14, 4th ed., by Chip Wood. Center for Responsive Schools, 2017.

    Offers age-by-age narratives and easy-to-scan charts that clearly and concisely depict children's typical social-emotional, physical, and cognitive developmental characteristics.

Yardsticks Guide Series: Common Developmental Characteristics in the Classroom and at Home, Grades K–8. From *Responsive Classroom*, 2018. Center for Responsive Schools, 2018.

    Child development pamphlets based on Chip Wood's *Yardsticks*. One pamphlet per grade, each covering the three ages typically seen at that grade level.

Classroom Management and Engaging Academics

Closing Circles: 50 Activities for Ending the Day in a Positive Way by Dana Januszka and Kristen Vincent. Center for Responsive Schools, 2012.

    Simple five-to-ten-minute end-of-day activities that reaffirm classroom community and enable students and teachers alike to leave school feeling encouraged and competent. Includes helpful tips on finding time for closing circles.

Empowering Educators: A Comprehensive Guide to Teaching Grades K, 1, 2 by Kirsten Lee Howard, Amy Wade, Becky Wanless, and Lisa Dewey Wells. Center for Responsive Schools, 2021.

Empowering Educators: A Comprehensive Guide to Teaching Grades 3, 4, 5 by Julie Kelly, Andy Moral, Jenni Lee Groegler Pierson, and Amanda Stessen-Blevins. Center for Responsive Schools, 2021.

Empowering Educators: A Comprehensive Guide to Teaching Grades 6, 7, 8 by Linda Berger, Emily Parrelli, Brian Smith, and Heather Young. Center for Responsive Schools, 2021.

Each of the books in this series is an introduction to best practices in education offering clear, practical advice, real-life examples, turnkey resources, and grade-specific strategies.

The First Six Weeks of School, 2nd ed., from *Responsive Classroom*. Center for Responsive Schools, 2015.

Comprehensive guide for structuring the beginning of school to help ensure a productive year of learning. Use the critical first weeks of school to establish expectations, routines, a sense of community, and a positive classroom tone.

Interactive Modeling: A Powerful Technique for Teaching Children by Margaret Berry Wilson. Center for Responsive Schools, 2012.

Provides step-by-step guidance on use of the *Responsive Classroom* strategy of Interactive Modeling. Includes classroom examples, tips for use in different classroom situations, and scripts that teachers can follow.

The Joyful Classroom: Practical Ways to Engage and Challenge Elementary Students, from *Responsive Classroom* with Lynn Bechtel and Kristen Vincent. Center for Responsive Schools, 2016.

Creating active, interactive, and exciting lessons through the use of collaborative learning structures, academic choice, the natural learning cycle, and student self-assessment that connect with students' lives and interests while helping them stretch and grow.

The Language of Learning: Teaching Students Core Thinking, Listening, and Speaking Skills by Margaret Berry Wilson. Center for Responsive Schools, 2014.

    An essential guide to teaching the core competencies every child needs to engage effectively in their academic work and develop into a confident, self-motivated learner.

Make Learning Meaningful: How to Leverage the Brain's Natural Learning Cycle in K–8 Classrooms by Kristen Vincent. Center for Responsive School, 2021.

    Offers a brain-based approach to sustaining student engagement and provides examples of what the natural learning cycle looks and sounds like for teaching academics, discipline, and social-emotional skills.

Responsive Classroom for Music, Art, PE, and Other Special Areas, from *Responsive Classroom*. Center for Responsive Schools, 2016.

    Practical advice, charts, planners, and detailed examples help special area educators seamlessly blend key *Responsive Classroom* practices into their daily teaching.

Games and Movement Activities

85 Engaging Movement Activities by Phyllis Weikart and Elizabeth Carlton. Wadsworth Publishing, 2002.

    Ideas for challenging and enjoyable movement experiences that develop academic and cooperative decision-making skills.

Energizers! 88 Quick Movement Activities That Refresh and Refocus, K–6 by Susan Lattanzi Roser. Center for Responsive Schools, 2009.

    Quick movement activities for Morning Meeting, transition times, movement breaks in the classroom, and the playground.

The Incredible Indoor Games Book by Bob Gregson. McGraw-Hill, 2004.

    Fun, creative group games and activities suitable for indoor play.

Morning Meeting

80 Morning Meeting Ideas for Grades K–2 by Susan Lattanzi Roser. Center for Responsive Schools, 2012.

80 Morning Meeting Ideas for Grades 3–6 by Carol Davis. Center for Responsive Schools, 2012.

    Twenty ideas for each component of Morning Meeting (greeting, sharing, group activity, and morning message) plus many tips for getting the most out of each idea.

99 Activities and Greetings: Great for Morning Meeting . . . and Other Meetings, Too! by Melissa Correa-Connolly. Center for Responsive Schools, 2004.

    Directions for greetings and activities for both primary and upper elementary grades.

Doing Language Arts in Morning Meeting: 150 Quick Activities That Connect to Your Curriculum by Jodie Luongo, Joan Riordan, and Kate Umstatter. Center for Responsive Schools, 2015.

Doing Math in Morning Meeting: 150 Quick Activities That Connect to Your Curriculum by Andy Dousis and Margaret Berry Wilson. Center for Responsive Schools, 2010.

Doing Science in Morning Meeting: 150 Quick Activities That Connect to Your Curriculum by Lara Webb and Margaret Berry Wilson. Center for Responsive Schools, 2013.

Doing Social Studies in Morning Meeting: 150 Quick Activities That Connect to Your Curriculum by Leah Carson and Jane Cofie. Center for Responsive Schools, 2017.

    The four books in the *Doing . . . in Morning Meeting* series offer a variety of lively activities that integrate academic content into all four components of Morning Meeting. Each book is organized by grade level, with activities designed to be easily adapted to other grades as well.

The Morning Meeting Book, 3rd ed., by Roxann Kriete and Carol Davis. Center for Responsive Schools, 2014.

    Classic guide to launching each school day with a twenty-to-thirty-minute meeting that brings students together to build positive classroom community, practice social and academic skills, and warm-up for a day of engaged learning.

Problem-Solving Strategies

Sammy and His Behavior Problems: Stories and Strategies From a Teacher's Year by Caltha Crowe. Center for Responsive Schools, 2010.

    Tells the story of the author's year-long journey with a challenging but charming student. Includes practical strategies and reflection on both successes and challenges.

Solving Thorny Behavior Problems: How Teachers and Students Can Work Together by Caltha Crowe. Center for Responsive Schools, 2009.

    Presents five practical strategies that will help teachers and children solve common behavior problems together. Includes information about problem-solving conferences, conflict resolution, role-playing, class meetings, and individual written agreements.

Rules and the *Responsive Classroom* Approach to Discipline

Responsive School Discipline: Essentials for Elementary School Leaders by Chip Wood and Babs Freeman-Loftis. Center for Responsive Schools, 2011.

    A practical approach to discipline based on deep respect for students and all school staff that cultivates positive behavior and learning, and a safe, joyful climate throughout the school.

Teaching Children to Care: Classroom Management for Ethical and Academic Growth, K–8, revised edition, by Ruth Sidney Charney. Center for Responsive Schools, 2002.

An in-depth look at classroom management. Includes information about setting priorities and expectations with children, establishing classroom routines, generating rules with students, using logical consequences, planning and conducting social conferences and class meetings, and avoiding power struggles.

Teasing, Tattling, Defiance and More: Positive Approaches to 10 Common Classroom Behaviors by Margaret Berry Wilson. Center for Responsive Schools, 2013.

Offers practical ways to prevent and respond to everyday classroom misbehaviors so the focus stays on learning. Explains why children misbehave, and gives tips for parent communication.

Teacher Language

The Power of Our Words: Teacher Language That Helps Children Learn by Paula Denton. Center for Responsive Schools, 2007.

Provides an in-depth look at the *Responsive Classroom* approach to teacher language with chapters on the use of envisioning language, open-ended questions, listening, reinforcing language, reminders, and redirections. Includes many examples of these as used in classrooms.

References

Alsaker, Françoise D. 2004. "The Bernese Programme Against Victimisation in Kindergarten and Elementary School." In *Bullying in Schools: How Successful Can Interventions Be?* edited by Peter K. Smith, Debra Pepler, and Ken Rigby, 289–306. Cambridge: Cambridge University Press. https://doi.org/10.1017/CBO9780511584466.016.

Alsaker, Françoise D., and Stefan Valkanover. 2012. "The Bernese Program Against Victimization in Kindergarten and Elementary School." *New Directions for Youth Development* 2012, no. 133: 15–28. https://doi.org/10.1002/yd.20004.

American Psychological Association. n.d. "Bullying and School Climate," last modified August 2017, https://www.apa.org/advocacy/interpersonal-violence/bullying-school-climate.

American Psychological Association Zero Tolerance Task Force. 2008. "Are Zero Tolerance Policies Effective in the Schools? An Evidentiary Review and Recommendations." *American Psychologist* 63, no. 9 (December): 852–862. https://doi.org/10.1037/0003-066x.63.9.852.

Astor, Ron A., Heather Ann Meyer, and Ronald O. Pitner. 2001. "Elementary and Middle School Students' Perceptions of Violence-Prone School Subcontexts." *Elementary School Journal* 101, no. 5 (May): 511–528. As reported in Susan M. Swearer, Dorothy L. Espelage, and Scott A. Napolitano, *Bullying Prevention and Intervention: Realistic Strategies for Schools*. New York: Guilford Press, 2009.

Axford, Nick, David P. Farrington, Suzy Clarkson, Gretchen J. Bjornstad, Zoe Wrigley, and Judy Hutchings. 2015. "Involving Parents in School-Based Programmes to Prevent and Reduce Bullying: What Effect Does It Have?" *Journal of Children's Services* 10, no. 3 (September): 242–251. https://doi.org/10.1108/JCS-05-2015-0019.

Bear, George G. 1998. "School Discipline in the United States: Prevention, Correction, and Long-Term Social Development." *School Psychology Review* 27, no. 1: 14–32. https://doi.org/10.1080/02796015.1998.12085894.

Berguno, George, Penny Leroux, Katayoun McAinsh, and Sabera Shaikh. 2004. "Children's Experience of Loneliness at School and its Relation to Bullying and the Quality of Teacher Interventions." *The Qualitative Report* 9, no. 3: 483–499. https://doi.org/10.46743/2160-3715/2004.1920.

Biggs, Bridget K., Eric M. Vernberg, Stuart W. Twemlow, Peter Fongay, and Edward J. Dill. 2008. "Teacher Adherence and its Relation to Teacher Attitudes and Student Outcomes in an Elementary School-Based Violence Prevention Program." *School Psychology Review* 37, no. 4 (December): 533–549. https://doi.org/10.1080/02796015.2008.12087866.

Bradshaw, Catherine P. 2015. "Translating Research to Practice in Bullying Prevention." *American Psychologist* 70, no. 4 (May-June): 322–332. https://doi.org/10.1037/a0039114.

Bradshaw, Catherine P., Anne L. Sawyer, and Lindsey M. O'Brennan. 2007. "Bullying and Peer Victimization at School: Perceptual Differences Between Students and School Staff." *School Psychology Review* 36, no. 3: 361–382. https://doi.org/10.1080/02796015.2007.12087929.

Bradshaw, Catherine P., Jessika H. Zmuda, Sheppard G. Kellam, and Nicholas S. Ialongo. 2009. "Longitudinal Impact of Two Universal Preventative Interventions in First Grade on Educational Outcomes in High School." *Journal of Educational Psychology* 101, no. 4 (November): 926–937. https://doi.org/10.1037/a0016586.

Bradshaw, Catherine, Tracey Evian Waasdorp, Lindsey M. O'Brennan, and Michaela Gulemotova. 2013. "Teachers' and Education Support Professionals' Perspectives on Bullying and Prevention: Findings from the National Education Association Nationwide Study of Bullying." *School Psychology Review* 42, no. 3: 280–297. https://doi.org/10.1080/02796015.2013.12087474.

Buhs, Eric S., Gary W. Ladd, and Sarah L. Herald-Brown. 2010. "Victimization and Exclusion: Links to Peer Rejection, Classroom Engagement, and Achievement." In Handbook of Bullying in Schools: *An International Perspective*, edited by Shane R. Jimerson, Susan M. Swearer, and Dorothy L. Espelage, 163–172. New York: Routledge.

Burke, Charity. December 2019. "Don't Rely on Peer Mediation to Resolve Bullying in School." Mediate. https://www.mediate.com//articles/burke-peer-mediation-bullying.cfm.

Card, Noel, and Ernest Hodges. 2008. "Peer Victimization Among Schoolchildren: Correlations, Causes, Consequences, and Considerations in Assessment and Intervention." *School Psychology Quarterly* 23, no. 4: 451–461. https://doi.apa.org/doi/10.1037/a0012769.

Chen, Liang, Shirley S. Ho, and May Lwin. 2016. "A Meta-Analysis of Factors Predicting Cyberbullying Perpetration and Victimization: From the Social Cognitive and Media Effects Approach." *New Media & Society* 19, no. 8 (March): 1194–1213. https://doi.org/10.1177/1461444816634037.

Cohen, Jonathan, Dorothy L. Espelage, Stuart Twemlow, Marvin W. Berkowitz, and James P. Comer. 2015. "Rethinking Effective Bully and Violence Prevention Efforts: Promoting Healthy School Climates, Positive Youth Development, and Preventing Bully-Victim-Bystander Behavior." *International Journal of Violence and Schools*, 15, 2–40. Retrieved from https://www.researchgate.net/publication/281593701.

Coloroso, Barbara. 2016. *The Bully, the Bullied, and the Not-So-Innocent Bystander: From Preschool to High School and Beyond: Breaking the Cycle of Violence and Creating More Deeply Caring Communities*. New York: William Morrow.

Common Sense Media. 2015. "Fact Sheet: Parents and Media." PDF file. Accessed April 26, 2020. https://www.commonsensemedia.org/sites/default/files/uploads/pdfs/census_factsheet_parentsandmedia_0.pdf.

Common Sense Media. 2017. "The Common Sense Census: Media Use by Kids Age Zero to Eight, 2017." Accessed April 26, 2020. https://www.commonsensemedia.org/research/the-common-sense-census-media-use-by-kids-age-zero-to-eight-2017.

Common Sense Media. 2019. "The Common Sense Census: Media Use by Kids Age Zero to Eight, 2019." Accessed April 26, 2020. https://www.commonsensemedia.org/research/the-common-sense-census-media-use-by-tweens-and-teens-2019.

Craig, Wendy M., and Debra J. Pepler. 1998. "Observations of Bullying and Victimization in the School Yard." *Canadian Journal of School Psychology* 13, no. 2 (June): 41–59. https://doi.org/10.1177/082957359801300205.

Crowe, Caltha. 2009. *Solving Thorny Behavior Problems: How Teachers and Students Can Work Together*. Turners Falls, MA: Center for Responsive Schools.

Davis, Stan, with Julie Davis. 2007a. *Empowering Bystanders in Bullying Prevention*. Champaign, IL: Research Press.

Davis, Stan, with Julie Davis. 2007b. *Schools Where Everyone Belongs: Practical Strategies for Reducing Bullying*. Champaign, IL: Research Press.

Davis, Stan, and Charisse Nixon. 2010. *The Youth Voice Project*. State College, PA: Pennsylvania State University. https://njbullying.org/documents/YVPMarch2010.pdf.

Depaolis, Kathryn J., and Anne Williford. 2015. "The Nature and Prevalence of Cyber Victimization Among Elementary Children." *Child and Youth Care Forum* 44, no. 3 (June): 377–393. https://doi.org/10.1007/s10566-014-9292-8.

Dillon, James. 2008. *The Peaceful School Bus Program: A Program for Grades K–12*. Center City, MN: Hazelden.

Divecha, Diana, and Marc Brackett. 2020. "Rethinking School-Based Bullying Prevention Through the Lens of Social and Emotional Learning: A Bioecological Perspective." *International Journal of Bullying Prevention* 2, June: 93–113. https://doi.org/10.1007/s42380-019-00019-5.

Duong, Jeffrey, and Catherine P. Bradshaw. 2013. "Using the Extended Parallel Process Model to Examine Teachers' Likelihood of Intervening in Bullying." *Journal of School Health* 83, no. 6 (June): 422–429. https://doi.org/10.1111/josh.12046.

Elledge, L. Christian, Allison R. Elledge, Rebecca A. Newgent, Timothy A. Cavell. 2016. "Social Risk and Peer Victimization in Elementary School Children: The Protective Role of Teacher-Student Relationships." *Journal of Abnormal Child Psychology* 44, no. 4 (May): 691–703. https://doi.org/10.1007/s10802-015-0074-z.

Englander, Elizabeth. n.d. "Cyberbullying and Social Networking." PDF file. Accessed May 16, 2020. https://www.englanderelizabeth.com/downloads.

Englander, Elizabeth. 2013. *Bullying and Cyberbullying: What Every Educator Needs to Know*. Cambridge, MA: Harvard Education Press.

Englander, Elizabeth. June 8, 2017. "Elizabeth Englander on Targeting the Behaviors That Feed Bullying." Interview with Laura Varlas. ASCD Express 12, no. 19. https://www.ascd.org/el/articles/elizabeth-englander-on-targeting-the-behaviors-that-feed-bullying.

Erikson Institute. 2016. *Technology and Young Children in the Digital Age: A Report From the Erikson Institute*. Survey. https://www.erikson.edu/wp-content/uploads/2018/07/Erikson-Institute-Technology-and-Young-Children-Survey.pdf.

Espelage, Dorothy L., and Lisa De La Rue. 2012. "School Bullying: Its Nature and Ecology." *International Journal of Adolescent Medicine and Health* 24, no. 1 (March): 3–10. https://doi.org/10.1515/ijamh.2012.002.

Espelage, Dorothy L., Joshua R. Polanin, and Sabina K. Low. 2014. "Teacher and Staff Perceptions of School Environment as Predictors of Student Aggression, Victimization, and Willingness to Intervene in Bullying Situations." *School Psychology Quarterly* 29, no. 3 (September): 287–305. https://doi.org/10.1037/spq0000072.

Faris, Robert, and Diane Felmlee. 2011. "Status Struggles: Network Centrality and Gender Segregation in Same- and Cross-Gender Aggression." *American Sociological Review* 76, no. 1 (February): 48–73. https://doi.org/10.1177/0003122410396196.

Freiberg, Jo Ann. 2009. *Confronting and Working to Reduce Bullying Behaviors in School Settings*. Medina, WA: Institute for Educational Development.

Gini, Gianluca, Tiziana Pozzoli, Francesco Borghi, and Lara Fianzoni. 2008. "The Role of Bystanders in Students' Perception of Bullying and Sense of Safety." *Journal of School Psychology* 46, no. 3 (December): 617–638. https://doi.org/10.1016/j.jsp.2008.02.001.

Gini, Gianluca, Tizianna Pozzoli, and Shelley Hymel. 2014. "Moral Disengagement Among Children and Youth: A Meta-Analytic Review of Links to Aggressive Behavior." *Aggressive Behavior* 40, no. 1 (January): 56–68. https://doi.org/10.1002/ab.21502.

GLSEN. 2012. "Playgrounds and Prejudice: Elementary School Climate in the United States." Survey. https://www.glsen.org/sites/default/files/2019-11/Playgrounds_and_Prejudice_2012.pdf.

Gottfredson, Denise C. 2000. *Schools and Delinquency*. Cambridge, England: Cambridge University Press.

Guo, Siying. 2016. "A Meta-Analysis of the Predictors of Cyberbullying Perpetration and Victimization." *Psychology in the Schools* 53, no. 4 (April): 432–453. https://doi.org/10.1002/pits.21914.

Henry, David, Nancy Guerra, Rowell Huesmann, Patrick Tolan, Richard Van-Acker, and Leonard Eron. 2000. "Normative Influences on Aggression in Urban Elementary School Classrooms." *American Journal of Community Psychology* 28, no. 1 (February): 59–81. https://doi.org/10.1023/A:1005142429725.

Hinduja, Sameer. 2018. "Cyberbullying and Social Media." Presentation, Federal Commission on School Safety, June 22, 2018. https://cyberbullying.org/federal-commission-on-school-safety.

Hinduja, Sameer, and Justin W. Patchin. 2014. "Cyberbullying Identification, Prevention, and Response." Cyberbullying Research Center. https://cyberbullying.org/Cyberbullying-Identification-Prevention-Response.pdf.

Hodges, Ernest V., Michel Boivin, Frank Vitaro, and William M. Bukowski. 1999. "The Power of Friendship: Protection Against an Escalating Cycle of Peer Victimization." *Developmental Psychology* 35, no. 1: 94–101. https://doi.org/10.1037//0012-1649.35.1.94.

Hodges, Ernest V., Maurice J. Malone, and David G. Perry. 1997. "Individual Risk and Social Risk as Interacting Determinants of Victimization in the Peer Group." *Developmental Psychology* 33, no. 6 (November): 1032–1039. As reported in "Review of Research," Steps to Respect Program Guide, Committee for Children, 2005, https://cfchildren.azurewebsites.net/wp-content/uploads/resources/previous-programs/steps-to-respect/STR_ROR.pdf.

Hoff, Dianne L., and Sidney N. Mitchell. 2009. "Cyberbullying: Causes, Effects, and Remedies." *Journal of Educational Administration* 47, no. 5 (August): 652–665. https://doi.org/10.1108/09578230910981107.

Juvonen, Jaana, and Elisheva F. Gross. 2008. "Extending the School Grounds?—Bullying Experiences in Cyberspace." *Journal of School Health* 78, no. 9 (August): 496–505. https://doi.org/10.1111/j.1746-1561.2008.00335.x.

Kasen, Stephanie, Kathy Berenson, Patricia Cohen, and Jeffrey G. Johnson. 2004. "School Climate and Change in Personality Disorder Symptom Trajectories Related to Bullying: A Prospective Study." In *Bullying in American Schools: A Social-Ecological Perspective on Prevention and Intervention*, edited by Dorothy L. Espelage and Susan M. Swearer, 187–210. Mahwah, NJ: Lawrence Erlbaum Associates, Inc.

Katz, Lillian G., and Sylvia C. Chard. 2000. *Engaging Children's Minds: The Project Approach*. 2nd ed. Stamford, CT: Ablex Publishing Corporation.

Kowalski, Robin M., Gary W. Giumetti, Amber N. Schroeder, and Micah R. Lattinner. 2014. "Bullying in the Digital Age: A Critical Review and Meta-Analysis of Cyberbullying Research Among Youth." *Psychological Bulletin* 140, no. 4: 1073–1137. https://doi.apa.org/doiLanding?doi=10.1037%-2Fa0035618.

Kowalski, Robin M., Susan P. Limber, and Annie McCord. 2019. "A Developmental Approach to Cyberbullying: Prevalence and Protective Factors." *Aggression and Violent Behavior* 45, March–April: 20–32. https://doi.org/10.1016/j.avb.2018.02.009.

Lambe, Laura, Victoria Della Cioppa, Irene K. Hong, and Wendy M. Craig. 2019. "Standing Up to Bullying: A Social Ecological Review of Peer Defending in Offline and Online Contexts." *Aggression and Violent Behavior* 45, March–April: 51–74. https://doi.org/10.1016/j.avb.2018.05.007.

Luxemberg, Harlen, Susan Limber, and Dan Olweus. 2019. Bullying in U.S. Schools: 2019 Status Report. Center City, MN: Hazelden. https://www.violencepreventionworks.org/public/document/des_obppbullyingtrends_2019.pdf.

Maran, Daniela Acquadro, Maurizio Tirassa, and Tatiana Begotti. 2017. "Teachers' Intervention in School Bullying: A Qualitative Analysis on Italian Teachers." *Frontiers in Education* 2, no. 36 (July). https://doi.org/10.3389/feduc.2017.00036.

McCain, Becky Ray, and Todd Leonardo (illus.). 2001. *Nobody Knew What to Do: A Story About Bullying*. Park Ridge, IL: Albert Whitman.

Menesini, Ersilla, Virginia Sanchez, Ada Fonzi, Rosario Ortega, Angela Costabile, and Giorgio Lo Feudo. 2003. "Moral Emotions and Bullying: A Cross-National Comparison of Differences Between Bullies, Victims, and Outsiders." *Aggressive Behavior* 29, no. 6 (October): 515–530. https://doi.org/10.1002/ab.10060.

Monks, Claire P., Jess Mahdavi, and Katie Rix. 2016. "The Emergence of Cyberbullying in Childhood: Parent and Teacher Perspectives." *Psiocolgía Educativa* 22, no. 1: 39–48. https://doi.org/10.1016/j.pse.2016.02.002.

Monks, Claire P., Susanne Robinson, and Penny Worlidge. 2012. "The Emergence of Cyberbullying: A Survey of Primary School Pupils' Perceptions and Experience." *School Psychology International* 33, no. 5 (September): 471–491. https://doi.org/10.1177/0143034312445242.

National Crime Prevention Council. 2020. "Information and Resources to Curb the Growing Problem of Cyberbullying." Accessed November 16, 2020. https://www.ncpc.org/resources/cyberbullying/.

National School Climate Survey. n.d. "Bullying Prevention." https://schoolclimate.org/services/bullybust/.

Notar, Charles E., Sharon Padgett, and Jessica Roden. 2013. "Cyberbullying: Resources for Intervention and Prevention." *Universal Journal of Educational Research* 1, no. 3: 133–145. https://doi.org/10.13189/ujer.2013.010301.

O'Brennan, Lindsey M., Tracy E. Waasdorp, and Catherine P. Bradshaw. 2014. "Strengthening Bullying Prevention Through School Staff Connectedness." *Journal of Educational Psychology* 106, no. 3: 870–880. https://doi.org/10.1037/a0035957.

Olweus, Dan. 1993. *Bullying at School: What We Know and What We Can Do*. Oxford, England: Blackwell.

Olweus, Dan. 2013. "School Bullying: Development and Some Important Challenges." *Annual Review of Clinical Psychology* 9, no. 1: 751–780. http://dx.doi.org/10.1146/annurev-clinpsy-050212-185516

Olweus, Dan and Susan P. Limber. 2007. *Olweus Bullying Prevention Program Teacher Guide*. Center City, MN: Hazelden.

Orpinas, Pamela, and Arthur M. Horne. 2010. "Creating a Positive School Climate and Developing Social Competence." In *Handbook of Bullying in Schools: An International Perspective*, edited by Shane R. Jimerson, Susan M. Swearer, and Dorothy L. Espelage, 49–59. New York: Routledge.

Ostrander, Jason, Alysse Melville, Janelle K. Bryan, and Joan Letendre. 2018. "Proposed Modification of School-Wide Bully Prevention Program to Support All Children." *Journal of School Violence* 17, no. 3: 367–380. https://doi.org/10.1080/15388220.2017.1379909.

Padgett, Sharon, and Charles E. Notar. 2013. "Bystanders Are Key to Stopping Bullying." *Universal Journal of Educational Research* 1, no. 2: 33–41. https://doi.org/10.13189/ujer.2013.010201.

Paley, Vivian Gussin. 1992. *You Can't Say You Can't Play*. Cambridge, MA: Harvard University Press.

Pellegrini, Anthony D., Jeffrey D. Long, David Solberg, Cary Roseth, Danielle Dupuis, Catherine Bohn, and Meghan Hickey. 2010. "Bullying and Social Status During School Transitions." In *Handbook of Bullying in Schools: An International Perspective*, edited by Shane R. Jimerson, Susan M. Swearer, and Dorothy L. Espelage, 199–210. New York: Routledge.

Pellegrini, Anthony D., Cary Roseth, Shanna Mliner, Catherine Bohn, Mark Van Ryzin, Natalie Vance, Carol L. Cheatham, and Amanda Tarullo. 2007. "Social Dominance in Preschool Classrooms." *Journal of Comparative Psychology* 121, no. 1: 54–64. https://doi.org/10.1037/0735-7036.121.1.54.

Pepler, Debra, and Wendy Craig. 2007. "Binoculars on Bullying: A New Solution to Protect and Connect Children." Voices for Children Report. https://www.researchgate.net/publication/255594121_Binoculars_on_bullying_A_new_solution_to_protect_and_connect_children/link/00463520cd4a586214000000/download.

Pepler, Debra, Wendy Craig, and Paul O'Connell. 2010. "Peer Processes in Bullying: Informing Prevention and Intervention Strategies." In *Handbook of Bullying in Schools: An International Perspective*, edited by Shane R. Jimerson, Susan M. Swearer, and Dorothy L. Espelage, 469–479. New York: Routledge.

Rimm-Kaufman, Sara E., and Yu-Jen I. Chiu. 2007. "Promoting Social and Academic Competence in the Classroom: An Intervention Study Examining the Contribution of the *Responsive Classroom* Approach." *Psychology in the Schools* 44, no. 4 (April): 397–413. https://doi.org/10.1002/pits.20231.

Rodkin, Philip C., and Scott D. Gest. 2010. "Teaching Practices, Classroom Peer Ecologies, and Bullying Behaviors Among Schoolchildren." In *Bullying in North American Schools*, edited by Dorothy L. Espelage and Susan M. Swearer, 75–90. New York: Routledge.

Rosen, Lisa H., Shannon R. Scott, and Kathy DeOrnellas. 2017. "Teachers' Perceptions of Bullying: A Focus Group Approach." *Journal of School Violence* 16, no. 1: 119–139. https://doi.org/10.1080/15388220.2015.1124340.

Salmivalli, Christina, Antti Kärnä, and Elisa Poskiparta. 2010. "From Peer Putdowns to Peer Support: A Theoretical Model and How It Translated Into a National Anti-Bullying Program." In *Handbook of Bullying in Schools: An International Perspective*, edited by Shane R. Jimerson, Susan M. Swearer, and Dorothy L. Espelage, 441–454. New York: Routledge.

Slonje, Robert, Peter K. Smith, and Ann Frisén. 2013. "The Nature of Cyberbullying, and Strategies for Prevention." *Computers in Human Behavior* 29, no. 1 (January): 26–32. https://doi.org/10.1016/j.chb.2012.05.024.

Smith, Peter K., Kirsten C. Madsen, and Janet C. Moody. 1999. "What Causes the Age Decline in Reports of Being Bullied at School? Towards a Developmental Analysis of Risks of Being Bullied." *Educational Research* 41, no. 3: 267–285. https://doi.org/10.1080/0013188990410303.

Sprung, Barbara, Merle Froschl, and Nancy Gropper. 2020. *Cybersafe Young Children: Teaching Internet Safety and Responsibility, K–3*. New York: Teachers College Press.

Starks, Geoffrey. 2010. "*Tinker's* Tenure in the School Setting: The Case for Applying *O'Brien* to Content-Neutral Regulations." *Yale Law Journal Online* 120, no. 65. https://www.yalelawjournal.org/forum/tinkers-tenure-in-the-school-setting-the-case-for-applying-obrien-to-content-neutral-regulations.

StopBullying.gov. 2017a. "Build a Safe Environment." Last modified September 8, 2017. https://www.stopbullying.gov/prevention/build-safe-environment.

StopBullying.gov. 2017b. "The Roles Kids Play in Bullying." Last modified September 28, 2017. https://www.stopbullying.gov/bullying/roles-kids-play.

StopBullying.gov. 2017c. "Set Policies and Rules." Last modified September 28, 2017. https://www.stopbullying.gov/prevention/rules.

StopBullying.gov. 2018a. "Cyberbullying Tactics." Last modified May 10, 2018. https://www.stopbullying.gov/cyberbullying/cyberbullying-tactics.

StopBullying.gov. 2018b. "Laws, Policies, and Regulations." Last modified January 7, 2018. https://www.stopbullying.gov/resources/laws.

StopBullying.gov. 2019. "How to Prevent Bullying." Last reviewed May 30, 2019. https://www.stopbullying.gov/prevention/how-to-prevent-bullying.

StopBullying.gov. 2020. "What Is Bullying." Last modified July 21, 2020. https://www.stopbullying.gov/bullying/what-is-bullying.

StopBullying.gov. 2021a. "Tips for Teachers." Last modified May 21, 2021. https://www.stopbullying.gov/cyberbullying/tips-for-teachers.

StopBullying.gov. 2021b. "Who Is at Risk." Last modified June 20, 2021. https://www.stopbullying.gov/bullying/at-risk.

StopBullying.gov. n.d. "Misdirections in Bullying Prevention and Intervention." https://www.stopbullying.gov/sites/default/files/2017-10/misdirections-in-prevention.pdf.

Swearer, Susan M., Dorothy L. Espelage, and Scott A. Napolitano. 2009. *Bullying Prevention and Intervention: Realistic Strategies for Schools*. New York: Guilford Press.

Swearer, Susan M., Dorothy L. Espelage, Tracy Vaillancourt, and Shelly Hymel. 2010. "What Can Be Done About School Bullying? Linking Research to Educational Practice." *Educational Researcher* 39, no. 1 (January): 38–47. https://doi.org/10.3102/0013189X09357622.

Sweeting, Helen, and Patrick West. 2001. "Being Different: Correlates of the Experience of Teasing and Bullying at Age 11." *Research Papers in Education: Policy and Practice* 16, no. 3: 225–246. http://dx.doi.org/10.1080/02671520110058679.

Thornberg, Robert, and Tomas Jungert. 2013. "Bystander Behavior in Bullying Situations: Basic Moral Sensitivity, Moral Disengagement and Defender Self-Efficacy." *Journal of Adolescence* 36, no. 3 (June): 475–483. https://doi.org/10.1016/j.adolescence.2013.02.003.

Ttofi, Maria M., and David P. Farrington. 2011. "Effectiveness of School-Based Programs to Reduce Bullying: A Systematic and Meta-Analytic Review." *Journal of Experimental Criminology* 7, (March): 27–56. https://doi.org/10.1007/s11292-010-9109-1.

Twemlow, Stuart, Peter Fonagy, Frank C. Sacco, and John R. Brethour Jr. 2006. "Teachers Who Bully Students: A Hidden Trauma." *International Journal of Social Psychiatry* 52, no. 3 (May): 187–188. https://doi.org/10.1177/0020764006067234.

U.S. Department of Education. 2020. "Family Educational Rights and Privacy Act (FERPA)." Last modified December 15, 2020. https://www2.ed.gov/policy/gen/guid/fpco/ferpa/index.html.

Vaillancourt, Tracy, Shelley Hymel, and Patricia McDougall. 2003. "Bullying Is Power: Implications for School-Based Intervention Strategies." *Journal of Applied School Psychology* 19, no. 2: 157–176. https://doi.org/10.1300/J008v19n02_10.

Vygotsky, L. S. 1978. *Mind in Society: The Development of Higher Psychological Process*. Revised edition. Cambridge, MA: Harvard University Press.

Wang, Cixin, Brandi Berry, and Susan M. Swearer. 2013. "The Critical Role of School Climate in Effective Bullying Prevention." *Theory Into Practice* 52, no. 4: 296–302. https://doi.org/10.1080/00405841.2013.829735.

Wessler, Stephen. 2003. *The Respectful School: How Educators and Students Can Conquer Hate and Harassment*. With contributing author William Preble. Alexandria, VA: Association for Supervision and Curriculum Development.

Wood, Chip. 2017. *Yardsticks: Child and Adolescent Development Ages 4–14*. 4th ed. Turners Falls, MA: Center for Responsive Schools.

Yerger, William, and Cliff Gehret. 2011. "Understanding and Dealing With Bullying in Schools." *The Educational Forum* 75, no. 4: 315–326. https://doi.org/10.1080/00131725.2011.602468.

Zych, Izabela, Anna C. Baldry, and David P. Farrington. 2017. "School Bullying and Cyberbullying: Prevalence, Characteristics, Outcomes, and Prevention." In *Handbook of Behavioral Criminology*, edited by Vincent P. Van Hasselt and Michael L. Bourke, 113–138. Springer.

Zych, Izabela, Anna C. Baldry, David P. Farrington, and Vicente J. Llorent. 2018. "Are Children Involved in Cyberbullying Low on Empathy? A Systematic Review and Meta-Analysis of Research on Empathy Versus Different Cyberbullying Roles." *Aggression and Violent Behavior* 45, (March–April): 83–97. https://doi.org/10.1016/j.avb.2018.03.004.

Zych, Izabela, David P. Farrington, and Maria M. Ttofi. 2019. "Protective Factors Against Bullying and Cyberbullying: A Systematic Review of Meta-Analyses." *Aggression and Violent Behavior* 45 (March–April): 4–19. https://doi.org/10.1016/j.avb.2018.06.008.

Acknowledgments

This book reflects many people's thoughts and experiences. Scores of teachers, guidance counselors, administrators, and paraprofessionals invited me into their schools, classrooms, and work sites. They shared teaching materials and student-written reflections with me. They spent time telling me about their experiences with bullying and its prevention. They described student responses to bullying prevention practices that they've used in the past and practices that they are currently using. Without their help and input, this book would not have been possible.

Some of the educators whose learning spaces appear in this book are: Heather Robatille Dion, Sarah Fillion, Peter Halsey, Tracy Mercier, Kimberly Myhre, Jamie O'Hare, Susan Pelis, Jill Pszeniczny, Maureen Russell, Ina Pannell-Saint Surin, Sherry Wood, and Ellen Zunick.

Some of the educators who supported me in my exploration of multicultural children's books are: Consuelo Hernandez, Sandra Patricia Cano Sorensen, Isolde Stewart, and Rebecca Wanless.

I learned such rich information from various workshops that I attended led by Stan Davis, Charisse Nixon, Jo Ann Freiberg, Marta Koonz, and Stephen Wessler. I appreciated Jo Ann's thoughts in conversations that we had while I was beginning to formulate my thinking about bullying. Her words, "If it's mean, intervene," echoed in my head every day and set the direction of my work. Stephen Wessler's descriptions of specific ways that disparaging words can escalate into violence guided my thinking from the early days of this project as well. Stan Davis's unique and thoughtful approach to bullying prevention has challenged my thinking and enriched my perspective throughout the writing of this book.

The webinars offered by the Olweus Bullying Prevention Program, the Committee for Children's Steps to Respect program, and Center for Responsive Schools were so helpful. I appreciate their generosity in offering them.

Thank you, Gayla Sullivan, for helping me keep my thinking about teaching and learning alive by inviting me into your classroom community in the Estes Park, Colorado, public schools. Thank you, Isolde Stewart and Consuelo Hernandez, for welcoming my volunteering at New Horizons, a multicultural and multilingual preschool that creates a welcoming and inclusive environment for all.

Many people who work at Center for Responsive Schools, home of the *Responsive Classroom* approach, reflected with me, suggested new ways of looking at bullying prevention, and helped me in numerous ways.

Amy Hildenbrand, former Director of Publications, encouraged me to revise and update the book. Emily Hemingway, the current editor in chief, continued to support this project. Kevin Bradley, project editor, helped me clearly express every thought. Cathy Hess and Noelle Serafino proofread the text to ensure everything was accurate. Carly Oddleifson reviewed current research on bullying prevention. Clara-Christina Gerstner reviewed research on cyberbullying.

Chip Wood's years of mentorship have sparked my thinking about children and their relationships. He has provided me with years of thought-provoking insights about teaching since long before I began thinking specifically about bullying.

My late mother, Frances Crowe, was a one-person cheering squad and a provider of articles and clippings both physical and electronic. My sister-in-law, Nancy Crowe, has been the source of rich and fruitful conversations about teaching and learning. My daughter, Rosa Dinelli, has been an enthusiastic partner in deep conversations about children and their families, informed by her perspective as a psychologist. My life-partner, Jerry Allison, has provided feedback, hot meals while I worked, and fun every day, whether I'm sitting at home at the computer or out in the mountains with him.

About the Author

Caltha Crowe's teaching career spanned thirty-eight years before she left the classroom in 2007. She taught a range of elementary grades and preschool in a variety of settings, including schools in urban New Haven, Connecticut, the Chicago suburbs of Winnetka and Glencoe, and Westport, Connecticut. During many of those years, Caltha was involved with Connecticut's Beginning Educator Support and Training (BEST) program, working as a mentor to new teachers, helping with mentor training, and serving on program advisory groups.

Caltha currently lives in Colorado and volunteers in the local schools there. As a *Responsive Classroom* consulting teacher, she travels around the country to present workshops and coach teachers on using the *Responsive Classroom* approach. Caltha has a BA from Smith College, a master's degree in early childhood education from Goddard College, and a master's degree in educational leadership from Bank Street College of Education.

Index

A
adult intervention, 2, 7, 10-11, 115, 181
anchor charts, 94-95
arrival time
    and teacher observation, 17, 119
audience for bullying
    as allies, 7, 12, 170
    and intervention, 28
    roles of, 7
    teaching tools for, 8

B
blaming the target, 102
body language
    as clue to bullying, 18
    and communicating respect, 86-87, 97
    on the playground, 117
    and pre-bullying, 23
buddy pairing, 139-140
bully personality profile, 5
bullying behaviors
    and assertion of power, 5
    explicit naming of, 71
    joking vs. bullying, 18
    pervasiveness, 3-4
    in preschool, 4
    reluctance of children to report, 11
    teasing vs. bullying, 18
bus behaviors
    providing inclusive structure for, 139
    and teacher observation, 119
bystanders. *See* audience for bullying

C
cafeteria behaviors. *See* lunchroom behaviors
children's literature
    on being a bystander, 247-248
    in bullying prevention lessons, 174
    on excluding and including, 250-251
    on respecting and appreciating differences, 251-255
    and rules discussion, 72
    on someone being bullied, 256-258
    on taking care of each other, 249
    on teasing, 259
classroom rules
    and application to daily life, 68-70
    and bullying behaviors, 70-71
    as bullying prevention, 8-9, 11
    creation process, strategy in action, 75-76
    and cyberbullying, 72
    importance of, 175
    and lunchroom behaviors, 124-125
    parent familiarity with, 81
    positive tone of, 67-68
    quick conversations about, 126-127
    and recess behaviors, 123
    and *Responsive Classroom* rules-creation process, 65-67
    and role-playing, 92
    and social media, 150-152
    structuring discussions about, 124-125
    student investment in, 64
    teacher reference to, 26-27
cliques
    and adult observation of, 116
    and cyberbullying, strategies in action, 162-163
    prevention of in the lunchroom, 137
collaborative work
    and coaching by teachers, 97-103
    factors in success of, 85-86
    modeling skills for, 89-92
    and role-play, 92-93
colleague collaboration, 141
community building
    as bullying prevention technique, 8
    and scheduling of bullying prevention lessons, 172-173
    and whole-group activities, 52
confidentiality
    and children's reporting to adults, 80, 240
    and parent communication, 38-39

conflict resolution meeting, 20
connecting children to one another, 48, 57–58
conversation skills, 88
    in the lunchroom, 138
    in small groups, 103
cyberbullying, 146
    and aspects specific to the electronic world, 157
    and clues to watch for, 159–160
    and connecting to the rules, 72–74, 150
    and explicit instruction of digital device use, 155
    inclusion as prevention of, 154
    the indirect nature of, 147
    laws against, 161
    and parents' role, 165–167
    and positive classroom culture, 149
    prevention of, 149
    in relation to traditional bullying, 146
    responding to a clique, strategies in action, 162–163
    and social skills instruction, 153–156
    teacher response to, 145, 160–161
    and teaching developmentally appropriate skills for internet safety, 157
    and teaching digital citizenship, 12
    and technology use among children, 148
    tools for children to cope with, 164

D

denial of bullying
    teacher response to, 32
development, children's
    in bullying prevention lessons, 173
    eight-year-old behaviors, 214
    eleven-year-old behaviors, 217
    five-year-old behaviors, 184
    nine-year-old behaviors, 215
    and readiness for small-group work, 103, 106–107
    seven-year-old behaviors, 172
    six-year-old behaviors, 186
    and social behavior, 21–22
    ten-year-old behaviors, 216
differentness
    as risk factor in being targeted, 5–6
direct relational aggression, 3

E

empathy, 42, 48, 51, 153, 154
    lack of and bullying behavior, 5
exclusionary behaviors, 3, 18
    logical consequences for, 31

F

fishbowl strategy, 96–97
friendly interactions, 87
    differentiating from being friends, 172
    and inclusiveness, 135

G

games and sports
    noncompetitive, 136
    and pre-bullying behavior, 116
    providing inclusive structures for, 135
gateway behaviors
    and adult intervention, 26
    children reporting, 77
    and classroom rules, 26
    logical consequences for, 30
    nonpunitive response to, 10
    outside the classroom, 113
    as pre-bullying, 11, 15, 101, 170
    responding to, strategy in action, 33–34
    watching for while coaching, 101
gender stereotypes
    as risk factor for being targeted, 5–6, 23
"getting to know you" activities, 44, 57–59
    and academic lessons, 57
    importance of, 41–42, 43
    integrating academics into, strategy in action, 58–59
"go public" technique, 29
greetings, 44–47
    samples of, 56
    teaching skills needed for, 46–47
group activities
    and inclusion, 53
    samples of, 56
    teaching of, 54
group work
    in bullying prevention lessons, 176
    teaching skills needed for, 88–107

H

"hot spots" in school
    in bullying prevention lessons, 177, 178

I

ideal behaviors
    in Interactive Modeling and role-playing, 94
inclusiveness
    as bullying prevention technique, 8
    on the bus, 139
    and classroom community, 10, 41
    and group activities, 53
    at lunch, 137
    for new student, 92
    providing structures for, 134–140
    at recess, 135
    and rules creation, 66
indirect relational aggression, 3
individual coaching, 98
Interactive Modeling, 9, 46, 55, 89–92
    and fishbowl strategy, 96
    and listening skills, 49
    and partner reading, strategy in action, 91–92
    for practicing safe and inclusive behaviors, 130–132
    for reinforcing ideal behaviors, 94
    skills for small-group work, 88–89
    for teaching conversation skills, 138
interviews for younger children
    in bullying prevention lessons, 178
isolated child
    and positive group climate, 42
    teacher intervention for, 20
    and teacher observation, 19
isolation
    and being targeted, 101, 117
    and pre-bullying behavior, 116

J

joking. *See* bullying behaviors

K

kindness
    the challenge of, 245
    creating a climate of, 44
    and rules creation, 66
    teaching examples of, 68

L

labeling
    and parent communication, 38
language
    for applying rules, 72
    for greetings, sharing, and group activities, 45–46
    reminding and redirecting, 27
    reminding and reinforcing, 133–134
    when coaching individuals, 100
learning goals
    student creation of, 65
listening skills
    in bullying prevention lessons, 175
    and small-group work, 103
    teaching methods for, 49
logical consequences, 29–32
lunch partners, 137
lunchroom behaviors
    and classroom rules, 133
    and structures to promote inclusion, 124
    and teacher observation, 18, 118

M

marginalization
    as risk factor for being targeted, 53
Massachusetts Aggression Reduction Center (MARC), 16, 26
mean behaviors. *See* gateway behaviors
modeling. *See* Interactive Modeling
moral disengagement
    and bullying behavior, 5
Morning Meeting, 9, 44, 47–48, 52, 110, 120

N

nine second rule, 26
noncompetitive games
    and inclusive behaviors, 136

O

observation
    outside the classroom, 116
    and small-group work, 87
Olweus Bullying Questionnaire, 4, 11, 177
Olweus Bullying Prevention Program, 3–4, 7, 28, 121, 159
open-ended questions
    in bullying prevention lessons, 179
other regulation
    and tattling, 77

P

parent-teacher communication
    about bullying prevention, 59–61
    about classroom rules, 81–83
    as component in bullying prevention, 12
    about cooperative learning structures, 108–110
    about misbehavior, 36–40
    about outside-the-classroom behaviors, 142–143
parents
    as classroom helpers, 110
    and learning goals for their children, 82
    tips for, 166
partner chats
    in bullying prevention lessons, 176
Peaceful School Bus program, 139
picture books. *See* children's literature
playground behaviors
    and adult intervention, 115
    and children's body language, 117
    classroom rules for, 123
    creating rules for, strategy in action, 127–129
    providing inclusive structures for, 134
    and teacher observation, 118
power. *See* social power
pre-bullying behaviors. *See* gateway behaviors
proportionate consequences, 31–32
punishment
    vs. logical consequences, 29–30

Q

question, talk, talk, talk, question format, 105

R

recess behaviors. *See* playground behaviors
relational aggression, 3
reminding and reinforcing language, 133–134
remorsefulness
    denial in bullying behavior, 32
reporting
    use of term with children, 78, 171
reporting mean behaviors, 11, 78
    and adult response, 78
    and other adult supervisors, 79, 121–122
resources
    on bullying and bullying prevention, 261
    on child development, 264
    on classroom management, 264–265
    on games and movement activities, 266
    on Morning Meeting, 266
    on problem-solving strategies, 268
    on rules and *Responsive Classroom* approach to discipline, 268
    on teacher language, 269
respectful behavior
    in collaborative work, 85–86
    during morning greeting, 45–46
    in small-group work, 87
    teacher modeling of, 31, 245
    teaching examples of, 68–69
Responsive Classroom, 9–10
role-playing
    in bullying prevention lessons, 179
    safe and inclusive behaviors, 92, 131
rules. *See* classroom rules
rumor spreading, 3, 4

S

safe areas
    vs. unsafe, surveys about, 121
safe classroom, 10
    and cocreating rules, 64
    communication with parents about, 59
    guidelines for, 22
schoolwide approach, 9, 114
sharing, 48–51
    sample topics for, 56
sharing materials
    in small-group work, 88
small-group work
    coaching, 98, 100–101
    and respectful behavior, 86
    and sharing materials, 88

and taking turns, 103
    and teacher observation, 19
    use of talking stick with, 104
social hierarchy
    and bullying behavior, 5
social power, 3, 5
special education, children receiving
    and bullying, 5
    as risk factor for being targeted, 24
state laws
    and bullying, 157
surveys
    and "getting to know you" activities, 57
    to identify safe and unsafe areas, 177–178
Olweus Bullying Questionnaire, 4, 11, 177

T

talking stick, 104–105
targeting
    children at risk for, 23–24, 42, 43, 53, 101–102
tattling, 11
    and bullying reporting, 76–78
T-chart
    use in creating outside-the-classroom rules, 126
teacher language. *See* language
teacher observations
    and outside-the-classroom areas, 115–120
    small acts of meanness, 16
    and small-group work, 87
    of social interactions, 18
team sports. *See* games and sports

U

unkind behaviors. *See* gateway behaviors

V

Venn diagrams
    and "getting to know you" activities, 57

W

witnesses. *See* audience for bullying

About the Publisher

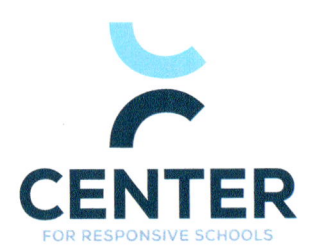

Center for Responsive Schools, Inc., a not-for-profit educational organization, offers professional development, curriculum, and books and resources to support academic, social, and emotional learning.

Center for Responsive Schools (CRS) is the developer of *Responsive Classroom*®, a research-based education approach associated with greater teacher effectiveness, higher student achievement, and improved school climate, and of Fly Five, a comprehensive social-emotional learning curriculum for kindergarten through eighth grade.

CRS Publishing, the independent publishing arm of Center for Responsive Schools, creates inspiring yet practical books for educators and students to support growth, learning, and success in and out of school.

Center for Responsive Schools' vision is to influence and inspire a world-class education for every student in every school, every day, and to bring hope and joy to educators and students alike. Visit us at crslearn.org to learn more: